WITHDRAWN

THE
SOURCEBOOK

THE SOURCEBOOK

Activities for Infants
and Young Children

SECOND EDITION

George W. Maxim

WEST CHESTER UNIVERSITY

MERRILL PUBLISHING COMPANY
A Bell & Howell Information Company
Columbus Toronto London Melbourne

To Libby, Mike, and Jeff
Together you made this possible.
Thanks!

Cover Photo: Andy Brunk

Published by Merrill Publishing Company
A Bell & Howell Information Company
Columbus, Ohio 43216

This book was set in Palatino.

Administrative Editor: David Faherty
Production Coordinator: Sharon Rudd
Art Coordinator: Ruth Ann Kimpel
Cover Designer: Brian Deep

Previous edition copyrighted 1981 by Wadsworth, Inc.

Library of Congress Catalog Card Number: 89–62919
International Standard Book Number: 0–675–21055–0
Printed in the United States of America
1 2 3 4 5 6 7 8 9—94 93 92 91 90

Preface

T his book is a collection of ideas designed to help preservice teachers, teachers, and aides provide appropriate experiences for infants and young children. It is by no means a complete collection, for thousands of ideas have been used by clever professionals through the years. Even up to the day of printing I debated with myself about additional suggestions or exercises that might make the book more attractive. However, I had to stop somewhere—and the result is a sourcebook of traditional ideas that have been informally passed from teacher to teacher, as well as original ideas that I have found successful in my teaching. I hope this combination of idea sources will enrich your child-care center, preschool, or kindergarten program, and stimulate you to adapt the ideas in new ways or to discover innovative ideas of your own.

The book is divided into three parts: "For Infants," "For Toddlers," and "For Young Children." Each presents activities that use the child's natural drive to explore and manipulate to help him or her grow in all areas of development. A final section, "How to Plan and Start an Early Childhood Program," offers detailed suggestions for those interested in originating their own nursery school or child-care facility.

In an effort to overcome the sexism implicit in the traditional use of the masculine gender pronoun, and to avoid the awkwardness of "he/she," I have alternated between masculine and feminine pronouns throughout.

I hope that those of you who use this book will share your reactions with me. Please send suggestions for specific activities to be added, and any comments or criticisms you may have, to: George Maxim, Department of Childhood Studies and Reading, 107C Recitation Hall, West Chester University, West Chester, PA, 19380. Your responses will be sincerely appreciated.

ACKNOWLEDGMENTS

A special expression of gratitude is extended to my wife Libby and to my sons Michael and Jeffrey. Their patience and encouragement made the project much more manageable than I had thought possible. They have been a "family" in every sense of the word.

David Faherty, administrative editor of education at Merrill Publishing, must be offered a special expression of thanks for his confidence in and enthusiasm for this project. Sharon Rudd, production editor, has taken the raw manuscript and transformed it into a handsome book—I thank her for that. Beth Franks performed her copyediting responsibilities with outstanding skill. She not only cleaned up my writing, she also demonstrated a keen insight into childhood while doing so. Ruth Ann Kimpel, art coordinator, was conscientious and helpful in overseeing the illustrations for the book. Phyllis Chorpenning also made an important contribution to this book with her adept typing skills and unfailing good spirit.

Contents

PART ONE

FOR INFANTS

One of the major challenges that child-care personnel face is finding suitable activities and materials for infants and toddlers. These professionals want to make the infant's experiences away from home profitable ones, but they often need some help and direction to work in developmentally appropriate ways.

This is complicated somewhat because the growth that takes place during the baby's first year is phenomenal. He or she progresses from a helpless being controlled primarily by reflexes to a standing, walking individual who expresses many emotions. At no other time in the life span do human beings experience a more dramatic increase in growth and development as during infancy. To provide effective care and guidance for infants, it is essential to understand the basic developmental stages for that period of life.

DEVELOPMENTAL STAGES OF INFANTS

The following section highlights some of the physical, sensorimotor, intellectual, and social development of the wondrous first year. It does not completely describe all the characteristics of any stage nor does it mean to imply that all babies should perform each when indicated. It will, however, provide guidelines for using the activities that follow later in Part One.

The First Week

☐ Average weight at birth is approximately seven pounds for girls and seven pounds, five ounces for boys (six-and-a-half to nine pounds is considered an average weight range).

☐ Average length at birth is from eighteen to twenty-one inches.

☐ Arm, leg, and hand movements are controlled primarily by reflexes.

☐ Maintains "fetal" position while sleeping (sleeps seventeen to nineteen hours per day and takes about 8 naps).

- ☐ Requires seven to eight feedings.
- ☐ Is an individual in terms of appearance, feelings, and activity level.

The First Month

- ☐ Holds hand in a fist or slightly open.
- ☐ Stares at but does not reach for objects.
- ☐ Grasps rattle or other object when fingers are pried open, but drops it quickly.
- ☐ Follows objects moved vertically if the object is held about eight inches from eyes.
- ☐ Responds to human voices (prefers mother).
- ☐ Begins a bonding and attachment relationship with parents and significant others.
- ☐ Expresses needs with unique cries.
- ☐ Daily patterns of eating, sleeping, and crying are disorganized.
- ☐ Is alert for about one in every ten hours.

The Second Month

- ☐ Reflex control is beginning to disappear; actions are becoming more voluntary.
- ☐ Holds head up for a few seconds when supported in a sitting position.
- ☐ Upper body is becoming more active—arms are waved about or used to bat at objects, and hands may hold objects.
- ☐ Can be pulled to a sitting position, but the head is wobbly.
- ☐ Stares at surroundings.
- ☐ Sucks at sight of bottle or breast.
- ☐ Visually prefers looking at people rather than objects.
- ☐ Turns toward the source of sounds.

The Third Month

- ☐ Moves arms and legs more vigorously.
- ☐ Raises head and upper body when on stomach.
- ☐ Eyes begin moving together and are able to follow a slowly moving object.
- ☐ Does not search for bottle or toy that falls from sight.
- ☐ Explores body with hands.
- ☐ Coos, gurgles, and squeals when awake.
- ☐ Smiles in response to a recognized face or voice.

The Fourth Month

- ☐ Rolls from side to side when placed on stomach.
- ☐ Turns head in all directions.

- ☐ Focuses on objects placed at different distances.
- ☐ Uses hands to grasp objects.
- ☐ Enjoys play and other forms of socializing.
- ☐ Interested in new sounds and in imitating others.
- ☐ Handles, shakes, and bats objects; puts everything into mouth.

The Fifth Month

- ☐ Rolls from back to stomach and stomach to back.
- ☐ Enjoys being pulled to a standing position.
- ☐ Plays with rattles or other objects placed in the hand; reaches for objects with one or both hands.
- ☐ Transfers objects from hand to hand.
- ☐ Bangs objects together playfully.
- ☐ Turns deliberately toward familiar voices or sounds.
- ☐ Knows parents and siblings; may resist strangers.

The Sixth Month

- ☐ Sits with support.
- ☐ Creeps forward or backward.
- ☐ Handles and explores objects in a variety of ways.
- ☐ Hands are directed by eyes while reaching for objects.
- ☐ Experiences abrupt mood swings.
- ☐ Babbles by repeating same syllable: "da-da-da."

The Seventh Month

- ☐ Begins to crawl.
- ☐ Sits alone for several minutes.
- ☐ Enjoys standing in upright position for a few seconds without support.
- ☐ Tries to imitate sounds.
- ☐ Understands some first words.
- ☐ Recognizes self in mirror.
- ☐ Likes rhythm—being bounced, jostled, and jiggled.

The Eighth Month

- ☐ Crawls either forward or backward, even with an object in hand.
- ☐ Uses finger and thumb in pincerlike grasp to pick up objects.
- ☐ Develops an interest in food and food utensils.
- ☐ Babbles a variety of sounds.

- □ Enjoys social games such as "peek-a-boo."
- □ Waves "bye-bye."
- □ Claps and waves hands.

The Ninth Month

- □ Learns to crawl up steps.
- □ Stacks objects and places objects inside one another.
- □ Sits in chair.
- □ May build a two-block tower.
- □ Feeds self cracker, holds bottle, or uses handles to drink from a cup.
- □ Uncovers a hidden toy.
- □ Wants a caregiver in constant sight.
- □ Gives a toy or object on request or gestures on request (waves "bye-bye," for example).

The Tenth Month

- □ Stands alone with good balance.
- □ Walks while holding onto a support with both hands.
- □ Sits down from standing position.
- □ Looks up when hearing own name.
- □ Enjoys playing with bath water or food.
- □ Understands simple commands or requests.
- □ Can point to some body parts when requested.
- □ Searches for a hidden object if it is seen being hidden.
- □ Seeks approval for accomplishments.
- □ Becomes attached to favorite toy or blanket.

The Eleventh Month

- □ Takes a step or two without holding onto support.
- □ Enjoys rhymes and simple songs.
- □ Climbs up stairs.
- □ Shows understanding of the word "no" by stopping when requested.
- □ Turns pages of a book.
- □ Enjoys social games like rolling a ball back and forth.
- □ Takes one afternoon nap.
- □ Fusses when diaper needs changing; may pull off soiled diaper.

The Twelfth Month

- ☐ Walks for short time; prefers crawling.
- ☐ May climb out of crib or play yard.
- ☐ Builds two- or three-block tower.
- ☐ Enjoys "caring" for teddy bear or doll.
- ☐ Searches for hidden object even if it wasn't observed being hidden.
- ☐ Groups objects by shape or color.
- ☐ Distinguishes self as separate from others.
- ☐ Experiments with many actions.
- ☐ Shows interest in what adults do.

All infants have a number of basic needs. These include *basic physical needs* such as shelter, food, warmth, adequate clothing, health care, rest, and activity; *basic psychological needs* such as affection, trust, and security; and *basic learning needs* such as freedom to explore, solve problems, and have access to developmentally appropriate materials. Infants also have a *basic need for respect of their personhood*, which is met by encouraging their efforts and celebrating their special accomplishments.

The activities in this section are designed to help child-care personnel meet the various needs of the infants in their care. These activities cover a wide range, but fall into five general areas: physical care, warm relationships, physical activity, mental growth, and language growth. They can be adapted for use in any center, and are based on contemporary research into appropriate educational encounters for infants and toddlers.

PHYSICAL CARE

Infant and toddler care can be very complicated if all the mechanics are picked up on a trial-and-error basis. I've included the following suggestions so the tricks of the trade will more quickly become a part of your repertoire, resulting in more pleasurable child-care experiences.

Diapering

Check each baby's diaper at least once an hour to see if it needs to be changed. Change diapers on a waist-high table; use a safety strap to keep the child from falling. Try hanging a mobile above the changing table to capture the baby's attention and prevent excessive squirming. Also, sing or talk to the baby as you change her. Make the situation one in which the baby feels comfortable and loved.

Use changing paper or other clean disposable material under a child who has had a bowel movement. Make a solution of $\frac{1}{4}$ cup bleach per gallon of water (or one tablespoon per quart if you want a smaller amount) and keep it handy in a spray bottle. After you discard the disposable cover, spray the bleach solution thoroughly over the surface. Also, some child-care workers prefer to use disposable gloves for diapering even though it is not essential.

Wash the child with a soapy cloth each time you change him. Rinse with clear water and pat dry. This helps control rashes and chafed skin caused by bacteria and the saltiness of urine, and is especially crucial if you are using waterproof pants or disposable diapers.

Think twice about using baby powder. Pediatricians now advise against it because of several cases of death by inhalation among infants. In addition, talc, the basic ingredient of most baby powders, has been shown to be chemically related to asbestos, a known carcinogen.

Place diapers soiled by bowel movements in small plastic bags and tie them prior to disposal. They should be disposed of in a covered waste container lined with a plastic bag and designated for soiled diapers only.

Adults should wash their hands and the baby's after each diaper change. This helps prevent the spread of such potentially dangerous diseases as hepatitis.

At about nine months, the baby may be changed while standing. Supply favorite toys for the child to hold in each hand for balance.

Bathing

Once the baby loses her umbilical cord (usually at about ten days), she is ready for her first sponge bath. Wash the baby in a sink or basin; you may want to cushion the bottom with a bath pad. (Bath pads are spongy mats made especially for infant tubs.) Add several inches of warm water—not much warmer than your body temperature—and gently lower the baby into the sink.

Offer firm support as you bathe the baby. Reach around behind the baby's neck with your *nondominant* hand and gently grasp the top of the opposite shoulder with your thumb, making sure you support the baby at the armpit and ribs with your fingers. The baby's head should then be resting on your wrist and inside forearm. Hold the baby's opposite thigh with the other hand, making sure the inside thigh rests on your wrist.

Wipe each eye with a ball of cotton dampened with warm, clear water. Wipe from the inside corner to the outside of each eye. Also wipe around the face and neck (especially mouth, nose, and ears) with a moistened washcloth. Soften any dried mucus or other material until it can be wiped off easily. Do not poke anything inside the baby's nose or ears—wash only what you can see.

To wash the baby's scalp, reach under the baby's back and hold his head in your hand. Tilt it backward so that excess water can trickle away from the face. Squeeze a few drops of water from a dampened washcloth onto the scalp and use the washcloth to massage the scalp.

Sometimes babies are washed with water alone. But when using a mild, baby formula soap, be sure to do one part of the baby's body at a time. Remove the soap with at least two separate rinsings with a clean, moist cloth.

Talk and sing to the baby during the bath. Make it a fun time. When the child is clean, pat her dry with a clean, soft baby towel.

After a few months, babies become more and more excitable in the water. They will kick, splash, and slap at the water as they exercise their muscles in this enjoyable medium. At this time you may want to protect yourself with a plastic apron, or move babies to a tub for their baths. (Oh, your sore back!)

Children have many fears in bathtubs. Always make sure you remove the child from the tub before you pull the drain plug. Otherwise, the youngster may fear going down the drain with the bath water. Some children fear having their hair washed, probably because they cannot see what's happening to them. If the child is able to sit alone (after about six months), pause momentarily as you work the shampoo into the hair, and hold a mirror in front of him as you joyfully sculpt sudsy forms on his head. He may want to join you after a while!

Bottle Feeding

Pediatricians usually advise parents on the formula to use for their babies; the formulas are usually commercially prepared. Parents should bring an ample supply of the formula each day to the center, making sure there is enough to meet the needs of the baby while she is in your care.

Be sure to clearly label each bottle with the babies' names so you know who belongs to what formula. Each baby operates on an individual feeding schedule, so be sure to determine their schedules and the amounts of formula consumed during each feeding. Ask the families for that information and keep a feeding schedule chart in the nursery for easy reference.

Be sure to wash your hands thoroughly before feeding an infant. Cuddle the infant and talk to him; make eye contact. Hum a simple tune or talk to the baby in a soft voice. Feeding time should be a close, pleasurable social encounter.

Keep the bottle nipple full of formula so the infant does not swallow air. And never prop up the bottle and leave a baby alone with it. The baby may not have the motor control necessary to remove the bottle from her mouth before she falls asleep and could aspirate the formula. You also risk "bottle mouth syndrome," a condition that fosters tooth decay by allowing the liquid to lie in the mouth and coat the teeth with sugar.

Hold the infant on his side to aid the passage of the formula into the stomach. Prop a pillow behind the baby's back to help him maintain the side-lying position.

Babies usually require "burping" after a feeding in order to bring up any gas bubbles. Hold the baby looking over your shoulder and gently tap her back, alternately starting at the lower back and moving up to the shoulders.

Allow at least twenty minutes per feeding. Infants should not be rushed.

Introducing Solid Foods

Between the ages of three and six months (six months now being recommended by many doctors), the baby is ready to begin exploring solid foods. Developmental signs inform you when infants are ready for solid foods. They are able to sit with support, demonstrate a chewing reflex, and manipulate the tongue in order to transfer food to the back of the mouth. They may also indicate interest by watching others eat and leaning forward with their mouths open.

Cooperate with the parents when introducing new foods to baby. Parents will let you know when their infant's need for formula is decreasing. Find out what foods can be tolerated and how much is usually given per feeding. Also, resist the temptation to add sugar or salt—these foods in their natural state are quite tasty to infants.

Infant cereal, usually rice cereal mixed with formula or breast milk, is the first food. Rice is the grain that is least likely to provoke allergies. From rice cereal, infants can comfortably move to single grains such as barley, soy, or oats. Try each for several days to test for potential allergic reactions. Wheat cereal, the most likely to cause allergies, should be tried last.

It is important to begin the transition to solid foods slowly. Chewing skills are not mastered in a single day. Feed two or three teaspoons of very thin cereal initially, gradually working up to a larger portion of several tablespoons. Then introduce small amounts of vegetables and fruits. Try mashing a banana, pear, or baked apple.

Protein-rich foods such as meat, chicken, fish, egg yolk, yogurt, or mild cheese should be introduced last. Egg white, a greater source of allergic reaction, should be the final infant food to be introduced. (Check with the child's parents to see if he has allergic reactions to certain foods. Children are most sensitive to milk, eggs, and citrus fruits.)

Each baby has an individual tolerance for amounts of food. So, whether you choose homemade baby food, baby food in jars, or dehydrated foods, put reasonable amounts into a serving dish and discard what is left over. (Start with a few baby-spoonfuls and gradually increase the amount as the need for solid food increases.) The baby will signal you when she is done.

Never feed an infant directly from an open baby food jar and return the unused portion to the refrigerator. Food-borne diseases as well as common illnesses such as colds and influenza are more effectively controlled with careful sanitary practices.

After about six to nine months, or when teeth begin to emerge, the infant begins to prefer chomping on a teething ring or some hard foods rather than sucking on a pacifier. Try biscuits, large, hard unsalted pretzels, or bagels for that purpose.

When the child begins eating solid foods, a new challenge awaits you—getting her to use eating utensils. Follow these suggestions:

1. Allow the child to use his fingers during feeding time, but remember that he will be messy. This is an important initial step in getting the infant to feed himself.

2. Give the infant a spoon to play with as you feed her. Soon you will be able to help her fill the spoon and put it into her mouth. Naturally, she will miss the target a few times at first, but have patience—she will slowly improve with practice.

3. Let the infant play with an unbreakable empty cup while you are feeding him. When he seems to gain control, fill the cup with a few drops of a favorite liquid and let him try to drink from it. Again, there is bound to be some spilling, so give only a small portion at a time and allow plenty of practice. You may want to put a rubber band around the cup to help prevent it from slipping.

Sleeping

Most babies in their first month or two sleep for about two-thirds of each day (fifteen to sixteen hours). That sleep does not take place all at one time, but during sporadic patterns of wakefulness and sleep. However, at about the third month of life and throughout the first year, the infant spends less time sleeping (thirteen to fourteen hours) and has begun to sustain long periods of sleep. Infants still will not get all that sleep at night, however, and will need opportunities for naps during the day so the nursery should have an area that is airy, clean, and quiet enough that babies can sleep undisturbed. Essential to the area is a safe crib, for the United States Consumer Product Safety Commission has estimated that 150 to 200 infants die each year in crib accidents and another 40,000 must be treated by a doctor because they have been injured. Thus the commission has developed a series of suggestions for cribs manufactured since 1974:

1. Buy a crib with narrow spaces between the crib slats. Make sure the slats are no more than $2\frac{3}{8}$ inches apart, which will prevent babies from slipping between them.

2. Use a mattress that fits snugly. If you can fit more than two fingers between the mattress and crib, the mattress is too small.

3. Make sure there is as large a distance as possible between the top of the side rail and the mattress support. This will discourage the infant from trying to climb out. Most crib accidents happen when infants fall out while trying to climb.

4. Attach bumper pads securely to the inside of the crib. Make sure the pad goes around the entire crib, ties or snaps into place, and has at least six straps. Use the bumpers until the baby can pull up to a standing position.

5. Check any metal hardware on the crib. No sharp or rough edges should be evident. Locks and latches on the drop side of a crib should be safe and secure from accidental release by an infant inside the crib.

Comforting a Crying Baby

Crying is normal behavior for all babies; it is a powerful signal of need. First you may hear a gentle whimper, followed by some thrashing of arms and legs and active fussing, and finally comes the spasmodic outcry. There are few sounds that concern caregivers more than a baby's cry. Picking up the baby, hugging, singing, rocking, feeding, diapering, or covering him are common responses.

"Why Is He Crying So Much?"

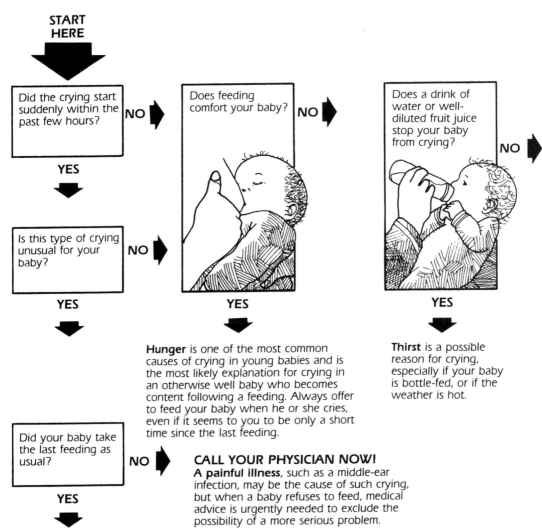

START HERE

Did the crying start suddenly within the past few hours? — **NO** ▶

YES ▼

Is this type of crying unusual for your baby? — **NO** ▶

YES ▼

Does feeding comfort your baby? — **NO** ▶

YES ▼

Does a drink of water or well-diluted fruit juice stop your baby from crying? — **NO** ▶

YES ▼

Did your baby take the last feeding as usual? — **NO** ▶

YES ▼

Hunger is one of the most common causes of crying in young babies and is the most likely explanation for crying in an otherwise well baby who becomes content following a feeding. Always offer to feed your baby when he or she cries, even if it seems to you to be only a short time since the last feeding.

Thirst is a possible reason for crying, especially if your baby is bottle-fed, or if the weather is hot.

CALL YOUR PHYSICIAN NOW!
A painful illness, such as a middle-ear infection, may be the cause of such crying, but when a baby refuses to feed, medical advice is urgently needed to exclude the possibility of a more serious problem.

An underlying disorder that is making your child feel sick is the most likely cause of unusual crying. If your baby is feeding normally, the problem is likely to be minor, possibly pain resulting from *gas* or *diaper rash*. Consult your physician if your baby becomes reluctant to feed or is still sick the next day.

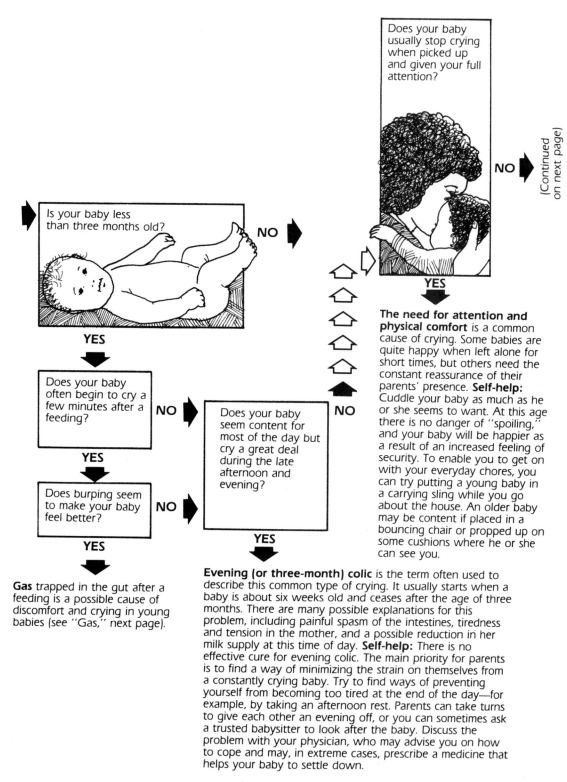

Does your baby usually stop crying when picked up and given your full attention?

NO (Continued on next page)

YES

Is your baby less than three months old?

NO

YES

Does your baby often begin to cry a few minutes after a feeding?

NO

YES

Does burping seem to make your baby feel better?

NO

YES

Does your baby seem content for most of the day but cry a great deal during the late afternoon and evening?

NO

YES

The need for attention and physical comfort is a common cause of crying. Some babies are quite happy when left alone for short times, but others need the constant reassurance of their parents' presence. **Self-help:** Cuddle your baby as much as he or she seems to want. At this age there is no danger of "spoiling," and your baby will be happier as a result of an increased feeling of security. To enable you to get on with your everyday chores, you can try putting a young baby in a carrying sling while you go about the house. An older baby may be content if placed in a bouncing chair or propped up on some cushions where he or she can see you.

Gas trapped in the gut after a feeding is a possible cause of discomfort and crying in young babies (see "Gas," next page).

Evening (or three-month) colic is the term often used to describe this common type of crying. It usually starts when a baby is about six weeks old and ceases after the age of three months. There are many possible explanations for this problem, including painful spasm of the intestines, tiredness and tension in the mother, and a possible reduction in her milk supply at this time of day. **Self-help:** There is no effective cure for evening colic. The main priority for parents is to find a way of minimizing the strain on themselves from a constantly crying baby. Try to find ways of preventing yourself from becoming too tired at the end of the day—for example, by taking an afternoon rest. Parents can take turns to give each other an evening off, or you can sometimes ask a trusted babysitter to look after the baby. Discuss the problem with your physician, who may advise you on how to cope and may, in extreme cases, prescribe a medicine that helps your baby to settle down.

Continued from previous page

Are you feeling tense or overtired OR has there been a recent major domestic upheaval?

 NO ▶

Consult your physician if you are unable to make a diagnosis from this chart.

YES

▼

Sensitivity to increased tension

in the home and particularly in the mother can make a baby unsettled and more likely to cry. **Self-help:** A baby will usually settle down to a new routine or in new surroundings within a week or so, although you will need to give more attention and reassurance than usual during this time. If you think that the cause of your baby's crying could be a reaction to tension in yourself, try to find ways of reducing any strain you are under. Discuss this with your physician, who may be able to suggest ways of helping. A crying baby is frustrating, and much child abuse starts when an overly tired parent must cope with an irritable baby. Seek advice from your physician or a child-abuse hotline if you think you could lose your temper and become abusive.

Gas

Young babies often swallow air during feedings, especially those eager feeders who gulp greedily at the start of every feeding. Excess gas in the gut causes regurgitation of feedings and may be linked to discomfort and crying, so it is a good idea to spend a little time helping your baby to bring up gas after each feeding. Some of the best positions for burping are shown below.

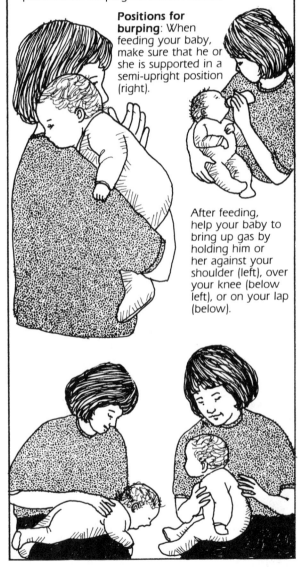

Positions for burping: When feeding your baby, make sure that he or she is supported in a semi-upright position (right).

After feeding, help your baby to bring up gas by holding him or her against your shoulder (left), over your knee (below left), or on your lap (below).

From *Children: How to Understand Their Symptoms,* by the American Medical Association. Copyright 1986 by Random House, Inc. Adapted with permission.

Sensitivity to pain, hunger, thirst, or physical distress are the most frequent causes of crying. Each seems to have a distinct pattern—a hunger cry is slow and rhythmic in nature, while a pain cry is sudden, loud, and long. You will learn to recognize these cries as an infant's desperate attempt at communication. You'll quickly become successful at translating cries such as the hunger cry and the wet cry, and learn to take the appropriate measures to supply necessary relief.

Sometimes, however, a baby just cries and cries and you can find nothing wrong; there is no apparent reason for it. This is acutally quite common. The screaming and thrashing may become difficult for you to accept, especially since the infant seems to be saying, "Try your best to get me to stop, but it just won't work!"

The most commonly expressed concern among caregivers is how to respond to such crying. "Will I risk spoiling the child if I respond to every whimper or cry?" "Will the baby feel rejected and unloved if I don't react?" No one knows the answers to these questions, but the advice I always offer is that if we are going to make a mistake, it is safer to offer more affection than less. The baby needs you, so respond positively with your calming efforts.

Keep in mind that, in most cases, crying is just a part of infancy—all babies cry. It does not mean that something is seriously wrong each time a baby cries. But if a baby cries more often than you think is normal or suddenly starts to cry in an unusual way or for no apparent reason, consult "Why Is He Crying So Much?" (pp. 10–12). Formulated by the American Medical Association for parents, its step-by-step approach to deciphering babies' cries may also be useful to other caregivers.

ESTABLISHING WARM RELATIONSHIPS

Some new parents tend to view their newborn as a helpless blob or lump of raw clay ready to be controlled, directed, and molded into whatever form adults wish. But the baby is a unique person right from the start with his or her own special rights, feelings, and needs. The new child is a complex bundle of genetic potential and what he will eventually become depends not only on that particular potential but also on the interactions he has with his world.

The infant's first need is physical care and comfort. This is the most basic necessity even before birth. Important as physical care is, however, it does not comprise the baby's only basic need. She may have all the physical care one can expect, but still may not develop normally if she is not given proper attention by warm, responsive adults. People are necessary! Adults must offer love and security to the child; she needs to feel protected, relieved when distressed, and confident that others care about her. The child must know that she is loved but also that she is respected. These special feelings provide infants with the emotional security necessary to develop well.

☐ Share as much body contact with the infant as possible. Nuzzle the baby, hug him, rock him in your arms, and offer other kinds of warmth and touching experiences.

☐ Communicate your love and respect through nonverbal means. Always make physical and eye contact when you interact with babies.

☐ Talk to the baby courteously and considerately. Let her know that she is valued as a person by treating her as courteously as you would an adult. For example, a mother carried her infant into a child-care center holding him so that he was facing away from her. The mother stopped to talk with an aide, all the while holding her baby in the same position and virtually ignoring him. Soon the infant began to fuss and whimper. A caregiver responded to the situation by selecting one of the baby's favorite rattles from the toybox and taking it to him: "Are you crying because you don't have your favorite toy to play with? Here it is. The next time you want it, just let me know." The baby immediately stopped crying and clutched the rattle. Reaching for the caregiver and accepted into her arms, the little boy showed clearly how he responded to the caregiver's positive attitude toward him.

☐ Lose any feelings of self-consciousness and offer the babies a little bit of "pizzazz." Get down on the floor, dance around, sing, and feel free to participate in the interactive play activities so loved by infants.

Interactive Play Activities

Mimicking

The caregiver encourages the baby to imitate gestures or sounds. Waving "bye-bye" or stretching out the arms to indicate "so big" are favorites. Coughing, sniffing through the nose, or making simple sounds such as "ahr-r-r-r" amuse the infant for great periods of time.

Drop and Fetch

Babies seem to drop things at first simply to see what happens. They hear the noise and turn to see what transpired. Their great joy comes, however, when the caregiver becomes involved and picks up the object. This soon becomes great entertainment; the baby drops and the caregiver fetches. To some caregivers, this repetition seems pointless and boring. However, when we consider the social play resulting from the interaction, we realize that this game is an important source of learning about the world.

Peek-a-Boo

Babies enjoy this traditional adult-infant participation game. The caregiver begins the game by hiding her face in back of her hands or a blanket, suddenly showing her face, and saying, "Peek-a-boo. I see you," to the baby.

Pat-a-Cake

Infants enjoy this simple rhyme game because of its joyful sounds and spirited physical activity. Be prepared to repeat the game several times with your engrossed partners! (Remember that your interest, or lack of it, will influence the level of baby's play. So if you get tired of the game, switch to another.)

Pat-a-cake, pat-a-cake, baker's man.
    (Clap baby's hands together)
Bake me a cake as fast as you can.
Roll it
    (Roll baby's hands)
And pat it
    (Pat baby's hands)
And mark it with B
    (Make a letter B on baby's tummy)
And put it in the oven for baby (*or baby's first name*) and me!

Action Games

Traditional favorites are jiggling the baby above one's head, swinging him from the chest to between the knees, tickling the baby's trunk, or bouncing him on a knee to a familiar rhythmic verse. Several examples are offered later in this section.

Give and Take

This is a popular favorite, which begins with the caregiver giving the child a favorite toy and saying, "Now I'll give it to you." Back and forth activity is encouraged as the caregiver says, "Now you give it to me."

Gotcha

Once babies are able to creep or crawl, they enjoy the challenge of moving away and being chased to a warning, "I'm gonna getcha." The caregiver should let the baby crawl for a while and grab him or her, exclaiming, "Gotcha!" The baby should be given a big hug or tickle after each episode.

Hide-and-Seek

Babies laugh with glee as their caretakers repeatedly call their names while searching behind doors or in wastebaskets or drawers for the "lost infant."

Facial Examination

Older infants punctuate their growing social awareness by showing an interest in a caregiver's facial features. The baby may grab the nose, grasp eyeglasses, touch an ear, or poke at your eyes. By guiding the infant with words such as "Easy, easy," the caregiver informs the baby that such exploration must be done carefully. You may want to name each feature as the child touches it, eventually encouraging the child to touch the same feature on his or her face. By continually following this pattern, the child may be able to respond appropriately by the end of the first year when asked to "Show me your nose (or other feature)."

PHYSICAL ACTIVITY

During the infant's earliest days, learning occurs mainly through sensory stimulation. Tease the infant's senses, for even a day-old child can follow moving objects, feel changes in temperature, and move the head in response to sounds. Infants move from these first reactions to exploring all the parts that make up their small bodies. They are fascinated with the realization that "Those wiggly toes down there are part of me, too, and I can make them move or stop!" Infants enjoy such new discoveries and revel in activities that help them master new knowledge. Capitalize and build on this natural curiosity for it helps support future desires to explore. The fingers wish to touch what the eyes see—the child wants to smell, taste, and squeeze everything in sight. The joy of every new discovery is an exquisite sensation for infants. So the earliest types of activities should be physical in nature. The following list offers some examples.

- ☐ Rub smooth satin on the child's cheek.
- ☐ Tickle the baby's lips with a soft piece of terry cloth.
- ☐ Hold a favorite toy in front of the baby and encourage him to reach for it. If the child does not participate, hold it closer and gradually pull it farther away as he learns to reach.
- ☐ Suspend a favorite toy above the baby with elastic so she can look at it, reach out and bat it, and watch it move. Help her hit it by moving her hand.
- ☐ Get a toy that can be attached to a flat surface by means of a suction cup. Encourage the baby to reach for it and grasp it.
- ☐ Hold the baby on your lap. Place a favorite squeaky toy in front of him so he must reach for it. Squeak the toy and reinforce the baby's efforts with praise and smiles.
- ☐ Hang a mobile over the crib so the baby can look at it while lying on her back. Occasionally place a brightly patterned sheet on baby's crib so she can be visually stimulated when she's on her stomach, too.
- ☐ Babies are attracted by bright objects. Move a bright object or penlight across the baby's line of vision until he follows the light with his eyes.
- ☐ Hold a safe, unbreakable mirror above the child in the crib. Place it about seven or eight inches from the baby's eyes.
- ☐ Lay the baby on a variety of surfaces during feeding, changing, rest, or play.
- ☐ Provide toys with different kinds of surfaces, such as plastic, cloth, furry, soft, smooth.
- ☐ Stimulate the baby's hearing by tying a bell to her bootie or around her wrist, putting a rattle in her hand, setting a metronome near her, talking or singing, rustling paper near her ear, or playing soft music periodically.
- ☐ Say a series of babbles (*ma, pa, ba, ga*) so the child hears them easily. Say these sounds or the baby's name in various situations. Reward his attempts to imitate you.

- ☐ Call the baby's name from the side of the crib opposite where she is looking. If she doesn't respond, gently turn her toward you and offer a bright smile.
- ☐ Call the baby's name over and over again. Sometimes sing it and sometimes vary your pitch and inflection. Try to get him to look at you when you do this.
- ☐ Smile and talk as you hold the baby. Hold her about twelve to eighteen inches from your face. Tickle her or toss her gently, trying to make her laugh and gurgle.
- ☐ Use a pull toy that makes some type of sound. Pull it slowly back and forth in front of the baby.
- ☐ Seat the child upright in a soft chair and support his head with pillows. Hold a toy or bright object in front of the baby and encourage him to initiate head support. Gradually reduce the support until you see how well the baby keeps his balance. Repeat the procedure.
- ☐ Place a soft, small object (a sponge or a piece of soft cloth) in the baby's hand and wrap her fingers around it. Take your hand away. Repeat the procedure if she drops it. Then vary the texture of the objects placed in the baby's hand.
- ☐ Seat the child on your lap facing you and pull him up by having him grasp your fingers.
- ☐ Stand the baby on your lap and bounce her up and down, smiling and saying a series of babbles.
- ☐ Help the child to stand by placing his hands on the corners of the crib.

Other games and activities appropriate for infants are discussed on the following pages.

Crib Toys

Use crib toys to attract the infant to new objects and to give her practice reaching and grasping. Toys varying in color, texture, and sound have great appeal to the young infant.

Crib Gym

Make a crib gym (as shown in Figure 1) to give the infant plenty of practice in reaching and grasping. Stretch a length of heavy-gauge elastic across the crib, and attach it on both sides. To that piece of elastic tie several shorter lengths so they hang down a short distance. Then securely tie a rattle, a plastic spoon, beads, bells, or other toys too large for the infant to swallow to each piece of elastic. The infant will begin to use his gym by hitting the toys and enjoying the bouncing action. Later, he will begin to grasp the objects with his fingers.

Cuddly Toys

Woolly or furry teddy bears, bunnies, kittens, and other soft toys increase an infant's feeling of comfort. Be careful that the infant cannot pull off and swallow eyes or other parts. Such features should be embroidered or painted on for safety.

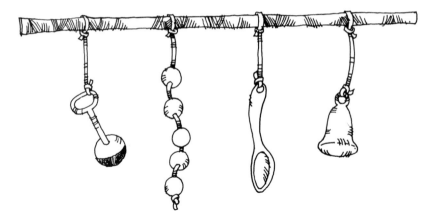

Figure 1

Caution: Some states do not permit soft cuddly toys in child-care facilities for sanitary reasons. Check with the appropriate agency to determine your state's regulations.

Music Boxes

The enjoyable sounds of colorfully decorated music boxes stimulate the child's developing hearing skills.

Rings and Rattles

Give the infant a variety of toys to explore. She will initially select the ones that are easier to grasp (such as plastic rings), but eventually she will move to ones that require greater finger control (plastic rattles). Vary the toys so that the child will be exposed to many textures, shapes, and sounds.

Pacifiers

One of the baby's most obvious pleasures is sucking. The sucking reflex is present at birth and remains strong until about nine months or a year. Many babies satisfy their need to suck through feeding or play; others require more prolonged sucking episodes. Check with the parents to determine babies' needs. Ask parents to send along the needed pacifiers when they bring their babies to the center.

Some people are opposed to pacifiers because they feel that prolonged sucking may influence the position of baby's teeth. However, most dentists agree that sucking on objects even into the second or third year has far less influence on the baby's teeth than was once supposed. If using a pacifier, remember that it is not meant to be stuck into the mouth to quiet a crying baby, but should be used to satisfy the child's strong urge to suck.

A word of caution: Infants tend to drop pacifiers. When they land on the floor or any other unsanitary surface, sanitize them by immersing them in boiling water for twenty-five minutes. Allow them to cool before giving them back to the babies.

Squeeze Toys

Make squeeze toys from vividly colored fabric stuffed with old pantyhose. A doughnut-shaped toy is probably the most appropriate. Babies enjoy holding the toy and squeezing it with their fingers. Variety stores sell such toys with noise-makers inside, but before selecting one, make sure it is safely constructed so the noisemaker won't fall out and be swallowed by the child.

Hand Chimes

Hang a bamboo chime within reach of the baby and watch her bat the tubes to enjoy the tinkly sounds. To make a bamboo chime, attach pieces of yarn or elastic to short bamboo tubes as shown in Figure 2. Tie each piece of yarn or elastic around a bamboo stick. To hang the chimes, thread a long piece of yarn through the stick and tie the ends together.

Puff Balls

Wad up some old fabric (shirts, legs of trousers, pajamas, skirts, etc.) and shove it into the toe of a stocking or sock. Tie a knot in the end and cut off the excess stocking material.

Pop-Beads

Show the infant or toddler some large pop-beads (large enough so the infant cannot swallow them if he puts them into his mouth). Pull them apart and hold the pieces close to each other. The child may at first only look at the two parts, but eventually he will attempt to grasp them and put them back together. Because infants enjoy placing new toys or objects into their mouths, avoid any toys that can be easily swallowed.

Figure 2

Exercises

Pedal Pusher

Exercise your infant while she is awake. Hold her feet while you pedal her legs gently. After a while she will return the pressure against your hands.

Bath Exercises

Bath time affords the child an excellent opportunity to exercise his fingers. Allow him to pick up the sponge or washcloth and try to squeeze out the water. Bath toys with pleasing sounds (such as a rubber ducky that squeaks) or delightful textures are valuable additions to baby's bath time.

Pull-Ups

Grasp the child's hands and pull her from a lying position to a sitting position. After a period of time, she will learn to pull herself up as you help by continuing to hold her hands.

Eye Got It

Hold an attractive toy about eight to ten inches from the infant's eyes. After you are sure that he sees it, move it slowly until he follows it with his eyes.

Creep and Crawl

Dress the child in loose clothing so she will be unrestricted in creeping, crawling, turning, or pushing activities. Provide a safe, clean area in which the child can freely crawl about. There should be several toys and books nearby for her to look at, explore, and grasp. Initiate exercise activities with the infant: move her arms and legs, hold her in a sitting position, encourage her to turn, push, creep, and crawl. Hold the child and toss her gently into the air. Hold her upright while giving her gentle support. Bounce her to music to give her initial feelings of motion.

I Can Stand

Pull the infant to a standing position and allow him to feel the weight on his legs. Support him by the hips or waist as he struggles to maintain balance. Later, the infant can be urged to pull himself up by holding on to the rail of his crib or playpen.

Floor Space

At about six months of age, babies begin to creep, roll, and crawl. They need space to kick, squirm, and work their busy arms and legs. Mattresses, pillows, or furniture cushions placed on the floor add interesting challenges for the babies as they go through, over, and under them. Offer such safe, easy-to-clean floor coverings as vinyl coated mats or pads for them to practice their emerging skills.

As they crawl, babies enjoy reaching for things and looking at moving objects or bright patterns, so infant-care facilities should offer stimulation related to these interests. Colorful floor coverings, large bright laminated pictures of people, animals, nursery rhyme characters, flowers, or popular childhood characters, and an unbreakable mirror mounted on the walls at floor level bring immense enjoyment to the baby's eager explorations.

The First Step

Place the baby in a walker where he can practice extending his legs and making walking movements without having to support his full weight. Gradually, he will learn to stand by himself. When this happens, squat in front of the infant, grasp both his hands, and encourage him to step toward you. He may be reluctant or scared—if so, don't force him. Stop and try again later. Slowly increase the distance as the child gains skill, comfort, and confidence. Soon he will be taking his first independent steps, usually clutching a favorite toy for security.

MENTAL GROWTH

Up to the time of between seven and nine months of age, an infant's perception of the world is quite limited. She perceives everything as being a part of her. Objects do not exist unless the infant is looking at, listening to, or touching them. When objects are at hand, the infant does not understand that they are independent of her. When she shakes a rattle, for example, the infant examines herself and her actions, not the rattle itself. In fact, she may not even glance at the rattle.

At about seven to nine months of age, babies experience huge mental progress. They begin to realize that the world exists beyond themselves; objects exist even though they cannot be seen, heard, or felt. Now, when a toy (or a person) leaves the infant, it does not disappear from existence; the baby may fuss or even cry to get the toy (or you) back again. Infants understand that objects can be explored actively as separate entities from their own existence. Now, when the baby picks up a rattle, he is not as much interested in his own actions but in the unique sounds, sights, or other pleasurable sensations the rattle brings. The baby seems to wonder, "I wonder what will happen if I shake this rattle harder." It makes a louder noise—what a fascinating discovery! At about twelve months, babies begin to remember names of the special objects or people in their environment. They remember what a "teddy" or "blankie" is and often are able to search for a "ball" when you ask, even if the object is not in the immediate environment.

At twelve months, then, babies will understand much of what is said to them. Chattering happily in response to adult initiated interactions, she lets everyone know that she is aware of objects and people. She seeks to discover everything she can about an object. She explores with her fingers, tastes, bangs, drops, and tests everything with all five senses. In order to foster this deep interest in the world around her, it is important to offer a stimulating environment. Provide a variety of new and interesting experiences so the baby will remain alert and curious for increasingly longer periods of time. The following ideas are but a small sample of the wide range of activities you can use to stimulate mental growth during infancy.

☐ *Offer a variety of toys.* Babies learn most easily by doing something with people or with objects such as rattles, balls, or large beads that respond to them as they act, not by just sitting and watching.

☐ *Use common safe household objects.* Babies appear to exercise all their senses with an object. They hold it and watch it as they turn it over or shake it. They try to put it into their mouths or rub it against their faces. Even while awaiting a meal in the high chair, the baby may bang objects endlessly to hear the sound or test the texture of the foods with his fingers. The world is a fascinating collection of sights and sounds! Pots and pans are especially interesting to infants. Their clang and clatter are a great motivator for baby as he gradually deepens his understanding of the relationship between his own actions and the results of those actions.

☐ *Provide a variety of experiences.* Place the baby in her stroller and take her for special walks, trips to the park, or on other short excursions. She will enjoy

---

Choosing Safe Toys

Yes   No

____ ____   1. Is it too large to be swallowed, stuck in the ear, or jammed into the nose?

____ ____   2. Can the detachable parts such as button eyes or bells be swallowed, stuck in the ear, or jammed into the nose?

____ ____   3. Can little parts easily break off?

____ ____   4. Are there sharp corners or dangerous points?

____ ____   5. Is the construction solid and durable?

____ ____   6. Is the material nontoxic?

____ ____   7. Can parts pinch or catch hair?

____ ____   8. Is it possible for long cords to accidentally strangle the child?

____ ____   9. Can a child use the toy independently?

____ ____   10. Can plastic bags or large containers suffocate the child?

SOUND SIGHT SMELL TOUCH TASTE

MAILBOX

BEADS

the stimulation of new experiences of all kinds, especially if the caregiver accompanies them with a verbal description. ("Look at the pretty flowers, Sharman. Let's see if they smell as good as they look.")

☐ *Let babies participate.* Infants enjoy listening to adult conversations. Some grow quite excitable when such communication takes place, many to the point of trying to join in. Let the baby listen to adult conversation and encourage him to sputter and gush while trying to talk along.

Play to Learn

Imitation and verbal stimulation help children to develop conceptual skills, so offer plenty of opportunities for good, old-fashioned interactive play. Respond to the baby's actions with warmth and encouragement. Babies learn from the reactions of significant people around them; they may learn to go forward and/or to avoid a sense of failure at all costs. Use a variety of mental and social games, verbally label objects ("Here is your *teddy bear.*"), read books to infants, sing songs, and let them explore during any activity. Some planned play activities include these.

☐ Allow the child to handle a rattle or some other toy for a short time. Put the toy under a blanket and see if the baby will search for it. If not, shake the rattle and make a sound to attract him. Take the blanket off if the baby does not respond. Continue until he begins to understand the idea of object permanence, that is, that an object still exists even though it is out of sight.

☐ Hold an attractive, colorful toy above the infant as she lies on her back. Keep it steady until you are sure she sees it, then move it slowly from one side to another to encourage her to turn her head and exercise her neck muscles as she reaches for the toy.

☐ Hold your forefinger so the baby can grasp it. Slip it away from the baby but hold it before him. As the baby tries to catch it, quickly bend your finger down at the middle joint. He'll laugh heartily when you let him win, which should be most of the time.

☐ Put a bright object about twelve inches from the baby, first on one side and then on the other. Encourage the baby to turn from side to side while following the object.

☐ Place the baby on the floor a few inches from a favorte toy. Make a sound with the toy to attract the child to it. Reward the baby if she is able to crawl and reach it. Gradually increase the distance between the baby and the toy.

Don't be frustrated if your efforts fail to result in immediate success. It takes much repetition and practice before a baby or toddler is ready to acquire specific skills. Don't always expect them to do something correctly the first time or to remember today what they were able to do the day before. Don't rush them. They love to experiment, but only in a relaxed, trusting, accepting environment.

The groundwork established during a child's first years influences the degree and direction of succeeding growth. By the time the child is two years old, he is ready for new challenges—experiences in which he tries to make further sense of the world he is getting to know. Every mind-stirring event he encounters only adds to his wonder. So it is vitally important that you extend the direct learning experiences of the earlier years and encourage the curiosity and desire to learn that can last for the rest of their lives.

LANGUAGE GROWTH

The acquisition of language is one of the most marvelous accomplishments of human beings. It starts during infancy, usually before four months of age, with babbling. Prior to that time, babies tend to make only certain nasal sounds such as the vowel sounds "ee" in "see," the "oo" as in "moo," or the "ah" as in "hot," and the consonant sounds formed in the back of the mouth such as "g" as in "go" or "k." But, at about four months, babies experiment with varieties of repetitious babbling sounds, such as "da-da-da-da." Babbling is characterized by repetitious syllables and vocal experimentation which continues in different forms until the child is about eighteen months old.

You can encourage your babies to vocalize by your eager responses to their attempts. Imitate their babbles, smile, talk, bounce them on your knee, or hug them for their efforts. You may not increase their babbling or change the sounds they utter until about six or eight months of age, but eventually your efforts do pay off. Babies will more often make sounds they hear than the ones they do not. The following suggestions are offered to help you provide a language rich environment.

Sound Games

Let the child know you are interested in her babbling or gurgling. Imitate her sounds and encourage the baby to alternate her sounds with yours. Eventually, you will become so engrossed in the game that it will be difficult to tell who is leading whom. After a period of imitating sounds, change your pronunciation of the sound. For example, if the child has been saying "ma, ma, ma" (as in "mama"), change the pronunciation after a while to sound like the "ma" in "make."

Babies enjoy playing with their fingers and toes, and this opens up many more game possibilities. "This Little Piggy Went to Market," "Thumbkin," and other games combining movements of fingers or toes with rhymes or simple tunes are fun for infants or toddlers.

This Little Piggy Went to Market

This little piggy went to market.
  (Gently squeeze thumb or large toe)
This little piggy stayed home.
  (Repeat on pointer finger or second toe)

This little piggy had roast beef.
> *(Repeat on third finger or toe)*

This little piggy had none.
> *(Repeat on fourth finger or toe)*

This little piggy cried, "Wee-wee-wee! I can't find my way home." [or]
This little piggy cried, "Wee-wee-wee!" all the way home.
> *(Repeat on small finger or toe)*

My Turtle

This is my turtle.
He lives in a shell.
He likes his home very well.
> *(Put palms together horizontally, bottom fingers folded under)*

He pokes his head out when he wants to eat,
> *(Poke middle finger out of bottom hand)*

And pulls it back when he wants to sleep.
> *(Put finger back in hand)*

Thumbkin
(Sung to the tune of "Are You Sleeping?")

Where is thumbkin? Where is thumbkin?
> *(Show fist with thumb folded in)*

Here I am! Here I am!
> *(Extend thumb only)*

How are you today, sir?
Very well, I thank you.
> *(Wiggle thumb)*

Run away. Run away.
> *(Hide thumb)*

Continue finger motions with the following verses:

Where is pointer?
Where is tall man?
Where is ring man?
Where is pinky?
Where are all men?

Talking with Baby

Early childhood specialist Alice Sterling Honig once commented:

> Caregivers must be great talkers. Babies may come silent into group care. Some families may not know how it is to nourish the early coos and babbles and words of infants and toddlers . . . A caregiver who

boosts language is giving the priceless gift of great power to babies. The power to communicate needs, wishes.*

Caregivers play an important role in early language acquisition. They can serve as a stimulator of and model for language whenever they interact with babies.

"Billy is getting dressed now. Now we'll put on his shirt—this arm goes through here and that arm through there. Now slip the shirt over Billy's head, peek-a-boo! Now we'll put on Billy's pants—one leg goes through here, and the other leg goes through there. Now Billy's socks—one on this foot and one on that foot. Now we're almost done. Whoops—we forgot Billy's shoes! One for this foot and one for that foot. Now Billy's all dressed!"

Similar language experiences can be shared during bath time ("Now wash Billy's tummy. Rub, rub Billy's tummy with soap."); feeding ("Here is Billy's bottle. Oh, Billy looks so hungry today."); diapering ("First we'll wipe Billy and get him all clean. There . . . now the dry diaper will feel much better."); or other routines. The main thing is to try to put all the child's actions into words. A word of caution, however: Many beginning child-care workers, especially those who are not parents, sometimes feel peculiar talking to babies. Because babies do not "talk back," these caregivers see infants as being essentially like plants and unresponsive to their talk. However, through increasing meaningful interaction, you are indeed helping the infant move from simple, random vocalizations to more effective means of communication.

Babies and Books

One of the most interesting discoveries verified over the past few years is that the first steps in learning to read actually begin shortly after birth, when infants hear language spoken around them. Whether it is during feeding time or at bath time, the gentle conversations, rhymes, songs, and other vocal experiences begin to set the stage for emerging literacy. When books are added to the warm physical encounters, the child associates pleasure with reading.

Hold the baby comfortably in your lap and turn the pages of a book that has large, simple pictures. Point to different objects in the picture and name them for the child. Tell the child something about the picture, such as, "Look, Heather, here is a doll. It looks just like your doll." Do so in a pleasant voice so that everything will add up to a comfortable experience. Remember that the baby's listening vocabulary will become much larger than her speaking vocabulary, so long before she is able to say the word herself, she will be able to point to a picture if you say the word for her. For example, if you say, "Heather, show me the kitty," she will proudly point to the picture.

*Honig, Alice Sterling (1981, November). What are the needs of infants? *Young Children*, 5.

By the time the baby is about a year old, he will be able to turn the pages of appropriate-sized books as he "reads" all by himself. Babies find books containing large pictures of familiar single objects, animals, or people most stimulating. Try making a *texture book,* a book that contains pictures and shapes made from materials of various textures. These books appeal to the infants' touch as well as to their sight, inviting them to explore and experience each page.

Sturdy picture books are most appropriate for infants, but their awareness of the printed word should not be limited only to such print media. Print surrounds the infant each day. Television commercials, cereal boxes, newspapers, billboards, letters in the mail, greeting cards, calendars, and a variety of other sources naturally introduce children to printed language. Of course, the baby will not read these things, but exposure to print greatly influences the child's eventual acquisition of reading skills.

Singing to Baby

Babies love being sung to, especially if the songs are accompanied by activity. Many caregivers hesitate to sing because they lack confidence in their voices. Don't worry about your voice—infants don't care if you sound like Barbra Streisand or a worn out foghorn. They simply love to hear you sing. Also, don't worry about finding a composed song for every situation. Make up the tune and lyrics as you go along based on whatever you happen to be doing at the moment. Sing to the baby as you feed her, change her, dress her, play with her, bathe her, and so on. Look directly at the baby while you sing. Smile, and try to get her to "sing" along with you.

Beginning songs and rhymes can help the child learn to associate word labels with her body and with familiar objects in her surroundings. Consider the enthusiastic response most infants will give when you start with the baby's big toe and grasp each toe in turn while reciting "This Little Piggy Went to Market." These games and rhymes not only establish special closeness and warmth between child and caregiver, but they also provide experiences in auditory sequencing, anticipation of outcomes, and imitation.

Mother Goose rhymes and other action songs or games are both stimulating and enjoyable for children of this age. Infants learn to listen and relate to new forms of language through these media. Some popular tunes and rhymes for infants include the following:

Row, Row, Row Your Boat

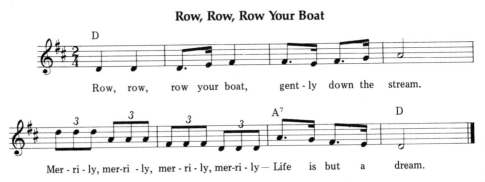

Old MacDonald

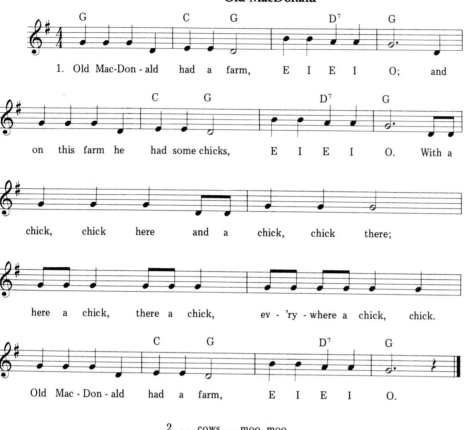

1. Old Mac-Don-ald had a farm, E I E I O; and on this farm he had some chicks, E I E I O. With a chick, chick here and a chick, chick there; here a chick, there a chick, ev-'ry-where a chick, chick. Old Mac-Don-ald had a farm, E I E I O.

2. ...cows...moo, moo...
3. ...pigs...oink, oink...
4. ...ducks...quack, quack...

Twinkle, Twinkle, Little Star

Twink-le, twink-le, lit-tle star; how I won-der what you are. Up a-bove the world so high, like a dia-mond in the sky. Twink-le, twink-le, lit-tle star; how I won-der what you are.

Are You Sleeping?

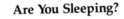

Are you sleep - ing, are you sleep - ing, Broth - er John? Broth - er John? Morn - ing bells are ring - ing, morn-ing bells are ring - ing. Ding, dong, ding. Ding, dong, ding.

Cradle Song

Sleep, ba - by, sleep. Thy fa - ther tends the sheep. Thy moth - er shakes the dream - land tree, and down come love - ly dreams for thee. Sleep, ba - by, sleep.

The Farmer in the Dell

1. The farm - er in the dell, the farm - er in the dell, heigh ho the der - ry oh, the farm - er in the dell.

2. The farmer takes a wife, the farmer takes a wife, heigh ho the derry oh, the farmer takes a wife.
3. The wife takes a child . . .
4. The child takes a nurse . . .
5. The nurse takes a dog . . .
6. The dog takes a cat . . .
7. The cat takes a rat . . .
8. The rat takes the cheese . . .
9. The cheese stands alone . . .

Because we often associate these special songs and rhymes with childhood, there is a tendency to think that they are the only forms of music to which infants should be exposed. However, babies should experience many forms of music, for they appear to greatly appreciate variety. Try some of the following:

□ *Folk music.* Babies enjoy the repeated verses and simple melodies.

□ *Jazz.* Bouncy rhythms are especially appreciated during active times.

□ *Classical.* Louder, fast-paced varieties attract most babies; try Bach's Brandenburg Concerto no. 2.

□ *Lullabies.* These soothe and calm babies during periods of quiet rest and prior to sleep.

SUMMARY

The infant's life is replete with dependencies that special adults must satisfy. The most important are physical care and comfort as well as emotional security. Babies need loving caregivers who meet these basic needs and help them establish a sense of security and well-being within the environment. Infants become attached to adults through these satisfying experiences and gain the confidence and enthusiasm to explore all the exciting new phenomena around them. Babies increase their power of concentration, mental skills, and sensorimotor development as they practice diligently over and over the actions necessary to master playroom toys. Helping babies in this process requires a caregiver's deep understanding of what toys are most appropriate for her babies; the caregiver chooses the most meaningful and worthwhile toys when she is able to match new toys to the level of the baby's already acquired skills. Appendix A summarizes the characteristics of infants at different stages of development and suggests appropriate toys and activities for each. Examine this appendix carefully and use it as a handy reference for the period of infancy as well as for the rest of the early childhood years.

PART TWO

FOR TODDLERS

From about one year until three, children are often referred to as toddlers. Many of their babylike characteristics remain, but new and more childlike behaviors emerge. Toddlers become walkers who practice their newfound skill with fervor. They become talkers who take great pride in communicating ideas with words. Toddlers grow aware of the new opportunities for exploration made possible by their emerging skills, so they meet new adventures with curiosity and determination. Their efforts are so zealous that it seems their very lives hinge on whether or not they can do a simple job like opening or closing a door by themselves. These delightfully spirited youngsters use their boundless energy to become involved in many things.

Like infants, toddlers require much physical care, so cribs, dressing tables, and play yards will still be found in their facilities. But, because toddlers become more advanced in all areas of development, they will need additional materials and equipment. They enjoy vehicles to ride on or in, toys to push or pull, and containers to put things into or take things out. They love to climb and crawl, too, so climbers and tunnels are necessary—even if you make your own from boxes, planks, pillows, or benches.

Toddlers would rather play alone than join in with other children; they must be offered opportunities to play with solitary materials: puzzles, blocks, books, crayons, markers, collage materials, and puppets are but a few examples. But, because they are becoming aware of other children around them, toddlers must be offered opportunities to engage in activities that hold the potential for involving others: dress-up clothes, blocks, sand and water play, and storytime, for example. They may play alone or watch others play, but the desire to play together has its roots in such a foundation.

The following outline of toddlers' basic developmental characteristics will help give you an idea of what they are capable of at different stages.

DEVELOPMENTAL STAGES OF TODDLERS

Twelve to Eighteen Months

☐ Walks with help; falls often.

☐ Stands alone with feet spread apart.

☐ Enjoys pulling or pushing toys.

☐ Stacks two to four objects.

☐ Repeatedly picks up objects and throws them.

☐ Enjoys scribbling.

☐ Likes looking inside containers.

☐ Searches for hidden objects.

☐ Enjoys stories.

☐ Explores and experiments with everything in the environment.

☐ Follows simple directions ("Give me the ball").

☐ Enjoys sharing rhymes and songs.

☐ Has about a ten-word vocabulary.

☐ Likes picture books.

☐ Plays alone; not interested in other children.

☐ Refers to self by name.

Eighteen to Twenty-four Months

☐ Walks without help; falls infrequently.

☐ Carries large toys while walking.

☐ Fits toys together; pulls toys apart.

☐ Feeds self.

☐ Stacks four to six objects.

☐ Scribbles energetically.

☐ Bowel control may be achieved.

☐ Enjoys pouring and filling.

☐ Regularly says "no" in response to requests.

☐ Still prefers to play alone, but watches others.

☐ Does not share well with peers.

☐ Craves adult attention.

☐ Openly affectionate; hugs and kisses abound.

☐ Invariably asks "Why?"

- Has a fifty to three hundred word vocabulary.
- Imitates adult actions in play.
- Refers to self as "I" or "me" instead of always by name.

Two to Three Years

- Controls hands and fingers much better.
- Jumps, hops, and gallops.
- Kicks a ball.
- Jumps in place.
- Enjoys swinging but cannot "pump."
- Pedals tricycles and other wheeled toys.
- Turns pages of a book one at a time.
- Can make vertical or horizontal lines.
- Stacks seven or more blocks.
- Attains control of bladder.
- Enjoys pounding, squeezing, and rolling clay.
- Asks many questions.
- Names and matches geometric shapes and primary colors (red, yellow, blue).

SUITABLE MATERIALS AND ACTIVITIES

The material that follows offers suggestions for good toys and activities for toddlers. Ideas were selected because they are inexpensive, easily made, or already available in most centers. (For more information on toys suitable for toddlers, see Appendix A.)

Twelve to Eighteen Months

Toys and games listed for infancy, plus:

- Low furniture to hold onto
- Wheeled toys to push and pull
- Surprise boxes; music boxes
- Record player and records
- Nontoxic crayons, markers, and drawing paper
- Blocks
- Balls
- Nesting toys; plastic containers
- Pounding toys

Eighteen to Twenty-four Months

The toys and games listed previously, plus:

- ☐ Large open spaces to walk and toddle (attempt to run)
- ☐ Plastic eating utensils
- ☐ Puzzles
- ☐ Sand and water toys
- ☐ Plastic pop-beads
- ☐ Containers with lids
- ☐ Nesting toys

Two to Three Years

The toys and activities listed previously, plus:

- ☐ Books
- ☐ Pegboards
- ☐ Dominoes
- ☐ Picture lotto
- ☐ Finger paint
- ☐ Tempera paint for easels
- ☐ Beads to string
- ☐ Trikes and other pedal toys
- ☐ Wagon and wheelbarrow
- ☐ Balls of all types
- ☐ Feely box or bag
- ☐ Shape sorters
- ☐ Clay and other modeling media
- ☐ Materials for dress-up, creative dramatic play
- ☐ Walks and short trips

Physical growth during toddlerhood is not quite as rapid as during infancy, but there are other areas of change that are quite significant. Advances in motor skills are phenomenal, speech skills blossom and grow at an astounding pace, and learning and thinking abilities are markedly advanced. Toddlerhood is a fascinating period of life; caregivers provide for its early months with activities and materials designed for infants and the latter months with those used by young children. Thus, suggestions for working with toddlers can be chosen from Part One of this book as well as from Part Three. Examine the preceding outline of developmental stages and choose the appropriate activities for your toddlers.

Most often, toddlers will be involved in free, unstructured play. However, there will be time for experiences where individuals or groups operate on a more structured basis, usually when exploring with the senses or comparing and contrasting objects. In such instances, your procedure should have a clear beginning, middle, and end.

Beginning

☐ *Have all the necessary materials ready.* For example, if you want the children to discriminate among objects on the basis of color, you can have ready a box full of plastic teddy bears colored red, yellow, and blue.

☐ *Allow children time to explore the materials freely.* Dump the box on the rug and say, "Let's see what we have here." Encourage the children to play freely with the objects.

☐ *Briefly describe the activity.* Say, for example, "Let's play a game with these teddy bears. Here is a *red* rug. We'll put the *red* teddy bears on this rug because they are the same color." Do an example of each of the other colors, too.

Middle

☐ *Involve the children.* Say, "Now you try. Show me a teddy bear. Where will you put it?"

☐ *Ask the children to describe what they are doing.* Ask, for example, "Why did you put that teddy bear on this rug?" If the children cannot explain, say, "You put the blue teddy bear on the blue rug. They are the same color?"

Ending

☐ *Have the children summarize what was done.* Ask, "What did we do with our teddy bears today?"

☐ *Encourage children to use the materials again when playing independently.* Say, "The teddy bears and rugs will stay at this table for awhile. Come back and play with them when you like."

The following activities may be appropriately shared with toddlers by using the suggestions above, or any reasonable adaptation.

Activities—Twelve to Twenty-four Months

Follow Me

Toddlers learn a lot by imitating adults. They demonstrate special cognitive skills when they imitate—concentrating, observing, and remembering. Sit on the floor with your toddlers and say, "I'm touching my nose. Now you do it." Add other skills and tasks: wave arms, clap hands, bang two toys together, and so on.

Name It

Toddlers are beginning to use words, so encourage their language development during daily routines. At snack time, for example, persuade a child to ask for food: "Here's a cup of juice. Now tell me what it is. Say 'juice.' " When sharing a book, say, "Here is a book. Look at the picture of the duck. What is the picture?"

Pouring Fun

Use two plastic containers; one should be small enough for the toddler to grasp. Show the toddler the larger container and allow her ample time to examine it. Then bring out the smaller container in which you've placed a wooden bead. Shake the container so the bead rattles. Show the child the bead and say, "Watch. I'll pour the bead into the big cup." Do the suggested action. Put the bead back into the smaller container, hand it to the child, and encourage her to try.

Straddle Ball

Sit on the floor with your legs spread out so that they form a V shape. Ask the child to sit about three to four feet away facing you in the same manner (you may have to help position his legs). Roll a ball between the legs of the child and encourage him to roll it back between your legs. Move back away a bit further after you've done this successfully several times. Continue as long as the child can aim accurately.

Toddler Bowling

Set up four or five plastic bowling pins in a row in front of the child. Sit on the floor with the toddler and demonstrate how to roll a ball toward the pins to knock them over. Have the child try. As a variation, place a cardboard box (about 12″ × 15″) on its side so the open top is facing the child. Stand about three to five feet away and take turns rolling the ball into the opening.

Picture Sounds

Collect a number of large, colorful pictures of common animals. Show the pictures one at a time, encouraging the children to tell you what they are. Ask the children to make the sound associated with each animal.

Activities—Twenty-four to Thirty-six Months

Auto Driver

Tape down a strip of construction paper (2″ × 24″) or lay fabric tape on the floor to serve as a pretend road. Sit on the floor with the child with the road in front of you. Have two small toy cars ready, one for the child and one for you. Show how you can push your car along the "road." Encourage the child to guide her car along the road, too. Make more challenging roads as the child becomes more skillful.

Lotto

Divide a master sheet of $8\frac{1}{2}'' \times 11''$ construction paper into six sections, three in each of two rows. Paste a picture of a familar object or living thing in each section (flower, ball, kite, tree, and so on). Make a set of cards, each of which is slightly smaller than the sections on the master sheet. On the cards, paste pictures identical to those on the master sheets. Give one card to a child and ask him to name it. Then the child searches for the matching item on the master sheet and places his card, picture up, on top of it. The child continues until all the sections of the master sheet have been covered.

It's Pouring!

Get two small plastic cups that can be easily held by the child. Fill one cup one-third full with uncooked rice and place it next to the empty cup. Demonstrate how to take the rice-filled cup and pour it back and fourth from one cup to the other. Call the child's attention to the pleasant sound made by the rice. Try pouring other items and compare the sounds; dried beans or water work well.

I Fooled You

Place three common objects in front of the child (block, doll, or ball, for example). Point to them and ask the child to name each. Then, as the child watches, take one object away and ask what's missing. Repeat the game several times, commenting, "I can't fool you!" each time the child identifies what was removed.

Make the game more challenging for those who are ready by asking the child to close his eyes as you remove the object. Show the child the actual removed object each time he makes a guess, whether the guess was right or wrong.

Basketball

Use a laundry basket and a ball for this activity. Demonstrate how to toss a ball into the basket. Encourage the child to stand as close to the basket as she needs and try it, too. To challenge the more able children, move the basket farther away or use smaller baskets.

Clothespin Trim

Gather some plastic bowls or containers with thin, firm rims and some regular clothespins (*not* the spring-type that must be squeezed open and shut). Show the children how to pick up a clothespin and push it onto the rim of the bowl. See if they can fill up the entire rim.

Milk Carton Trains

Save plastic milk cartons. Make a train by punching holes through the tops and bottoms and threading them with string so they are connected as shown in Figure 3. Half-gallon cartons are handy for the engine, quarts and pints for the cars. You can cut the sides out of some so that toddlers can haul things such as blocks, balls, pieces of cloth, and so on. The train slides easily across the floor because the cartons are covered with a waxy type of plastic.

Figure 3

PART THREE

FOR YOUNG CHILDREN

By the time children turn three, they have a solid foundation of language. The rules of grammar are "understood" even though the youngsters don't consciously know it. They love to use the word "why" and count on its effect to bring out a variety of responses from adults. Young children are inquisitive; they need freedom to explore and be curious about their world. Their growing small and large motor skills enable young children to get about and manipulate things; these skills help extend their field of learning as well as their ability to control and influence their world. The caring ways significant adults react to young children's efforts to control and influence their world, in turn, gives young children self-confidence and a positive self-concept. With these positive feelings, the young children strive to reach their fullest potential through activities designed to encourage individual success.

As children grow in mind and body, they become eager to experiment and interact with all the new phenomena confronting them within their expanding environment. The following activities were designed to encourage a spirit of confidence, creativity, and curiosity. They can be used in a variety of ways—with a high degree or a minimum of teacher direction, as child-centered, free, exploratory experiences, or as a combination of these. The choice is yours.

PREPARING FOR THE FIRST DAY OF SCHOOL

Few events are as profound in any child's life as the first day of school. Saying good-bye at the door and leaving behind the secure hands of a parent or other trusted adult is a time filled with a variety of emotions. For some, it is a stressful time; many children are not sure what is going to happen and greet their new challenges with great apprehension. For others, it is an earnest time; these children possess the self-assurance and trust necessary to enter most new situations with calm confidence. Teachers or caregivers are not free of emotion, either, even though they may have experienced this initial encounter several times before during their teaching careers. Most are eager to greet their new charges and make their school entrance a positive one. Others may be opening the year for the very first time and face the uncertainty with fear or anxiousness. Parents, too, experience a variety of emotions. They are concerned about how their child will be treated, about whether the teacher will be nice, about their child's behavior away from home, or even about losing a central place in their child's life. Children's concerns, teachers' concerns, and parents' concerns all must be addressed prior to and during the first day of school if we are to make the first step to a successful year a steady and confident one.

Days before the children arrive, early childhood caregivers and teachers prepare the environment so that the setting is warm, comfortable, and productive. Colorful mobiles are hung from the ceiling, the walls are decorated with fanciful childhood characters, and the room is arranged with inviting bulletin board displays that provide a secure, comfortable environment. Designed to elicit smiles and other positive signs of acknowledgement, this setting will be a joy to return to each day. Accommodations focus on the children who will be entering the classroom and are intended to help promote self-concept as well as an understanding and respect for others.

Individual Name Tags

Prepare individual name tags for your children. If your school offers parent-child visitations prior to the opening of school, give your children their name tags then and ask them to wear the tags when they come back on the first day of school. If your school does not have early visitations, mail a tag home to each child and ask that it be worn to school on the first day. Remember, children bring something special with them to school—their names—so the tags will help you greet them by name and emphasize just how important they are to you.

Children often worry when meeting a new group that may be different from any they have experienced before. They wonder if anyone will want to take care of them, if anyone will really like them. A letter to the child from the teacher is very reassuring. Offering some words of affection and encouragement along with a very personal item with his name on it lets the child know that he has definite recognition from you; he will treasure his name tag and keep it safely to wear to school on the first day. Have extras on hand, however, in case a child shows up without one.

Name tags should be attractive and appealing to the children. They can be cut from colorful construction paper and taped or carefully safety-pinned on the children, they can be threaded with yarn and worn around the neck, or they can be worn as headbands. (See Figure 4 for ideas.)

Displays to Welcome the Children

Choose a child-oriented, attractive bulletin board theme that corresponds to your name tags. Bears, animals of all kinds, nursery rhyme characters, cartoon figures, storybook favorites, and common objects with human attributes (a pencil with facial features, for example) all offer interesting possibilities. Samples are shown in Figures 5 through 9, but ideas are limitless—use your imagination.

Figure 4

Notice that the displays feature one large central character and related name tags in two parts. In Figure 5, for example, the scoop of ice cream bearing the child's name can be separated from the cone (also displaying the child's name). This makes it possible for the child to wear half of the tag and keep the other half on the bulletin board for further learning activities. (See the section ''The Children Arrive'' for detailed suggestions on how to carry out those related activities.)

In Figure 5, the ''Big Scoop'' welcomes the children to the room. Make the background, small cones, and title from colored construction paper. ''Big Scoop's'' head is fashioned from cotton decorated with construction paper features. ''Big Scoop'' becomes the class mascot and the leader of all introductory activities.

In Figure 6, Humpty Dumpty greets all the incoming ''good eggs'' from his precarious perch. Cut out a white paper or cloth Humpty Dumpty, decorate with marking pens, and place him on a colorful paper background. Cut out small eggs, one for each child, and cut each in half. Each half has the child's name printed in bright colors. Humpty Dumpty becomes the class mascot and the leader of all introductory activities.

Freddie Frog croaks out a welcome to his new classroom family as each member is displayed on matching miniature frogs and lily pads. To create the bulletin board illustrated in Figure 7, cover it with blue paper, make a green construction paper title, and draw Freddie Frog on tagboard, then decorate him with felt-tip markers and tempera paint. Freddie's lily pad is made from green construction paper and the flower with pink paper. The children's frogs are small, green versions of Freddie with names printed on both them and the lily pads. Freddie Frog is the class mascot and leader of all introductory activities.

Or ''Nutty'' Squirrel, the classroom mascot shown in Figure 8, can welcome your children to their new room. Create a cut-paper squirrel; attach it to the bulletin board next to a large construction paper acorn that has a tan top and yellow bottom. Print Nutty's name on each part. Each smaller, cutout acorn also has two parts, each with a child's name printed in black. Nutty is the class mascot and leader of all introductory activities.

Figure 5

Figure 6

Figure 7

Figure 8

Ask parents to send a photograph of their child to be featured on a bulletin board with bright construction paper picture frames. Write a name tag for each child and place it beneath his or her photo, as shown in Figure 9. "Flash," the classroom photographer, welcomes your children to the room and leads them through the introductory activities.

Bus Identification Tags (Kindergarten)

The first few days of school are hectic for all kindergartners, especially those who ride the bus. You can help prevent children from getting on the wrong bus or from getting dropped off at the wrong stop by duplicating the pattern illustrated in Figure 10. Write the child's name, bus number, bus driver, and bus stop on the tag and string it around his or her neck as the children leave your room each day.

Decorate Doorways

Decorate the inside or outside of your door so that the children can be attracted to your classroom in a very special way. A large character with a welcome sign never fails to win attention, while any display that includes the children's names adds to their enjoyment. (See Figure 11.)

Organizing the Physical Space

The classroom should be not only bright and cheerful, but must also be effectively organized so that all children can experience joy and success with materials suited to their particular interests and needs. Divide your room into several clearly defined areas or centers which are organized thematically and filled with an appropriate number and type of related materials. The activity areas common to most early childhood programs include dramatic play, block-building, group circle, art, woodworking, books, manipulative toys and games, rumpus, science, sand and water play, learning centers, and possibly a computer center. These areas provide for the critical needs and interests of young children; the wise teacher should provide for each in the classroom. Each area contains materials that are openly and invitingly displayed, enticing the children to examine and experiment on their own. Activities and materials appropriate to each area are provided later in the book, but for now, let's look at the areas themselves.

Dramatic Play Area

The best play of young children happens spontaneously, when the youngsters are relaxed and receptive. The dramatic play corner houses equipment for play activities such as dress-up or housekeeping, and it is one center that has traditionally offered a wealth of opportunities for spontaneous play. Usually organized as a separate "room" within the classroom, the dramatic play center is often located in an alcove or set apart by walls of low screens or shelves. This gives the children a degree of privacy, but their play is still visible to the teacher.

Figure 9

Basic equipment for the dramatic play center includes child-sized furniture such as a wooden or plastic sink, table, refrigerator, stove, and cupboard. Sometimes doll beds, cradles, doll-sized carriages, a chest of drawers, rocking chairs, ironing boards, or play telephones are added. Unbreakable dolls, simple doll clothes, doll blankets, and other accessories are often included. Male and female clothing, as well as purses, briefcases, and other dress-up items provide endless opportunities for play enhancement.

Block Center

Blocks are essential for any classroom where play, physical exercise, social skills, and learning are valued. They are enjoyed equally by the toddler who can barely place one block atop another and by the kindergartner who builds elaborate projects.

A well-equipped block center should be allotted generous space in the classroom. The most popular blocks are the solid, uncolored hardwood *unit blocks*. These blocks get their name because they begin with a basic unit (5½ " × 2¾ " × 1⅜ ") and then scale smaller or larger blocks in exact multiples or fractions of that unit. Unit blocks are expensive but almost indestructible; a quality set will last until you retire! *Hollow blocks* are large, hollow, wooden blocks. Usually more popular with children at the beginning of the year than unit blocks, these blocks are light enough to handle and stack and can be used to build large enough

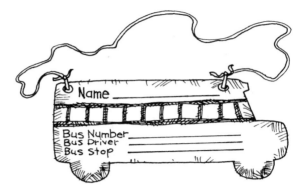

Figure 10

Figure 11

structures for the children to get into: "garages" or "railroad stations," for instance. The basic hollow block is called the "square"; measuring 5½ " × 11" × 11". Multiples of the basic square block provide children with a variety of components for their large structures. "Red brick" *cardboard blocks* of different sizes and shapes offer the same possibilities as hollow blocks. Other popular building toys include interlocking blocks such as *bristle blocks* (small plastic blocks covered with stiff bristles which allow them to stick together), *Tinkertoys, Lincoln Logs,* and *Duplo* or *Lego* blocks.

Group Circle

Because of their unique contributions to the children's program, the block corner and dramatic play area should be set up first when arranging the room. Your next decision will be where the children should come together for discussions, stories, music, or any other whole-group activity. Like the block and dramatic play centers, this area must have clearly defined boundaries so the children know where they are supposed to stay. Teachers normally paint or tape a circle on the floor or place a rug where they want the children to meet. Others become highly creative; one teacher, for example, referred to her large group area as the "Happy Circle." She painted a smiley face on a large sheet of circular yellow oilcloth. For group time, she laid out the oilcloth on the carpet and asked the children to seat themselves cross-legged around the smiley face. (Although the children will sit in such a manner on a rug, the teacher usually finds it more comfortable to sit on either a low chair or stool.)

Art Center

The art center is another very popular area of the room where children have lots of opportunities to explore, experiment, and create. Provide materials that allow the children to paint, draw, color, mold, cut, paste, or build.

The art center should have easels with space for two to four children, primary color paints in plastic containers, and large brushes with either flat or round bristles. Place the easels near a water source so that accidental paint spills can be cleaned up quickly and brushes washed easily. Other art materials can be spread out on low tables or shelves so they are easily accessible to the children: pencils; crayons; felt-tipped marking pens; chalk; scissors; paste or glue; paper for cutting, pasting, and drawing; old magazines, fabric scraps, glitter, string, macaroni, etc. for making collages; and modeling materials such as clay or Play-Doh.

Woodworking Area

As three-, four-, and five-year-olds gain more accurate control of their muscles, working with real tools two or three times a week can be an important experience for boys and girls alike. Real tools are necessary; toy tools such as a die-cast light metal hammer only insult or frustrate the enthusiastic builder. The following tools are recommended for an active woodworking area:

- [ ] Sturdy workbench with two vises
- [ ] Hammers
- [ ] Saws (crosscut), 12- and 16-inch
- [ ] Assorted nails (large heads)
- [ ] C-clamps to hold wood steady
- [ ] Hand drills and bits
- [ ] Sandpaper (wrapped around a wood block)
- [ ] Child-sized cotton work gloves, cap, and carpenter's apron
- [ ] Rasp or smoothing plane
- [ ] Nuts and bolts
- [ ] Wrenches

Provide plenty of soft wood (pine is especially good), which is easily obtainable as scraps from lumberyards, home builders, parents, or even high school shop classes. Have a large pegboard near the area and paint outlines of the tools available in the center on it. Mount hooks above the outlines and direct the children to replace the tools on the appropriate hooks when they are finished using them.

The children's initial interest will probably not be to construct something; they simply enjoy the physical and sensory sensations of pounding nails into wood, sanding or sawing the wood and smelling the fragrance of the sawdust, turning the hand drills to make holes, and performing other jobs they have seen adults do.

Book Center

Cozy chairs, cushions, stuffed animals, a couch, a rocking chair, and/or carpet squares help make this area cheerful and inviting. Located as far as possible from the distraction of the noisy activity areas, the book center contains a wide variety of reading materials that arouse curiosity and stimulate imagination. Books, magazines, and other reading materials can respond to the many "whys" of your children as well as to their rich fantasy. Books offer children a host of characters facing frustrations, concerns, and problems similar to those they must solve. Good books grab the attention of young children because they reflect so well the hopes, joys, fears, anger, and sorrow in their own lives and offer the spirit and encouragement to revel in successes and overcome failures.

Your book center should have racks or shelves on which books can be displayed with their covers showing so the children can readily see what is available. If you are among the lucky ones, your room will have a record player or tape recorder with a set of earphones. This makes it easy for the children to listen to commercially produced or teacher-made audio tapes whenever they feel like hearing a story.

It is best not to organize your book corner as a "library" by displaying your entire collection. Children become confused when confronted by too many choices, so provide only twenty to thirty books at one time. Change them periodically; each month, for instance, you might supplement your own collection with new choices from the public library. Keep four or five books your children particularly enjoy on permanent display.

Manipulative Toy Area

Most early childhood classrooms have special areas for activities designed to build small muscle skills, eye-hand coordination, and cognitive abilities. A few of the possible options are illustrated in Figure 12, but *puzzles* are among the most popular manipulative toys available. Simple wooden or durable cardboard puzzles should be matched to the children's development level; one- or two-piece puzzles are appropriate for two-year-olds, while five-year-olds will be able to complete twenty-four-, sixty-, or even one-hundred-piece puzzles. *Dressing frames* that help children develop skills such as lacing, tying, buttoning, zipping, and snapping are challenging to most young children. *Commercial table toys* such as Tinkertoys, Duplo or Lego blocks, stacking toys, wooden beads for stringing, plastic pop-beads, shape sorters (illustrated in Figure 12), lotto games, parquetry, pegboards, and other manipulative games or activities are not only inherently pleasing for young children, but also serve as the raw material for intellectual growth. Before young children can be expected to hold a pencil to write, for example, they must be able to control the movements of their wrists and finger muscles. They gain this control as they pour, cut, build, drill, mix, paste, button, zip, grasp, and lace. As these small muscle skills evolve, children learn to coordinate the movements of the hand and eye. Children who easily thread a wooden bead on a string, for example, demonstrate eye-hand coordination because they are able to make the eyes and hands work together.

Display manipulative materials in a way that encourages children to arrange, rearrange, put together, take apart, match, handle, and sort. Keep games, puzzles, and toys on open shelves or in cupboards at the children's level with an invitation to ''Please Touch'' rather than ''Do Not Touch''; that way the children can take the items off the shelves themselves and play with them at a low table or a nearby rug. As with books, rotate these materials periodically, maintaining an average of about two items for every child in the class.

Be sure to check your materials daily—nothing is more frustrating than trying to complete a puzzle with pieces missing. Many teachers code puzzle pieces by placing small numbers or letters on the back of each puzzle piece that correspond to a number assigned a particular puzzle. Other teachers carefully label plastic margarine tubs with pictures for storing toys with many small parts. By doing so, teachers not only help maintain the materials, but help children develop effective organizational skills.

Rumpus Area

The young child's day is full of active movement, for these little bodies house boundless energy. Young children need plenty of time during the day to release this energy as well as to learn what they can do with their bodies and practice

Figure 12

developing large muscle skills: climbing, jumping, sliding, crawling, and walking freely. If they have room, most classrooms provide indoor wooden climbers with mats underneath for protection. Some classrooms have lofts where children are able to crawl through small passages, climb ladders, jump down elevated platforms, or glide down slides or poles.

If you are not fortunate enough to have this equipment, crawling tunnels can be made from planks and small crates, cardboard boxes could be used for an obstacle course, and other ordinary equipment can be adapted for active use by the children. Just think of the possibilities young children will invent if you offer a refrigerator box with holes cut in it, some milk crates, packing cartons, hoses, barrels, or even old tires. Secret hiding places, special adventures, and challenging physical endeavors emerge from the children's creative fabrications.

Science Center

Young children prefer active exploration with real things, so the classroom should offer an environment where they can physically interact with a variety of novel materials. Such materials exist in many forms, colors, weights, textures, and states. Plants and animals fascinate children and caring for them opens up new vistas of understanding. Ordinary objects such as wood, stone, feathers, seeds, leaves, and seashells invite active exploration. Magnets, scales, and machines suggest interesting experiments. Offer a world of things for seeing, touching, hearing, smelling, and tasting.

Arrangements of real things are treated much like exhibits in the best child-oriented museums—not with a "hands-off" policy, but one that invites touching and exploring. Children's natural curiosity must be allowed to surface in the classroom. By arranging opportunities for this to happen, you let the children know that you value and welcome their curiosity, an important prerequisite to further learning.

Sand and Water Play Areas

Sand and water are great play materials because there are no wrong ways to use them. Children play with sand and water for sheer pleasure—they dream, explore, and invent new ways of using these materials every day.

Sand and water play can take place either indoors or out. Indoors, a sand or water table, tub, or converted wading pool can be used to house the materials. Sandboxes, hoses, and a variety of other equipment are suitable for outdoor play. There is no need to purchase expensive equipment such as the plastic buckets, shovels, molds, and rakes found in supply catalogs—many "junk materials" such as empty pump-spray bottles, plastic food containers, old combs, corks, and spools help children express their ideas creatively. However, absolutely no glass or other material that might shatter or splinter is acceptable.

Try not to be overly restrictive in the use of materials for sand and water play. This kind of play gives children a chance to explore, create, and even destroy—sometimes this too is emotionally important. Good teachers present sand and water play possibilities in such a way as to ensure proper supervision while encouraging free expression.

Learning Centers

These areas contain materials and activities designed to independently reinforce or extend cognitive learning. All of the other centers we have discussed up to this point contained truly creative opportunities—to build, to originate, to pretend. These free play activities allow children to be challenged by real problems. Now, however, the teacher may plan a number of independent activities where the children sit down at special tables to carry out instructions in step-by-step fashion. Used primarily in kindergartens, this type of work period often lasts from fifteen to thirty minutes. Learning centers are normally organized around a central theme and include card matching activities, manipulative materials, audio tapes, and other items designed to teach or reinforce specific learning objectives, especially in reading or math. Learning centers are not found in all early childhood programs—only those that place an emphasis on learning specific skills and concepts.

Computer Center

Of all the centers described so far, this is the most contemporary. Even ten years ago only a few early childhood methods books would have recommended using computers in a setting for young children, because many people felt they were too difficult for youngsters to manage. But computers are on the scene today and even some of the most vocal early skeptics have been convinced that computers can deliver useful learning experiences. A wealth of excellent, age-appropriate software is available for children today, and very few youngsters fail to become captivated by their action-oriented, fast-paced games.

Floor Plans

Choosing thematic equipment for the classroom centers is just the beginning—it is also important to consider how the centers will be arranged so that young children will obtain the most benefit.

Look at the floor plan pictured in Figure 13a, designed by a teacher of four-year-olds. Note that the storage shelves are placed against the walls and the tables are located in the middle of the room. Many beginning teachers approach the design of their first classroom similarly. If we examine the drawing closely, however, we find that the room may actually be counterproductive to the goals of the program. For instance, the open spaces in the middle invite children to run around from one activity to another. The easels are open to the rest of the room and in a direct line to the door. The block center is right next to the storage cubbies—you can imagine the anger generated as block structures are toppled by eager youngsters leaving their cubbies to visit another classroom center.

Arrange the centers to cut down on running space; children also need well-defined areas in which to work and play. In Figure 13b, notice how the shelves were brought away from the walls and used as dividers to set off as many specific areas as possible. By doing so, the children playing in the highly active areas such as blocks or housekeeping will feel secluded from other activities while the children choosing a quiet area such as books will not be distracted by the others. The new arrangement should also make it easier for children to get from one area to another without interfering with others as they play. The advantages of well-organized space are that it eliminates unproductive behavior and helps children pursue activities with a sense of security, confidence, and trust.

Organizing and Displaying Materials

The quality of your classroom environment, then, depends a lot upon how the space is arranged into centers, but there is yet another organizational factor involved—the techniques used to organize and display materials within the centers. If the materials are not displayed properly we run the risk of the children misusing them. What message do we send, for example, when we clutter shelves with as many toys as possible? The most obvious is, "Here you go, children. Use these in any way you wish!" Good teachers understand the unspoken messages communicated to children through the ways items are displayed, so they follow some very important guidelines:

Introduce equipment and materials deliberately. It can be dangerous to overstimulate young children with too many new materials. The children become literally overwhelmed by everything around them and may demonstrate two basic behaviors: withdrawal from all activity because of too much stimulation too soon, or uncontrolled darting about from one part of the room to another in an attempt to experience as much as possible in the shortest amount of time.

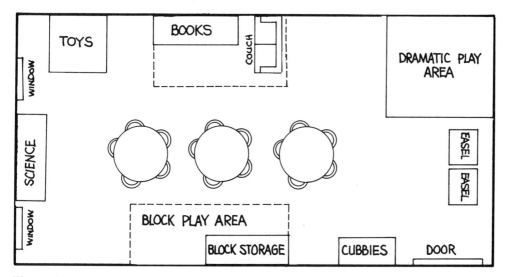

TOYS

BOOKS

COUCH

DRAMATIC PLAY AREA

WINDOW

SCIENCE

WINDOW

EASEL

EASEL

BLOCK PLAY AREA

BLOCK STORAGE

CUBBIES

DOOR

Figure 13a

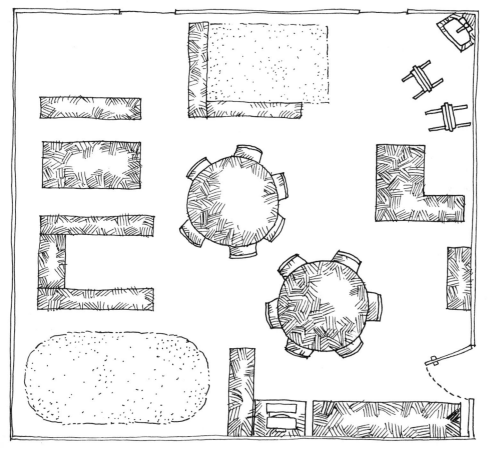

Figure 13b

Introduce only a few materials at the beginning of the preschool year and gradually add others as time goes by to maintain a comfortable, challenging environment.

Encourage children to understand that every item has its place.   Draw pictures or take photographs of each item, mount them on durable cardboard, and laminate them for protection. Tape these labels to the appropriate storage shelves and place each item at its represented place. All materials now have special storage locations, and children will learn to return things to their appropriate locations when they are finished with them. The child begins to feel that "this is my classroom and I care about it."

Older children do not need photographs or pictures to help them; gross outlines of items such as cooking utensils, cleaning utensils, eating utensils, or art supplies will be enough. This way, the children not only contribute to classroom organization, but practice the skill of matching and grouping as well.

Give young children time to adjust to group life outside the home before you expect them to share.   As you know, young children are egocentric. We cannot expect their self-centeredness to disappear the moment they set foot in your classroom, so let them enjoy a period of time when they know their desire to use certain materials can be satisfied. By providing duplicates of basic materials such as table toys or kitchen utensils, we help children adjust to a new situation without fear of being left out or disciplined for taking something another child is using.

Help children plan what they want to do.   Construct a planning display at the beginning of the year to help the children make choices about what they want to do. Mount close-up photographs of each child on tagboard cards and glue a clothespin to each card. (If you don't have photos, write the children's names on separate cards and let them decorate the cards however they wish.) Large tagboard signs depict the various areas within your classroom. After a conference with you, the child takes her photo and clips it to a picture representing the area where she will play. (See Figure 14.) Your personal educational philosophy will determine the method of movement from center to center, but it will probably follow one of these four patterns:

1. The teacher assigns all children to the centers by pinning their pictures to the center designations.

2. The teacher provides the child with two or three alternatives and the child chooses from among them.

3. The children and the teacher confer and choose jointly from among all choices.

4. The children have free choice of all center possibilities.

The most appropriate planning strategies for preschoolers appear to be those in which the children can make choices. Those choices can be as simple as pointing to the reading area or as complex as picking out the props and costumes desired for some fantasy play. The important thing is that the children get some chance

Figure 14

to select activities that interest them, and, with the help of an adult, plan how they will proceed.

Allow the room to be the children's.   The physical space should reflect the interests, needs, and talents of the children. The room becomes theirs when shelves, tables, chairs, and storage facilities are at the children's eye level, when displays and materials are easily accessible. It becomes theirs when their artwork and other creations are prominently displayed. It becomes theirs when individual lockers (*cubbies*) are designed for the children's personal use. (Youngsters take comfort in knowing that a special part of the room is for them and will enjoy assuming responsibility for keeping it neat and orderly.) The space becomes theirs when it has an aesthetically pleasing decor—warm colors, draperies, flooring appropriate to the activity area (i.e., tile for the art center, carpeting for the book center), and washable, durable surfaces. It becomes theirs when the children feel at home!

Establishing a Tie Between Home and School

Perhaps the most sensible way to introduce your facility to parents and children is to plan for school visitations a week or two before school actually starts. Usually done on an appointment basis, this visit helps parents and children to become familiar with the new setting and to feel at ease in the teacher's presence. (For more general advice on parent-teacher conferences, see pages 294–296.)

Call the parent on the telephone to set up a time for the meeting. This direct contact establishes a personal tone for the visit and invites questions or comments in a way that a written invitation can't.

Arrange a comfortable seating area where you can sit and talk with parents. Don't sit behind a desk with a parent seated on a chair in front of you—this sets up roadblocks to good communication by establishing an artificial barrier between you. Instead, arrange two or three child-sized chairs facing each other or sit around a children's table. Try to have a beverage (coffee, tea, or milk) for the parent along with a small snack. A small nutritious snack along with juice or milk should also be available for the child.

Arrange the room with displays, materials, and furniture, much as they will be seen on the first day of school. Since the purpose of this meeting is to establish a smooth transition between home and school, you want to assure the child that the new environment will look the same upon his or her return to your room. A drastic change from this meeting day to the first day will only create confusion in the young child.

Arrange a separate display area for the parents. Include photographs of activities from the school program, advertising brochures, program descriptions, and information on policies regarding health, field trips, meals, fees, and so on. These "hands on" items often serve as an excellent resource to break the ice conversationally.

When the parent and child arrive, emphasize the idea that the program and setting are there for the *child* by directing your first comments to the child: "Good morning! You must be Charles and this is your dad. Hello, Charles, and good morning, Mr. Goodwin. Please come in; I've been expecting you. This will be where you'll be coming to school, Charles."

Direct your next few comments to the parent. This will give the child a little while to size you up and take a quick glance around the room. This also informs the parent that he is an important part of the child's experience away from home, too.

Extend your initial comments to the child by calling his or her attention to the play materials arranged about the room. Try not to overwhelm the child with too much, but have popular materials such as puzzles, books, crayons, blocks, or other items that require a minimum of supervision. Say something such as, "Children come here to use crayons, paint, Play-Doh, or other art materials." Lead the parent and child on a short walking trip around the room pointing out these items for the child. End the tour at your prearranged conversation area, inviting the child to return to an area he seemed to be attracted to on the walking tour: "Charles, your dad and I will sit at this table and talk for a few minutes. We have a Mickey Mouse puzzle you can play with or you might like to draw with crayons. They're right here at another table. These are two kinds of things children like to play with at school. Your dad and I will be right at that table if you need us."

If the child appears distressed when asked to leave his parent (most will leave willingly), do not force him to go. Just say, reassuringly, "Charles, if you would like to stay and listen to us talk, that's okay, too. But, if you want to play with the puzzles or crayons after a little while, we'll all go over and you can use them." When you actually do this, try to get the parent to help interest the child. If that fails, simply bring a puzzle, book, or toy to your conversation area and let the child play there as you talk. Or walk from one display to the other as you speak with the parent; the child may become interested in one or another as you move along. Don't force participation, though. Your objective during this meeting is to get to know the child and parent, and to establish a sense of trust.

Briefly discuss your program along with special policies (health, field trips, birthday celebrations, meals, fees, and so on). Most of this information should have been shared with the parent through the mail, but you may want to review important points. The visit should focus on questions parents may have about the mailed information, and on the child—special needs, interests, hobbies, talents, and so on.

Many parents hope you will be particularly sensitive to their child, so let them see that you are a caring person who enjoys working with children. Share your ideas about childhood with them, for they need to know you are a trustworthy person who will make sure their child gets the best care possible.

Encourage parents to discuss positive aspects of the child at this initial meeting. Some will criticize the child or want to talk about a special problem. Indicate your interest in such concerns, but schedule a later meeting when they can be explored at greater depth, without the child being present.

Allot about one hour per visit. Plan to spend a half hour to forty-five minutes in conversation, keeping at least fifteen minutes free to summarize the meeting and make any preparations for the next. You may want to jot down a few special notes while the parent talks with you or wait until after the visit. On the one hand, taking notes during the visit formalizes the process; on the other, waiting until the end of the day often causes confusion and incompleteness. You may want to decide on a case-by-case basis.

End your visit on a personal note. Go with the parent to the area where the child is playing and say, "Charles, I know you are having fun, but it's almost time to leave. You may play with the crayons again when you come back to school." Have the child's cubby ready and direct him to the special place that will be all his own. Have a variety of cutout shapes ready, all related to your classroom theme (cartoon characters, farm animals, vehicles, and so on—for an example, see Figure 15.) Invite the child to choose the shape he would like to have for his cubby. Print the child's name on the tag, explaining what you're doing: "I'll start at this end of the tag and use a capital C because I'm writing a name. Then I use lowercase letters to finish your name: . . . h . . . a . . . . r . . l . . . e . . . s. There! *Charles.*" Attach the tag to the child's cubby and let him know that this is a special place for any items brought from home such as coats, hats, or boots.

Invite the child to bring a favorite "security" item from home—a special blanket, stuffed animal, doll, or toy. These can be talked to, cuddled, "read" or sung to—they give children feelings of comfort and safety during those important first days away from home. Assure the child that his special toy can be kept safely in his cubby.

Invite the parent to send along one or two family photos that can be displayed at the children's eye level or in a special book of photographs. These will help the children, especially the reluctant ones, feel more comfortable in their new environment by reminding them that their family still exists even though they are not here now.

Before the parent and child leave, give the child a name tag to wear when he or she returns on the first day of school. This not only refreshes your memory as all the children enter on that busy day, but it gives the child something special to take home from the visit. Most children become strongly attached to their name tags and eagerly anticipate wearing them on the first day.

Figure 15

A Letter Home

If your facility does not provide a visitation day, you will still want to personalize the beginning of the year. Write your children a get-acquainted letter that their parents can read to them. Tell them about such things as your hobbies, interests, family, and plans for the forthcoming school year. You may even want to enclose a small photograph of yourself. (A sample letter is included in Figure 16.)

Provide a stamped, self-addressed envelope which the children can use to send back a letter that they dictate to their parents telling about themselves; also invite them to make drawings about something special in their lives. The drawings would make an interesting bulletin board for the opening of school.

Don't forget to send a letter to the parents, too. One similar to the example shown in Figure 17 would be appropriate.

Parent Newsletters

It is important not only to open lines of communication with letters to your parents at the beginning of the school year, but to keep in touch throughout the year. Regular newsletters should be sent weekly or monthly. These newsletters help achieve the following goals:

1. Inform parents of special school policies.
2. Highlight special events such as field trips or school visitors.
3. Offer special hints for follow-up activities that can be done at home, such as storybooks or art projects.
4. Suggest helpful advice for child-rearing.

5. Clarify school projects or activities by sharing such things as recipes, words to songs, or fingerplays.

6. Inform parents of special school needs and suggest how they might contribute.

A sample midyear newsletter is shown in Figure 18 (page 64).

Meet the Teachers

Display large photos of each teacher with information about special hobbies, interests, teaching experiences, educational background, personal background (hometown, family, etc.), and special awards. Be sure to also include your director and other staff members. (See Figure 19 on page 65 for one possible treatment.) Put the display where it can be easily seen and enjoyed by the parents and/or other visitors as they wait to see you.

The Children Arrive

Use a thematic approach to the opening of school. Choose a popular, child-oriented theme as an integral part of this introduction to school. Let's say you have chosen bears as your theme. You then decorate the room with stuffed bears, pictures of bears, and books about popular, likable bears such as teddy bears, Winnie-the-Pooh, Paddington, Corduroy, or the Berenstain Bears. The children should come to school wearing brown bear-shaped name tags they received during their earlier visit or in the mail. Bring the children together in a circle and introduce them to a special bear puppet, wearing a name tag similar to the children's: "Teddy the Magnificent" or "Teddy" for short. Have Teddy greet the boys and girls with a nonthreatening roar, then say: "Good morning, boys and girls. I am so happy to see you today. You all look so nice. I was lonely without you. We'll have fun each day playing, talking, and learning." Then, making Teddy look surprised, direct his attention to the children's name tags. Have Teddy feign an inability to read the words on the tags. "Good gracious," roars Teddy. "I've never seen so many names in all my life! A room full of bears that all look the same . . . please help me out quickly. Will you please tell me their names?" The teacher should then turn to the children and say, "Boys and girls, Teddy has a real problem. He'd like to know your names but he can't read." Then ask the children to introduce themselves individually to Teddy.

The bear tags worn by the children become excellent learning tools at the end of the day. On the bulletin board, provide a honey pot for each child with his or her name on it, as shown in Figure 20 (page 65). The children will be asked to match their tags to the appropriate honey pot. Some children will be able to match their tags with the related honey pots with no trouble; others may experience great difficulty. Regardless, this activity serves to reinforce the skills of some children and introduce new skills to others.

After about two or three weeks, when you are satisfied that the children have learned to recognize their names, you may wish to substitute last names for first names on the honey pots and encourage children to match bears and honey

Dear

    Summer is going by so fast and soon you will be
coming to kindergarten. I'm glad you will be in my
room. We will have many interesting things to do
this year.

    Did you find a name tag in this envelope?
Please wear it to school on the first day. All the
other children in our room will have one, too.

    My photo is at the bottom of this letter. I am
with my family. I will tell you about them when
you come to school. Please bring a photo of you
with your family to school. We would love to hear
about your family too.

    Enjoy the rest of the summer. I am looking
forward to seeing you in school.

Best wishes,

Mrs. Colegrove

Figure 16

Dear Parents,

It is a pleasure to welcome you and your child to Happy Day Nursery School. Being four, your child is among a group of other children at the magical age when they are full of questions, just loving to get into things. They are full of boundless energy! We want to capitalize on that spirit and encourage the children to explore and to solve problems. To meet this goal, they have to experience things, so there are times your child may become wet, or dirty, or messy, or rumpled. Becoming involved often means these things.

To help the children, we ask that you send them to school in play clothes. Please don't dress them in good clothing with instructions not to get dirty. Send them to school in durable wash-and-wear items that will withstand the challenges of childhood.

[Other policies, such as attendance, health and safety, schedule, and financial arrangements inserted here.]

As a final note, occasionally your child will be asked to bring home special messages like this one, perhaps pinned to his or her clothing. Please read them in the company of your child so that he or she will understand your interest in the school. By the way, please compliment your child on being a good messenger!

Thanking you in advance, I remain

                              Sincerely yours,

Figure 17

Dear Parents,

   In planning our preschool program, we use many
"happenings"--things children can do--to help them
learn about their world. Cooking and planting
seeds are examples of these kinds of activities.
Our food unit is another.

   This week, the children prepared a fruit salad.
They worked in groups of five. First, they washed
their hands. Each child then chose at least one
fruit to help prepare. Everyone cut up fruit on a
paper plate, then put it in a large bowl. We
examined the fruit very carefully. We compared
the colors, discussed the various tastes, found
which was the juiciest, and even sorted the seeds.
The children then took turns stirring the fruit
and spooning it into paper cups to serve at snack
time. Everyone enjoyed the "fruit salad
happening" very much.

   A REMINDER: Dr. Elizabeth Beckley of State
University will speak on the subject of
"Nutrition" at our monthly parents' meeting this
Thursday, March 16, at 7:00 p.m. The subject
should be of interest to all parents. Hope to see
you there.

                    Sincerely,

Figure 18

Figure 19

Figure 20

pots to form a complete name. From there, substitute addresses, phone numbers, or any other personal information you consider important.

Possibilities for opening day themes are limitless. Be aware of what interests children and turn it into a lively introduction to school.

Gingerbread Boy Excursion

Read the story of the gingerbread boy to the children. As a follow-up activity, make a gingerbread boy with the class, then take him to the kitchen where he can be put into the oven to bake. While you are there, introduce the children to the kitchen staff who can explain the various aspects of the kitchen. Return to your classroom while the gingerbread boy is baking. When he is done, return to the kitchen where the children will find the oven empty. Only a short note from the gingerbread boy is found—it tells the children to look for him in the director's (or principal's) office where, once the children arrive, the secretary and director introduce themselves and explain their major responsibilities. The gingerbread boy is not there either, but has left a note inviting the children to look in the nurse's office, library, hallways, custodian's room, and other important places. Finally, the children are led back to their room by the gingerbread boy where (at about snack time) they find him hiding.

If your facility does not have a kitchen, bring along a gingerbread boy purchased at a bakery. Show it to the children after you've read the story, explaining that when they return from outdoor play, it will be shared by all. Of course, the gingerbread boy will have "disappeared" while the children were out. Feigning surprise, lead the children on the excursion previously described.

Play an Action Game

Introduce a short action game, keeping your opening theme intact. Tell the children that bears are lots of fun and that school will be fun this year, too. Ask Teddy if he is happy to be in this classroom and have him respond a cheery, "Roar, roar!" Then, encourage the children to join you in the action song, "If You're Happy and You Know It" by using these phrases: " . . . say roar, roar . . . clap your paws . . . do them both!"

Now, while the children are together in a group, you may wish to read a book related to the theme of bears as well as to the situation of a first day at school. *The Berenstain Bears Go to School* by Stan and Jan Berenstain is one possibility. Some teachers prefer to extend group time during this first day of school by helping the children become familiar with each other through an enjoyable nursery rhyme or fingerplay. Such activity helps develop a spirit of camaraderie on this very important day. For example, say, "Let's have some fun together. Listen and watch what I do." Before you start, make sure the children are all seated and facing you. Place your hands behind your back and sing the popular tune "Thumbkin."

Where is Thumbkin?
Where is Thumbkin?
    (Hands behind back)

Here I am.
  (Right hand out, thumb up)
Here I am.
  (Left hand out, thumb up)
How are you today, Sir?
  (Right thumb "bows")
Very well, I thank you.
  (Left thumb "bows")
Run away.
  (Right hand behind back)
Run away.
  (Left hand behind back)

"Now, where are your thumbs? Can you make them Thumbkins by pointing them up like this? Very good! Let's sing the song together and this time you be Thumbkins, too."

Repeat the song as many times as the children show interest. Be sure to allow extra time for the children to move their thumbs to the song's actions. As the children gain confidence in future sessions, add verses for "pointer," "tall man," "ring man," and "pinky," using the appropriate fingers and following the actions indicated.

On the second day, some teachers prefer to adapt the initial "Thumbkin" activity by using children's names. For example:

Where is _____?
  (child's name)
Where is _____?
  (child's name)
There she is.
  (Child stands up)
There she is.
How are you today _____?
                  (sir or ma'am)
Very well, I thank you.
  (Child bows)
Run away.
  (Child sits down)
Run away.

Repeat the song several times, using each child's name and inviting the children to stand and sit according to the verse. The introducing phase of the routine can be extended on the third day with an activity called "This is My Friend." The game begins with the children seated in a circle, holding hands. Teddy starts things off by covering his eyes with his hand and saying: "Peek-a-boo! Who are you?" Uncovering his eyes, Teddy looks at a child as the child gives her name. The game continues until all the children are introduced.

Extending First Day Introductions

A primary goal of preschool settings is helping young children develop a positive view of themselves as people. Before any learning can effectively take place, the child must see himself as a worthy, loved individual. Growing directly from this feeling is an emerging awareness of other people and a willingness to understand relationships between himself and those people.

Following is a list of suggested activities designed to help foster children's understanding and appreciation of themselves and others.

Bear Hugs. Help the children learn more about each other by preparing a box with a bear illustration on the outside. Write a variety of questions on small bear cutouts, then place them in the box. Sample questions include:

"What is your favorite thing to eat?"
"Do you have a pet?"
"What makes you happy?"
"What toy do you like to play with most?"

The child chooses a "Bear Hug" from the box, you read it, and the child shares the information with her peers.

Introduction Name Game. Recite the following chant and encourage the children to join in when they are ready.

Please think hard.
Look real well.
Who is this . . .
Can you tell?

Move around the circle of children with your special bear puppet or other thematic character as you say the rhyme, stopping directly in back of a different child each time the rhyme ends. In unison, the children should shout the child's name to your theme character.

Two Little Children. Give children physical exercise as well as practice in learning each others' names by personalizing the old favorite, "Two Little Blackbirds." Here is the traditional version.

Two little blackbirds
Sitting on a hill.
One named Jack,
The other named Jill.
Fly away, Jack.
Fly away, Jill.
Come back, Jack.
Come back, Jill.

Arrange your children in a circle. Say (or sing) the following lines, filling in the first blank with a word that rhymes with one of the two children whose turn it will be to act out the song. "Two little children sitting on a _____ . One named
(gate)

_____ and one named _____ ." As the children hear their names, they come
(Mike)   (Kate)
to the center of the circle and get ready to move outside the circle by flapping
their arms as the next lines are spoken or sung: "Fly away, _____ . Fly away
                                                        (Mike)
_____ ." They come back inside the circle as the final lines are spoken or sung.
(Kate)
The rhyme can be repeated by substituting other actions such as hop, skip, run,
jump, gallop, and so on as other children are involved.

Action Name Rhymes.   Have the children form a circle. Tell them to examine their
name tags and tell you the first letter of their names. If they can't, help them.
Then, introduce this action rhyme and ask the children to listen carefully for their
first letter. Repeat the rhyme and ask the children to join in with the relevant
action.

If your name starts with A, B, or C,
Stomp your feet and count to three.
If it starts with D or E,
Pretend you are dancing like a flea.
If it starts with F or G,
Wave your hands and look at me.
If it starts with H or I,
Raise both hands way up high.
If it starts with J or K,
Shake one foot, yes you may.
If it starts with L, M, or N,
Walk like a bear coming out of its den.
If it starts with O, P, or Q,
Bend way down and touch your shoe.
If it starts with R, S, or T,
Flap your wings like a busy bee.
If it starts with U, V, or W,
Hop around like a kangaroo.
If it starts with X, Y, or Z,
Point your finger and shout, "That's me!"

Who's Who?   Ask three or four children to stand before the rest of the class.
Blindfold each or ask them to close their eyes. Give a spoken description of the
clothing each is wearing and see if they can identify themselves based upon your
descriptions. As the children become comfortable with that process, make a
transition to other characteristics, i.e., "This child loves to eat nachos."

Happy Handshakes.   Play some lively music and encourage the children to move
freely to its rhythm. When you stop the music, the children must stop and give
the nearest child a handshake and the greeting, "Hi. I'm (child's name)." The
music continues, the children move freely, and when the music stops again, the

children exchange greetings with a new partner. Continue until the children had a chance to exchange greetings several times.

Police Officer and Lost Child.   Select one child to be the police officer and another child to be a parent. The parent calls, "Police officer, police officer, please help me find my lost child." The police officer asks, "What does your child look like?" The parent describes any one of the other children in the class. The police officer tries to find the child based upon the parent's description. When the child is found, the parent becomes the police officer and the missing child becomes the parent.

Hens and Chicks.   Designate one child as the hen. She leaves the area as her chicks are seated in a circle. Choose two or three children to be chicks who make "peep-peep" sounds. Upon returning, the hen attempts to identify her chicks (the ones making the sounds).

Shadow Profile.   Tape a sheet of construction paper onto a smooth wall or the chalkboard. Have a child sit in a chair as close to the paper as possible. Set up a lamp with a 100-watt bulb so that it casts a sharply defined shadow onto the paper. Then trace around the outline with a pencil or crayon. Cut around the outline and have the child glue his silhouette to a contrasting shade of construction paper. This is a great activity, but it takes much patience (or some extra help) to get the child to sit still for a minute or so.

   You may wish to discuss facial features and special aspects of each child, such as glasses, hair, and so on. Children often enjoy playing a "Guess Who" game with the silhouettes.

Guess Who.   A "Guess Who" game enjoyed by young children involves taping their voices and then giving them some time to listen to themselves. When the initial excitement wears off, see if the group can identify the voices of different individuals on the tape.

Guess Who #2.   "Guess Who" games can often be played by describing the physical appearance of any particular child. For example, you may say, "I see someone with black hair, a white sweater, and a gold necklace. Can anyone guess who it is?" Add further clues if the children cannot tell who is being described. Try to include each child in this game.

Who's Missing?   Ask all the children to close their eyes while you choose one child to go and hide somewhere in the classroom. On signal, the others open their eyes and try to guess who is missing. If they have difficulty, furnish clues such as, "The missing person's name begins with the same sound as *ball*."

Me Poetry.   Provide a full-length mirror and several small hand mirrors for the children to use as they investigate their own bodies—hair, skin, clothing, and so on. Guide them in this activity by discussing their image, by using poetry, or by singing a short tune such as the following, "Mirror, Mirror."

Mirror, mirror on the wall,
Look at me when I call.
See my _____ hair;
     (color)
See my _____ eyes;
     (color)
See my _____ skin;
     (color)
And my _____ size.
     (tall, short)
Mirror, mirror, you're the best;
Now I'll let you take a rest.

I Am Special.   (Sung to the tune of "Are You Sleeping?") Sing this tune often and make sure each child has an opportunity to be described. Add verses that describe special friends, favorite foods, and other characteristics that make each child special.

I am special,
I am special;
Look and see,
Look and see;
I have _____ hair;
     (color)
I have _____ eyes.
     (color)
They belong to me,
They belong to me.

Fingerprints.   Use finger paints and finger-paint paper to make handprints, fingerprints, and/or footprints. Encourage the children to press their palms or other body parts into the finger paint and then onto the paper. Label each child's paper and discuss the likenesses and differences of each person's prints.

Cognitive Possibilities.   Lead children through basic cognitive activities using the name tags. Ask the following questions:
    "Whose name begins with the same letter?"
    "Can you find a name that ends with the same letter?"
    "Which names are exactly alike?"
    "How many names start with B?"
    "Which name has the fewest letters? the most?"
    "Whose names have the same number of letters?"

People Puzzles.   Take a close-up photograph of each child. Prepare several templates by cutting holes in sheets of tagboard large enough to cover the photos. Place a template over a child's photo and ask the children to guess who the child is by using the clues showing through the holes. A sample template is shown in Figure 21.

Figure 21

Talking Books.   Tape a short, private interview with each child in your group. The process may take up to two or three weeks, depending on the number of children you have. Ask questions such as these:

"What is your name?"
"How old are you?"
"When is your birthday?"
"What is your favorite toy?"
"What story do you like to hear most?"
"What is your favorite food?"
"What gives you a very happy feeling?"
"What do you like most about school?"

While you are involved in the process of taping, take close-up photos of each child and organize them into booklet form. Once these tasks are completed, gather the children together and tell them you have a special tape to play for them. As the tape is played, show the photo of the child being interviewed. Discuss each interview, emphasizing the idea that many likenesses and differences exist among the group members. Offer the children an opportunity to independently look at and listen to the talking book by making it available at an interest center.

Who Can It Be?   Follow an interview procedure similar to the one described in the preceding activity, except that you will not ask the child to give her name. When all have been interviewed, call the children together and randomly play one of the interviews. Go over the information offered during the interview and ask the group to identify the interviewee. Offer only about two or three interviews per day, focusing on likenesses and differences of the children's responses.

Me Books.   Have the children draw pictures to show special things such as those illustrated in Figure 22. Add other pages, allowing the children to complete one page each day. Then compile the pages into booklet form and create a special treasure for the classroom and for the parents.

Figure 22

Body Portraits.   Place a large sheet of butcher paper on the floor. Ask each child to lie down on the paper as you trace around his body. Encourage the children to fill in various body components and articles of clothing for the picture. Cut out each portrait and hang them all up together as a room display.

A variation of this popular activity is to cut out two body shapes for each child. Set out crayons and/or paint and ask the children to fill in body components and articles of clothing as they would appear from the front for one outline and from the back for the other. Put the two outlines together and punch evenly spaced holes all around. Sew together the two segments with colorful yarn, leaving a small section into which the children may stuff crumpled newspapers. Once they finish and the body tracing begins to assume a three-dimensional appearance, finish sewing and tie up the yarn.

With either option, be sure to discuss various body parts and items of clothing the children are adding or should think about adding.

Me Badges.   Take close-up photographs of each child. Cut out the face and mount it on a cardboard circle with rubber cement. Laminate or cover the photos with clear contact paper. Print the child's name on construction paper or scrap ribbon. Tape or glue the ribbon onto the back of the circle as shown in Figure 23 (left side). Also, tape a safety pin to the back of the circle. The badge is a great source of pride since it identifies each youngster as a very special child.

Snack-Time Placemat.   Mark each child's place at snack time with a personalized placemat. Glue the child's photograph (or a self-portrait) to a 9″ × 12″ sheet of construction paper, and print her name in large letters beneath the photo as shown in Figure 23 (right side). Laminate the placemat or cover it with transparent adhesive paper for protection. Knowing others are looking at her placemat will

Figure 23

give the child an increasing awareness of herself, as well as a knowledge that her classmates are aware of her as an individual.

Chalk Trace.   Have one child stand on the pavement so that he casts a shadow in front of him. Trace around the shadow and print the child's name under it. Allow the children to add facial features or other details with colored chalk.

Body Part Puzzles.   Take full-length photographs of your children and mount them on tagboard. Cut the figures into simple body parts and place them (in groups of five) into a box. The children try to put them back together. This may be an expensive activity if you cannot print the photos yourself, but it is a very positive experience for the youngsters.

Personal Pillows.   Ask the children to bring to school an old T-shirt or any other short-sleeved shirt in decent shape that they may have outgrown. Sew up the neckline and sleeves, then have the children stuff their shirts from the bottom and finish sewing. Keep the pillows at the circle area where the children can use them at special times. (See Figure 24.)

Look How I've Grown!   Soon after the start of the school year, give the children each a large sheet of drawing paper and ask them to draw a picture of themselves. Measure each child, weigh him or her, and record these measurements on the drawing along with the date. Repeat the procedure in January and at the end of the school year. Put the three pictures in a folder to be taken home at the end of the year. The parents will enjoy seeing their child's growth in physical growth and mental maturity.

SPECIAL DAILY ROUTINES

Young children enjoy participating in activities at the start of the school year that emphasize the concept of everyone being special. These daily events may contribute to the child's sense of self-worth and help build a framework for group responsibilities. One of the traditionally popular special routines includes choosing classroom helpers. Individual contributions to group welfare can be effectively demonstrated by assigning helpers for specific classroom duties. Appointing helpers can be done on a daily or weekly basis, but it should be a consistent part

Figure 24

of the schedule. There are several ways to organize this facet of your program; the following suggestions may prove helpful. (See Figure 25 for an illustration of these ideas.)

Start off the year by utilizing concrete materials to indicate individual responsibilities. For example, a child's photograph and a sponge may be placed next to each other on a "Our Helpers" bulletin board to indicate who is responsible for cleaning the table after a snack. A straw and a photograph indicate the straw arranger, a photograph and napkin for the napkin passer, and so on.

As the children begin to recognize their names, print them on smiley faces and follow the preceding procedure by associating the smiley faces with the labeled concrete object. A "Happy Helpers" bulletin board is an attractive way of organizing the materials.

As a final stage in this developmental process, organize a special "Busy Bees" or "Helping Hands" bulletin board, on which one hand is labeled with the classroom responsibility and the other identifies the child assigned to it. To avoid disagreements as to whose turn it is to do what job, print the job completed by each child on the back of the hand showing her name.

One of the most perplexing aspects of job assignments is planning a system by which all children have an opportunity to perform the responsibilities they enjoy most. A way to do this is to move down the alphabet, alternately giving each child a chance to make a first choice, second choice, and so on. Record the child's name and date on the back of each "busy bee" to ensure fairness. Another way to address the fairness issue is to provide a job chart that changes daily (see the example, "Calendar-Based Job Chart" in the following section).

Calendar Concepts

Because children experience great difficulty with the concept of *time*, we often unwittingly offer time-related experiences where children are forced to act as if they know something, when in fact they don't. Lilian Katz, a respected early childhood specialist, offers the following example:

> Imagine it's Thursday the 19th. The teacher asks her 5-year-old students what day it is. One child answers "Tuesday." Now that won't do. So the teacher asks, "What day was it yesterday?" This is not teaching, it is coaxing. "Can anyone point to Thursday on the calendar? What letter does it begin with?" The children have a one-in-seven chance of getting it right—and they eventually do. But 10 minutes are wasted, and the children still don't understand why it's Thursday the 19th. What does it mean when children have to behave day after day as though they understand something when they haven't got a clue?*

How do you translate such an abstract concept as "time" into the concrete, meaningful experiences required by young children? Certainly you don't do it by

---

*Katz, Lilian (1987, October). "Lilian Katz: Let's not underestimate young children's intellects," *Instructor*, 92(3), 16.

  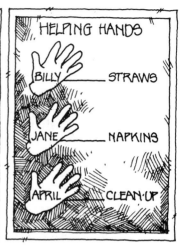

Figure 25

simply putting up a large calendar displaying clearly marked dates, the names of the month and days, and a colorful illustration appropriate for the particular month. Although this careful construction will attract the children's initial attention, it will not continue as a worthwhile learning activity. Young children may be able to adapt to a routine of selecting the numeral that stands for the day's date, but they do so only as that numeral follows the previous one in sequence. It is doubtful that such a routine can help them acquire the following basic calendar concepts:

☐ Calendars tell us the number of days in a year—365.

☐ Calendars divide the 365 days into groups of twelve, called months.

☐ Many of the months have the same number of days, but some do not.

☐ Calendars divide months into weeks, and each week is made up of seven days.

☐ Days of the week are given special names.

☐ Calendars help us know when special days are coming.

☐ January 1 begins a new year. The last day of the year is December 31.

The following activities have been designed to help you translate abstract calendar concepts into concrete learning experiences for young children.

Daily Schedule

Because calendars are basically abstract, it is best to approach the teaching of related skills by helping to clarify the sequential nature of time. A good way to do this is to illustrate and discuss the normal classroom routine. Make a chart of the daily schedule out of a long horizontal strip of tagboard. Divide it into sections and illustrate a major activity associated with each time block in the sections. Be sure to use simple, clear illustrations so the children can "read" them. Storytime, for example, can be a simple drawing of a book, snack time can be a drawing of a juice pitcher and cracker. For more ideas see Figure 26.

Discuss the illustrations during the group meeting to make sure that all the children understand what they depict. Each day, discuss the routines in sequence, pointing to the relevant sections of the chart. Be sure to stress activities that come "first," "next," and "last."

As the children internalize the daily routine, you may wish to cut apart the sections, shuffle them, pass them out so that each child gets a section, and ask them to arrange the activities in sequence, explaining why the daily routine is correct.

Ask the children to draw their own illustrations whenever any changes in the classroom's daily routine are in store (field trip, guest speaker, rain cancelling outdoor play, etc.).

Building a Calendar

To extend this beginning concept of sequence as it relates to time, capitalize on the personal routines of each child. Label a 10" × 14" piece of oaktag with the name of the day (*Wednesday*, for example). Say the word while pointing to it, making sure to emphasize left-to-right progression of the letters. First talk about what goes on in school on Wednesdays by using the daily sequence chart. Then, talk about the things that make this a special day for your children. For instance, it might be Francine's birthday or Arthur has an eye exam later in the day. As the children contribute, you may want to illustrate, print, or encourage the children to draw their own pictures of what they said, as shown in Figure 27.

Kindergarten and child-care children will be able to help you construct a chart each day, while most preschoolers will not because of their common two- or three-day schedules. For the preschoolers, label a chart for each day even though they are not there, but leave the chart blank under the daily label. Make blank charts for the weekend days, too. Arrange the daily charts in sequence so that the children begin to sense the order of the days of the week and to understand that a week is a collection of seven days. (See Figure 28.) Try to include the concept of *yesterday, today,* and *tomorrow* in your daily discussions. Discuss what

Figure 26

happened *yesterday* while recalling the significance of the illustrations focus on *today* and determine what *tomorrow* will be called. When the children understand the days for each week you may wish, at the start of a new month, to introduce the numerals of each date. Do so carefully, for when you're a child—so small and new to the world—even the most seemingly insignificant changes can be alarming.

Cut out the numerals from colorful construction paper and paste them beneath the name of the day as you introduce the name of the day. Print the name of the month (let us say *November*) on a separate card and hold it in your hands so the children can focus on it. Pronounce its name and ask the children to do

Figure 27

SUNDAY	MONDAY	TUESDAY	WEDNESDAY	THURSDAY	FRIDAY	SATURDAY
①	②	③	④	⑤	⑥	⑦
NO SCHOOL	FIRST FLOWER	ALICE				

Figure 28

the same. Review that a collection of seven days is called a week and explain that now the children are going to make a collection of weeks that will be called a month. But, because a month is made up of several weeks, we will need to give each day a second name (number name) so, for example, we can keep track of which Tuesday of the month we might be talking about. Put the children in this situation: "Suppose a child was born six years ago on a Friday. Someone asks her when her birthday is. She says, 'Friday.' Would that be a good answer? When is your birthday?" Children will typically answer with a month and date designation: "June eight." Show how a week is a collection of days and how a month is a collection of weeks, both of which help people keep track of time. Use a page from a real calendar to show this.

Say to the children, "Today is Monday and it is also the first day of the month of November. We call it Monday, November one (or first)." Ask a child to place the numeral on the rectangle and continue your discussion in the manner previously described. Keep your daily chart collection up on the wall as the month progresses, making sure to physically arrange the weeks as a calendar.

Extending Calendar Concepts

As the children construct calendars and understand the concepts of day, week, and month, continue to provide concrete, meaningful activities. Introduce the name of each month with a separate printed card so the children can focus on it. Then it can be attached to a sturdy attractive calendar base such as a sheet of pegboard or bulletin board. The days of the week could also be placed on smaller cards and attached to the calendar base by the children themselves. Instead of using a rectangular sheet of paper each day, the numerals could be placed beneath the day names much as a regular calendar. The children see the calendar grow this way. (See Figure 29.)

Many teachers prefer seasonal themes when making calendars, using numeral cards with acorns, pumpkins, turkeys, or Christmas trees. Other teachers

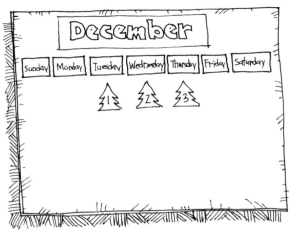

Figure 29

choose to expose all the dates at the beginning of the month and ask the children to take turns covering each day with an illustrative card as the days pass by. Initially, the entire month may be covered with identical shapes, but after a while you may choose to vary your technique to develop other concepts. For instance, you may alternate colors for each row on the calendar; red apples for the first row, green for the second, red for the third, and green for the fourth. Or you may wish to alternate symbols for each column—for example, corn shucks for one column, cornucopias for the second, pilgrims for the third, and turkeys for the fourth. Think of the patterning skills being developed as you take advantage of the calendar in these ways. (Patterning skills involve the ability to predict the symbol that will follow in sequence.)

Calendars and Your Curriculum

Some teachers prefer to exploit the many possibilities of calendars by concentrating on different academic areas for each month. For example, on a specific date, a child removes the correct numeral from the calendar and turns it over. On the reverse side he will find a basic shape (square, circle, triangle, rectangle) attached with Velcro or a magnetic strip, as illustrated in Figure 30. The child removes the shape, identifies it by name and color. He then examines a large silhouette on the calendar display whose component shapes contain one pattern exactly like the one he has. After finding the appropriate match, the child attaches it so that, by the end of the month, the outlined shape will be alive with a variety of colorful shapes. Similar activities could be associated with any area of your curriculum—colors, beginning sounds, rhyming sounds, numbers, and so on.

The following section describes a variety of calendar activities. Try them out on your preschoolers and see which ones work best for you.

Calendar-Based Job Chart.   For the purpose of illustrating the sequence of days, especially as it relates to the concepts of *yesterday, today, tomorrow,* and *week,* you may wish to associate your job chart with your early calendar activities. Attach library pockets to a large piece of oaktag, with one pocket for each child. Draw a picture and print words on each pocket to specify particular classroom jobs as illustrated in Figure 31. Place a card containing a child's name into each pocket so that the name is visible over the top of the pocket. Each day, move the cards over one place, emphasizing what each child's job was *yesterday,* what it is *today,* and what it will be *tomorrow.* Some children may even want to count the days until they finally get a highly desired job.

Season Dial.   Make a large wall display as shown in Figure 32. Divide a circle into twelve segments. Label each segment with the name of a month, starting with January at the top. Make your winter months' labels from white paper, spring from green, summer from yellow, and fall from orange. Illustrate a person standing in seasonal attire holding the name for each season next to its appropriate months. Have the children draw seasonal illustrations in each segment.

In the center, add a smaller circle. Draw hatch marks on the outer part of this inner circle, one each to indicate the number of weeks that occur during the

Figure 30

Figure 31

months. Use a push pin to attach a movable arrow, and turn it each time a new week begins. This gives the children a good idea of how the progression of weeks, months, and years are cyclical in nature.

Today Song.   Sing the following song by inserting the appropriate name of the day as you introduce each day of the week. (To the tune of "If You're Happy and You Know It.")

If you're happy that it's Thursday, clap your hands.
    (Clap hands twice)
If you're happy that it's Thursday, clap your hands.
    (Clap hands twice)
If you're happy that it's Thursday,
If you're happy that it's Thursday,
If you're happy that it's Thursday, clap your hands.
    (Clap hands twice)

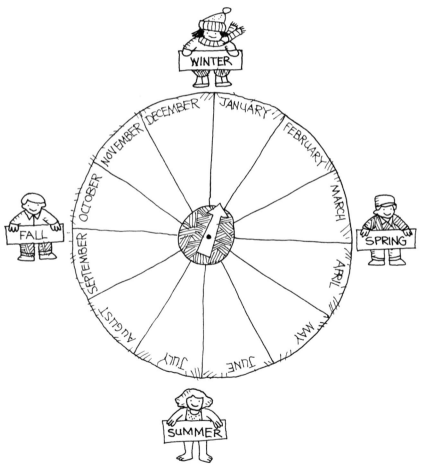

Figure 32

You may wish to sing the song a second or third time substituting other movements such as "stamp your feet," "slap your knees," "nod your head," or "raise your thumb." Or, you may wish to sing the song only once each day, but daily change the movement as well as the name of the day of the week.

Days-of-the-Week Bears.   Cut out seven bear shapes like the one illustrated in Figure 33—each wearing a different shirt for each day of the week. Glue each bear to a tongue depressor. Ask each child to take one, hold it up as she hears her day of the week recited in this rhyme and line up in sequence. After the rhyme is complete, the children call out the days of the week in order.

Monday Bear watches stars at night.
Tuesday Bear smiles warm and bright.
Wednesday Bear gobbles globs of honey.
Thursday Bear's fur is soft as a bunny.
Friday Bear hums a happy song.
Saturday Bear's paws are big and strong.
Sunday Bear loves to say this rhyme,
And thank you for a wonderful time!

Days of the Week Rhyme.   Recite the following rhyme with your children to help them remember the name and order of the days of the week.

Monday alone,
Tuesday together,
Wednesday we walk
When it's fine weather,
Thursday we kiss,
Friday we cry,
Saturday's hours
Seem almost to fly.
When we know that Sunday has passed,
It will be another new week at last.

Months of the Year Chant.   Children enjoy rhythm and rhyme, so help them remember the order of the months by repeating the following chant. (To involve the children in more action, you may wish to clap instead of pause where indicated.)

January (pause), February (pause), March, April, May (pause),
June (pause), July (pause), August and September (pause),
October and November (pause), and then there comes December(pause),
and then we start all over again. January (pause),
February (pause), etc.

Weather Chart.   Construct a bulletin board display on which you have made a young child, a tree, and the bright sun out of flannel. (See Figure 34.) Introduce the weather child to your children and ask them to help supply a name for him or her. Show the children some clothing you have made for the child, appropriate

Figure 33

for the yearly weather characteristics of your geographic region, i.e., short-sleeved shirt, shorts, swimming suit, long pants, long-sleeved shirt, shoes, sandals, sweater, jacket, boots, umbrella or raincoat, hat, gloves, and so on. Explain that the children are going to help dress the weather child each day based upon what it is like outdoors.

Your daily routine will start with a discussion of the weather. The sun always shines during the day so it is a permanent part of your display. If the day is sunny, the bright sun remains. If it is cloudy, the children select a flannel cloud and cover up the sun. Flannel raindrops or flakes of snow can be added if those conditions exist. A bare-branched flannel tree is also a permanent part of the display. Simply cover up the branches with light green buds for springtime, a large dark green leafy shape for summertime, a yellow-orange leafy shape for fall, and allow the branches to remain bare for wintertime. Daily discussions should focus on the influence of weather upon the physical environment and upon the ways people dress for comfort.

Attendance Recording

Use photographs or outline shapes of boys and girls to count the number of children in attendance each day. (See Figure 35.) Glue small pieces of Velcro on the backs of your figures and attach as many pieces of Velcro on your chart as

Figure 34

you have boys and girls in your classroom. Ask your children to place their figures above their appropriate name tags as they enter the room. Then everyone, in unison, counts the number of girls, the number of boys, and the total number of children in attendance. Ask a child to attach the appropriate numeral tags to the summary sentence. Count the number of absent children and have another child place that numeral card in the second summary sentence.

If you prefer a display format rather than a chart, many additional possibilities for attendance charts exist. Farmer Brown's Apple Orchard is one example, shown in Figure 36. Use a large construction paper apple tree, and again attach Velcro at various places at the base of the tree, in the leaves of the tree, and on the backs of paper apples (one for each child in your classroom). Print the children's names on the apples and attach them randomly to the Velcro strips at the bottom of the tree. As the children come into your room, they select their apples and put them on the tree. (If you'd like to extend math concepts as the first chart did, use yellow apples for the girls and red for the boys. Then count the number of children as you did in the earlier exercise.

Birthdays

One of the major highlights of the school year is the celebration of special days, but no party or experience seems to bring as much excitement as the planning and execution of a birthday party. Most preschool teachers set aside a special time during the day when the birthday child is allowed to share her special day with the others. Some suggestions for this special day follow.

Birthday Chair.   Paint a special chair with bright paint and decorate it. This is a "Birthday Chair" to be used by the birthday child only on his birthday.

Birthday Boxes.   Wrap a large shoe or hat box, top and bottom separately, with festively decorated paper and glue a bright bow to the top. Inside the box, place a packet of materials for making a special birthday hat (paper, stickers, buttons, ribbons, glitter, glue, etc.).

Bring out the box ceremoniously on each child's birthday and let the child choose the materials for the birthday hat which you (or an aide) and the child can make together. Decorate a box similar to the one described above and fill it with small trinkets—erasers, pencils, small cars, or animals. Have the birthday child choose a gift from the box.

Special Day.   Offer special privileges to the birthday child—being first in line, running errands, leading a routine, and so on. (Be sure to mention that the child is getting special treatment because she's "the birthday girl.")

Birthday Capes and Crowns.   The "royal birthday crown" is a variation of the birthday hat described earlier. Cut a crown shape from colorful construction paper for the children to decorate and wear on their special day. Decorate it with glitter, sequins, and other bright materials. (See Figure 37.) The birthday child wears the crown during the "official" birthday ceremony. If you can find some old velvet or

Figure 35

other appropriate material, fashion it into a royal cape for the birthday king or queen. Such royal treatment will certainly highlight these special days.

Royal Birthday Declaration.   Send each child home on his or her special day with a citation of recognition. Design a birthday salute such as the one illustrated in Figure 38 and fill it in with the suitable information.

Hip-hip-hooray! It is declared that _____
                                          (child's name)
is awarded_____ big birthday cheers on this date
              (age)
of royal birth, _____ . Happy birthday
and long live the king (or queen)!

Summer Birthdays.   If your school year is based on a ten-month calendar, some children will not be able to celebrate their birthdays during the school year. Rather

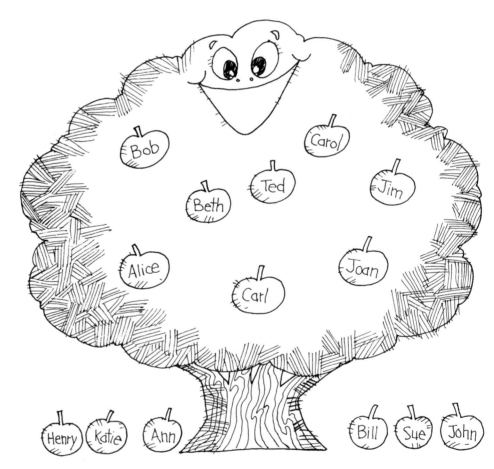

Figure 36

than celebrating all of these during the last week of school, try to celebrate them as "half birthdays." If a child was born on July 15, for example, her birthday would be celebrated on January 15—she would be four-and-a-half years old.

Birthday Flags.   Fly a special birthday flag on the day any child in your classroom celebrates a birthday. Cut a large rectangle from an old bed sheet. Hem the edges and then sew or paint an illustration of a birthday cake and the words "Happy Birthday" on the flag. Staple or glue the flag to a dowel stick or old broom handle and display it on the special day! (See Figure 39.)

Birthday Train.   Ask each child to bring in a photo. Attach the photos to cutout construction paper train cars, making one car for each month of the year. Design different size cards for each month, depending on the number of birthdays in each. Print the children's names and birthdays below their photos, as shown in Figure 40.

PLAY

Anyone who has ever spent time with young children knows the pleasure and enjoyment they derive from play. The smiles and expressions of glee are proof of its naturally enjoyable character. Play is an inseparable part of childhood and should be considered an essential component of quality early childhood programs. In this section we will look at activities to enhance the traditional categories of play: (1) *sociodramatic play* (involving two or more children assuming roles in a make-believe situation), (2) *constructive play* (using materials such as blocks or woodworking tools), and (3) *art and music* (expressing oneself creatively through these two media).

Figure 37

Figure 38

Figure 39

Sociodramatic Play

Sociodramatic play involves the use of creative thinking while enacting roles that are familiar to the children. By participating in such a process, children are able to experience growth in all areas of development.

☐ *Social.* By sharing and planning with others, children learn to cooperate.

☐ *Emotional.* Sociodramatic play allows children to savor pleasurable experiences and may also arouse emotions such as anger, hostility, and aggression.

☐ *Affective.* Children can explore their own likes and dislikes, and notions of good and bad.

☐ *Physical.* Typically, children exercise both small and large muscles in socio-dramatic play.

☐ *Cognitive.* Children express their thoughts in play actions.

☐ *Creative.* Children come up with their own solutions to the problems they encounter.

The Housekeeping Center

Perhaps the most common feature (in addition to blocks) of most early childhood programs is the area where the toys and objects related to household/family themes are stored and arranged. Toys commonly found in this center include:

☐ Miniature tables, chairs, stoves, refrigerators, sinks, and used adult furniture

☐ Household utensils (pots, pans, disks, cooking tools, eating tools, ironing board, iron)

☐ Dolls and doll accessories (carriages, cradles, crib)

☐ Cleaning supplies (mops, brooms, dustpans, empty spray bottles)

☐ Adult clothing (shoes, hats, dresses, pants, coats)

☐ Adult accessories (handbags, briefcases, gloves, scarves)

The housekeeping center should be partitioned off as a separate space in the setting. This reduces the incidence of problem behaviors and increases the amount and degree of cooperation among the children.

Figure 40

Theme Centers

Some early childhood professionals choose to supplement their housekeeping center with settings that suggest specific themes for sociodramatic play. These centers have theme-related props to spark interest and encourage creative expression of experiences in places the children may have visited. Some examples follow.

Restaurant

Chef's hat, apron
Menus
Table
Chairs
Sign
Eating utensils
Table cloth, placemat, napkins
Cash register
Telephone
(Locate near housekeeping
    center. The stove, sink, etc.
    can serve as the restaurant's
    kitchen.)

Doctor's Office

White shirt
Nurse's cap
Medical kit
Stethoscope
Tape, gauze, cotton
Scale and measuring chart
Glasses without lenses
Smock
Bed or cot
Eye chart, tape measure
Telephone

Fire Station

Hat
Badge
Boots
Telephone
Toy truck or wagon
Hose (or rope)
Walkie talkies
Megaphone

Service Station

Rubber hose connected to a box
    decorated like a gas pump
Empty oil cans
Air pump
Toy gas pump
Sponge, bucket and rubber
    wiper
Rags
Old tire, air filter
Cash register and play money
Spark plugs
Play automobiles
Tools
Flashlight
Cap
Keys

Plumber's Shop

Pipes that fit together
Wrenches and other tools
Hose
Plunger
Bucket
Sponge
Cap

Grocery Store

Cash register
Play money
Food cartons, boxes
Empty cans
Shopping bags
Plastic food
Telephone
Toy shopping carts
Calculators
Coupons

Beauty Parlor

Broken hair dryer
Curlers
Plastic scissors
Plastic basin
Comb
Hair nets
Apron or bib
Towels
Brushes
Empty plastic shampoo
     containers
Empty hair spray containers
Magazines
Mirror

Post Office

Telephone
Stamps
Envelopes of all sizes
Paper
Mailbox and mailbag
Rubber stamp
Packages, postcards, letters
Cash register and play money
Scale
Sign

Shoe Store

Shoe boxes
Old shoes
Chairs
Cash register and play money
Foot measuring device

Railroad Yard

Cap
Lunch box
Coveralls (bib types)
Lantern (no glass)
Neckerchief
Work shoes
Chairs (lined up for "cars")

Ice Cream Store

Empty ice-cream containers
Ice-cream scoop
Cap
Apron
Cash register and play money
Construction paper cones

*Other Suggestions for Dramatic
     Play*

Astronaut
Veterinarian
Baker
Painter
Police Officer
Fisherman
Tailor or Seamstress
Telephone Operator
Circus Performer
Forest Ranger
Ranch Hand
Airline Pilot
Underwater Explorer
Sports Figure
Television Star/Newscaster

Store the props in cardboard boxes with a picture of the character on front so the children can select whatever they wish to portray.

My Day. Invite your children to take turns making a dramatic play corner into an area that represents their life-style, hobby, interest, or fantasy by bringing in materials from home. This activity offers a child a chance to share something personal about herself with the other children. Creative play is one of the most effective forms of children's communication.

TV Stars.   Make a television set from a used packing box or look for a discarded television set from which the screen has been removed. Secure a large mirror to the inside of the set so that when the children look at the "screen" they see themselves as the actors or actresses. (See Figure 41.)

Hide-a-House.   Sew four pieces of old sheet to a fifth one so that you have a large top-to-floor cover for a table as illustrated in Figure 42. With permanent marking pens, draw different houses, stores, or buildings on the four side squares. The children can enter the structure through the slits in the corners and assume any roles they desire.

Simple Hand Puppets

Use common household items such as wooden spoons, spatulas, dish mops, strainers, or hair brushes to form the base for simple hand puppets. Decorate the items with wiggle eyes, yarn, felt, ribbon, sequins, pan scrubbers, and so on, and create a bunch of lovable characters for your classroom. (See Figure 43 for examples.)

A plastic detergent or bleach bottle makes a creative puppet head. Use an old mop head, yarn, or a discarded doll's wig for hair, a piece of cloth attached to the bottle's opening with a rubber band for a body, and paints or marking pens to create a face. Hold the bottle from underneath the body or by the bottle handle at the rear.

You can easily make puppets with moving mouths out of a sock. Cut a slit through the toe of the sock and turn it inside out. Fold open the mouth and pin an oval piece of felt to the slit. Stitch the felt to the sock. Turn the sock right side out and add buttons, scraps of yarn, or fabric for facial features.

MIRROR

PAPER (CARDBOARD BOX)

CONTROL KNOBS MADE FROM PIECES OF WOOD OR PLASTIC

Figure 41

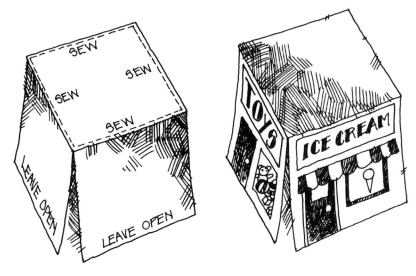

Figure 42

Paper plates form the beginning of interesting puppet friends. Fold a plate in half and glue two Ping-Pong balls to the top. Decorate the paper plate creature with fabric, yarn, or paper. Operate the puppet by placing your fingers on the top of the plate and your thumb beneath.

Puppet possibilities are limited only by your imagination, but a few more options are illustrated in Figure 44.

Peanut Puppets.   Carefully cut one end of the peanut shell away. Hopefully the peanuts will fall out—don't forget to eat them! Use paint or marking pens to draw the puppets' faces. Have the children place the puppets on their fingers and perform a peanut puppet production.

Puppet Stage.   Make a handy stage for your puppets and use them in a variety of ways, or just enjoy them out in the open! Two puppet stage ideas are illustrated in Figure 45 (page 98).

Constructive Play

Children enjoy using objects (blocks, tools) or materials (sand, water, wood) to make something. They take great pride in creating things by themselves under the careful guidance and support of a sensitive adult. Some of the most popular constructive play areas follow.

Blocks

Blocks are found in just about every early childhood setting. Children enjoy working with blocks and welcome the daily experiences they provide. These

WOODEN SPOON   SPATULA   DISH SCRUBBER

STRAINER   BLEACH BOTTLE   PEANUT SHELLS

FELT
OVAL

SOCK   PAPER PLATE

Figure 43

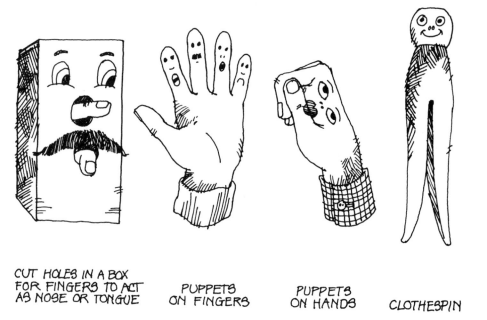

CUT HOLES IN A BOX
FOR FINGERS TO ACT
AS NOSE OR TONGUE

PUPPETS
ON FINGERS

PUPPETS
ON HANDS

CLOTHESPIN

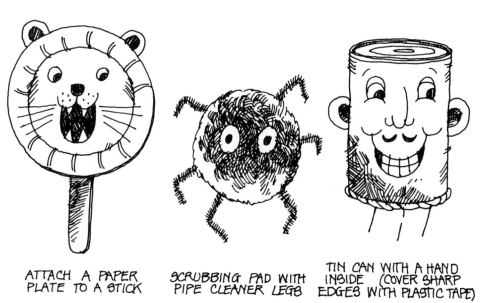

ATTACH A PAPER
PLATE TO A STICK

SCRUBBING PAD WITH
PIPE CLEANER LEGS

TIN CAN WITH A HAND
INSIDE (COVER SHARP
EDGES WITH PLASTIC TAPE)

Figure 44

AN OPENING IN AN OLD SHEET

A LARGE, STURDY BOX

Figure 45

blocks are normally arranged on a low shelf that's easily accessible to the children. The children are encouraged to use the blocks in creative ways to build airports, railroads, shopping centers, rocket ships, or whatever else they choose to bring to life with their rich imaginations. Basically, these blocks are of three types:

☐ *Unit blocks.* These hardwood blocks begin with a basic block 3½ inches square and 1½ inches thick; other blocks are multiples or fractions of the basic unit, usually increasing in size to quadruple units. In addition, wedges, triangles, cylinders, and other shapes help children construct homes, barns, stores, and so on. The most common unit block shapes are illustrated in Figure 46.

☐ *Hollow blocks.* Hollow, wooden blocks may be as large as 15 inches square and 6 inches thick. They are usually constructed of a soft, light wood that enables the children to build large structures such as forts, hideouts, private clubs, houses, and other buildings that are roomy enough for several children to enter. The constructions are usually kept up for several days.

☐ *Table blocks.* Smaller, solid blocks, usually no more than a few inches long, table blocks demand greater small muscle control and thus are usually used by more advanced children. These include bristle blocks, Lego, Tinkertoys, and Lincoln Logs.

In addition to these basic blocks, the creative early childhood teacher may wish to consider the following possibilities.

Styrofoam Toys. Save the loose macaroni-type styrofoam bits used for packaging. Place them on a table along with a generous supply of toothpicks. The children can pierce the styrofoam bits with the toothpicks, connect them, and create many unique structures.

"Junk" Block Play.   Collect a variety of pieces of junk. For example:

cans	straws	spools
cardboard tubes	fabric scraps	sponges
cardboard boxes	styrofoam	string
milk cartons	egg cartons	newspapers
paper cups	carpet scraps	plastic pails
wood scraps	paper plates	shells

Find these items in your garage and basement, or solicit help from the parents of your children. Place all the "junk" in a quiet corner of the classroom and encourage your budding engineers to make any design they wish by fastening the pieces together with glue or hammer and nails. A picture of a typical "invention" is found in Figure 47.

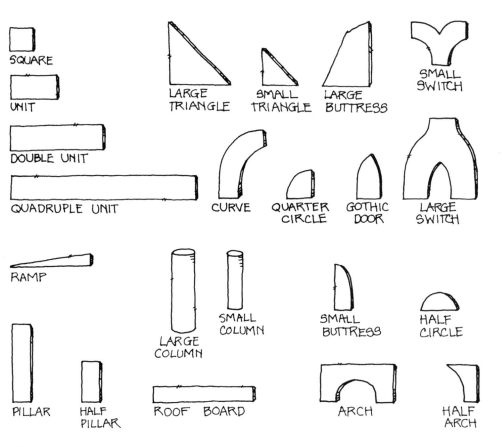

Figure 46

Figure 47
Several of these ideas were suggested by F. Charlene Fink.

Styrofoam Carpenter. Collect a number of large styrofoam scraps such as those used as packing material for radios or televisions. Children who experience difficulty putting screws into wood will find styrofoam blocks much less frustrating to work with.

Stages of Blockbuilding Interest and Skill. Maja Apelman condensed Harriet Johnson's description of the stages of development children seem to pass through as they play with blocks. Such knowledge can help you establish realistic expectations as the children play. Children progress through the stages regardless of whether the blocks are introduced to them at age two or six. The only difference is that older children go through the early stages much more quickly as they move toward the stage appropriate for their age.*

1. Blocks are carried around, not used for construction. This applies to the very young child.
2. Building begins. Children make mostly rows, either horizontal (on the floor) or vertical (stacking). There is much repetition in this early building pattern.
3. Two blocks are arranged with a space between them, connected by a third block to form a bridge.
4. Blocks are placed so as to enclose a space.

*Apelman, Maja (1984). Appendix 1: Stages of block building. In Elizabeth S. Hirsch (Ed.), *The block book*. Washington, DC: National Association for the Education of Young Children.

5. When children acquire facility with blocks they begin making decorative patterns. Much symmetry can be observed, though buildings, generally, are not yet named.

6. Naming of structures for dramatic play begins. Before that children may also have named their structures, but the names were not necessarily related to the function of the building.

7. Children's buildings often reproduce or symbolize actual structures they know, and there is a strong impulse toward dramatic play around the block structures.

The values children derive from block play were lucidly expressed by Harriet Johnson, a pioneer in early childhood education. She made three major points: (1) "The power to deal effectively with the environment accrues to a child through the free use of constructive material"; (2) "Possibilities are offered by blocks and similar materials for expressing rhythm, pattern, design"; and (3) "By means of these materials, children may review, rehearse, and play out their past experience."*

Woodworking

Woodworking is a wonderful experience—a process that offers children many benefits: creative expression, emotional release, and opportunities for small- and large-muscle growth and coordination.

The tools most often used in a preschool woodworking program include claw hammers, large-head nails, hand drills, crosscut and backsaws, miter box, clamps, sandpaper blocks, and wood glue. These must be quality tools. Toy tools frustrate children because they constantly break or fail to do the job efficiently.

Safety in the Woodworking Area. Children move impulsively and quickly when engaged in stimulating activity such as working with tools. If we allow their energy to go unchecked, they may be harmed through the misuse of materials they had hoped to enjoy. Our role is to help the children enjoy working with tools but at the same time to respect what they are doing.

The tools in an early childhood program should be chosen because they are safe if properly used. Items such as screwdrivers or pliers, for example, have no place in a program because they can harm, even if used properly. Before allowing any child to work with the tools, design a careful, deliberate introduction. Plan to introduce only one or two at a time to groups of no more than three children. Demonstrate proper use of the tools, explaining each step as the children watch. Let the children try, one at a time, making sure they follow directions very carefully. It is advisable to have the children wear unbreakable goggles whenever they work with tools.

Proper introduction to and use of the tools will help prevent most accidents. However, you should never leave the children alone when they are working.

*Johnson, Harriet (1972). *Children in the nursery school* (pp. 183, 189). New York: Agathon Press.

Children should never be allowed to use the tools without adult supervision. The activities in which the children use the tools are outlined below, but you must stop whatever the children are doing if you feel the tools are being used improperly.

Hammering.   Children love to hammer. They will spend up to half an hour at a time hammering if they are given the opportunity. But in order to hammer well children must be deliberately introduced to the proper technique. Two-year-olds are not yet ready to use real tools, so their carpentry experiences should be of the "readiness" type, that is, hammering wooden pegs into holes with mallets. These experiences help children to control eye and hand movements as well as to practice the vertical wrist action necessary to hammer. Another experience appropriate for this initial hammering stage is using the mallet to drive golf tees into pieces of styrofoam. But watch that the golf tees go into the styrofoam and not the mouth. Be sure to show the child how to use the mallet or hammer properly if she is having trouble. It should be grasped about two or three inches from the end of the handle. Instruct the child to keep her eye on the head of the object to be hammered. Tap it lightly until it has been started and take the helping hand away. Then the object can be hammered more forcefully. Be sure to emphasize the importance of using the vertical wrist movement as the main source of power. It is much easier to hammer with the wrist than with the elbow or shoulder, and the children will be able to control their hammering motions to a finer degree.

Once the children have shown a basic skill in the proper use of a toy hammer, let them use a real one. The typical hammer weighs about sixteen ounces, much too heavy for most preschoolers, so look for one that weighs between eight and ten ounces. The handle should be small enough for the child to grip easily, and the face should be free of any pit marks or dents. Some hammers have sharp claws on top that help remove nails. Ball peen hammers are favored by teachers who are concerned about the unrefined hammering skills of their inexperienced children. Ball peen hammers have a rounded, ball-shaped top in place of the claw and are not as dangerous if the child is accidentally struck.

A common method to help children drive their first nails is to start the nail yourself by tapping it lightly into the wood (make sure the nail is straight). Soon the children will want to try by themselves. Advise them to tap the nail lightly a few times while holding it straight. Then tell them to move their fingers out of the way and drive the nail into the wood, using the recommended vertical wrist action described earlier. A second useful technique for starting nails (especially small ones) is to first push the nail through some heavy paper. The paper will hold the nail in place as it is started with a few light taps. Rip the paper away after the nail becomes firmly embedded in the wood. Nails should have large heads and very narrow shanks for ease of driving. Be sure that shanks are strong enough to drive the nail into the wood without bending easily. Flooring or wallboard nails are especially good.

Old tree stumps are interesting objects for hammering practice. Remember, the children are just beginning to learn how to use a hammer, so they are not yet interested in actually using it to make something. They are quite thrilled simply at their ability to use a hammer to drive a nail into wood. As a result, they are content to spend concentrated amounts of time just hammering large numbers of nails into wood—your tree stump will be totally covered with nails in a very short time. A major advantage of the tree stump is that children hammer their nails into the end grain, which makes it easier to drive the nails without bending them. Other than tree stumps, only softwoods should be used for driving nails. Pine, fir, cedar, or redwood are ideal choices. The 2″ × 4″ size should be used for initial hammering practice, and scraps of one-inch thick lumber work well when children want to nail pieces of wood together.

Sawing.   Most preschool programs generally offer two types of saws for their children: the *crosscut saw* and the *backsaw.* Both are easy to use if introduced properly and provide countless hours of enjoyment for young children.

Perhaps the safest way of initiating practice with a real saw is to attach a miter box securely to the work table with C-clamps (4-inch clamps work best). Miter boxes are three-sided (the top is open), U-framed, box-shaped devices generally made of solid hardwood. (See Figure 48.) They have two sets of grooves cut into the side for guiding straight cuts and two sets for guiding cuts at a 45-degree angle. Miter boxes are good for young children because they are relatively safe and help children learn to saw correctly. To use the miter box, place the wood to be cut into the box and either hold it against the edge closest to you with your nonsawing hand or clamp it securely. Insert the backsaw (it has a reinforced top that ensures a straight cut) into the pair of miter box grooves that will give your desired cut and begin a slow back and forth stroke to get the cutting groove started. The stroke can then be speeded up, but be careful not to put too much pressure on the saw, or it may pinch or bind in the wood. Let the saw do the work; pressure is more of a hindrance than a help. You should cut smoothly and safely in this manner.

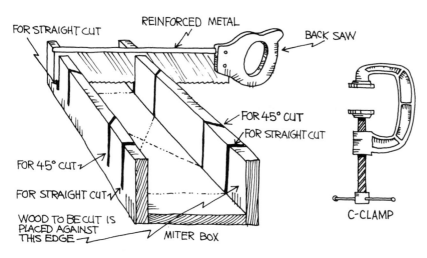

Figure 48

Once the children have acquired confidence by sawing successfully with miter boxes, you can introduce the crosscut saw. Crosscut saws have teeth much like the backsaw's but are somewhat longer and lack the reinforcing strip of metal on the top of the blade. (See Figure 49.) Look for crosscut saws that are sixteen to twenty inches long; they are the easiest for young children to handle. As with all sawing, the wood to be cut must be clamped to a secure base. *Vises* that are permanently mounted to the work table can be used by the children to hold the wood steady. Stanley brand WorkMates also work well. They offer a secure base for sawing and an adjustable top that can be easily adapted to hold almost any size or shape of wood.

Children often have a more difficult time starting a cutting groove with a crosscut saw than with a backsaw. Two major reasons for this are that the crosscut saw lacks the reinforced top, so its blade tends to bend as the children exert pressure sideways, and the grooves of the miter box no longer guide the saw, so the children tend to force the crosscut saw against the edge of the cutting groove. This results in troublesome binding against the wood and a sporadic, rather than a smooth, cutting motion. You may want to start a cutting groove for the children and remind them to hold the saw straight without forcing its direction. Again, let the saw do the work.

Drilling. Turning hand drills to make holes in wood is an enjoyable activity that fascinates nearly all young children. A good hand drill should have a handle that the child can grip comfortably and, if possible, a convenient removable cap that stores various sizes of drill bits. Children are not able to change the bits, so the teacher must do that when necessary.

Before drilling, secure a thick 2″ × 10″ × 30″ plank painted bright red to the top of a work table. Clamp the piece being drilled to the red plank, and tell the children that when they see red sawdust they should stop drilling. Make a starter hole with a large nail. Then the child can guide the bit to the starter hole and begin drilling. The child should hold the drill handle with one hand and turn the pinion with the other. Be sure the child's body is well above the drill so he is able to exert ample downward pressure. The drill should be in a straight vertical position at all times and the drilling movement should be rhythmic and smooth.

A second tree stump might be designated as a drilling station. The hammering stump will not work because the driven nails will tend to dull the drill bits. A word of caution as the children drill into the stump, however: *always make sure the child's body is above the drill and that the drill bit is pointed away from the body.*

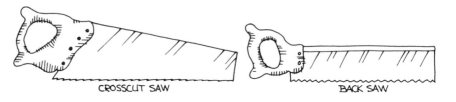

CROSSCUT SAW   BACK SAW

Figure 49

Constant supervision and adherence to firmly established safety standards is critical to a successful woodworking center.

Gluing.   Before being given opportunities to glue together pieces of wood, young children must have ample opportunities to glue and paste other materials. With such experiences they should understand some basic gluing considerations: the table surface must be protected with newspapers, the glue should be applied sparingly (too much results in a longer drying time), and a damp washcloth or sponge should be kept nearby to remove glue from hands while the child is working.

Yellowish wood glue in squeezable plastic containers is the best glue to use on wood, since it is water-resistant. Once children begin gluing or nailing pieces of wood together, their imaginations often become engaged, and they use their creations in other activities. A child's block of wood with a spool glued on becomes a much more long-lived "ocean liner" if the proper glue is used. In order to achieve the best bonding, the pieces should be clamped together or weighted until dry. Drying time varies, but it's best to allow the project to dry overnight before using.

Sanding.   Sanding a piece of wood is an absorbing experience for young children, especially because the wood constantly changes appearance as the grain is brought out. Choose a coarse grade of sandpaper—it is much less difficult to use. Sanding will be much more successful if the children attach the sandpaper to sanding blocks. Fold a piece of sandpaper around a wooden block large enough for the children to grip easily. Tack the sandpaper to the block so it will not slip. Clamp the wood to be sanded to a worktable and show the children how to make smooth, steady sweeps of the arm along the grain of the wood.

Because sanding involves much rhythmic movement, it is fun to make up songs to accompany the sanding strokes. Here is one I have used, sung to the tune of "London Bridge." Make up your own.

Sanding, sanding blocks of wood,
Blocks of wood, blocks of wood,
Sanding, sanding blocks of wood,
Making it smooth if I could!

Children progress through a sequence of interest and skills beginning with the sensory pleasure derived from woodworking to the desire to make things. Of course, their creations will be primitive, but just imagine the joy when a child realizes that the piece of wood she just sawed would make an excellent train engine just by driving a nail in the right place! The values of experimentation, creativity, muscular coordination, emotional pleasure, planning, and social exchange far outweigh the need for accuracy in the final product.

Two excellent resources that provide information about tools and offer suggestions for woodworking projects are *Woodworking for Young Children* by Patsy Skeen, et al. (Washington, D.C.: National Association for the Education of Young Children, 1984) and *Easy Woodstuff for Kids* by David Thompson (Mount Rainier, MD: Gryphon House, 1981).

Water Play

Perhaps no area of the preschool curriculum is so attractive to young children as the water and sand play areas. These areas provide relaxation, experimentation, and conversation, and allow manipulation and, most of all, just plain fun. This list outlines general ideas for water play, followed by some specific applications. You and the children will undoubtedly come up with your own. (Sand play will be covered in the next section.)

1. Play with water in a wading pool or other large container.
2. Play with water and soap (making bubbles or washing).
3. Play with water and colors (tempera paint or food coloring).
4. Play with water and various utensils (funnels, sponges, corks, boats, eggbeaters, cups, etc.).

Water Drums.   Place some pots, pans, lids, cake pans, pie tins, flower pots, plastic containers, and anything else that will make a unique sound in an area outside near a source of water. Lean the objects against trees, stones, walls, or other supports. Adjust spray bottles to the fine needlepoint spray. Have the children spray all the objects to make different noises.

Water Magic.   Get a number of jars with watertight lids. Fill the jars halfway with water, and have the children choose different food colorings to add to the water. Carefully fill the rest of the jar with vegetable oil. Have the children screw the lids on, checking to see that they're tight. The children then hold the jars sideways and rock them back and forth to see the designs change.

Strong Bubbles.   Add excitement to your water play activities by mixing ⅓ cup glycerine and ⅔ cup liquid soap with a quart of water. (The glycerine makes it possible to create larger and stronger bubbles while increasing the bubbles' survival time.) Put a drop of solution on waxed paper, insert a straw into the drop, and blow. Explore the many possibilities of this technique.

Water Slides.   Spread an old shower curtain on a grassy hill. Anchor the corners with plastic jugs filled with water. Spray a steady fine mist of water on the curtain and when it is completely wet, the children can jump on it and begin sliding.

Shooting Gallery.   Use plastic spray bottles, blasters, or squirt guns for this activity. Line up a series of plastic bottles weighted with water on a table or carton and place a Ping-Pong ball on the top of each. Have the children stand back a short distance and fire at the targets until all the Ping-Pong balls are knocked off.

Sailboats.   Children can enjoy pleasure cruises and stirring races or participate in many other creative experiences by making and sailing a variety of boats. Boats can be constructed from junk materials found around most early childhood facilities. (Some possibilities are illustrated in Figures 50 and 51.)

Stretch string along the length of a large pan of water to make sailboat racing lanes. Allow the children to choose one of the lanes for a race. They try to win the race by blowing their boats with straws.

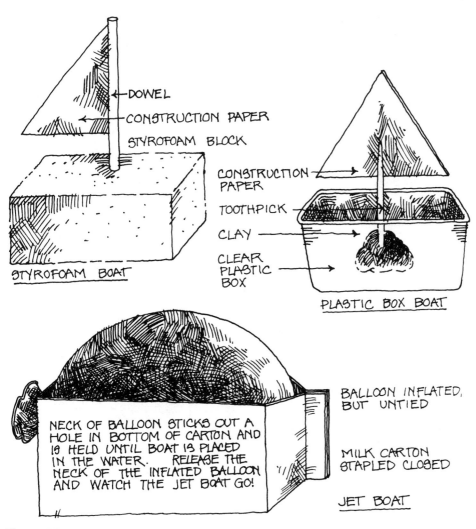

DOWEL

CONSTRUCTION PAPER

STYROFOAM BLOCK

STYROFOAM BOAT

CONSTRUCTION PAPER

TOOTHPICK

CLAY

CLEAR PLASTIC BOX

PLASTIC BOX BOAT

NECK OF BALLOON STICKS OUT A HOLE IN BOTTOM OF CARTON AND IS HELD UNTIL BOAT IS PLACED IN THE WATER. RELEASE THE NECK OF THE INFLATED BALLOON AND WATCH THE JET BOAT GO!

BALLOON INFLATED, BUT UNTIED

MILK CARTON STAPLED CLOSED

JET BOAT

Figure 50

Sand Play

The sandbox is another ideal area for informal creative play. As with water, the children find great sensory pleasure in manipulating this appealing material. Roads, airports, and cities are created by engineers and builders while cookies and cakes are created by cooks and bakers—all in the same sandbox. Imagination runs wild during such activities—the children almost always accompany their construction with the "brrm, brrm" of a steam shovel, a "whoosh" of a jet plane, or other more language-oriented exchanges. The following section describes some popular sand play activities.

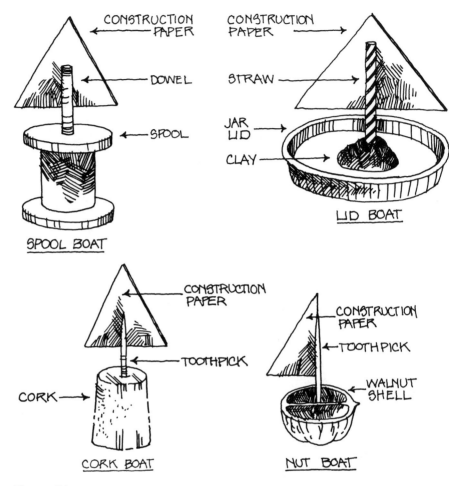

Figure 51

Sand Sculptures.   The children pack wet sand into various containers and these forms are transformed by their imaginations into houses, automobiles, space-ships, skyscrapers, and other objects. Try these containers as molds:

cans of all sizes	plastic containers, all sizes and shapes
buckets	shoe boxes
milk cartons	cardboard tubes
funnels	pie tins
matchboxes	cake pans
cookie cutters	Jell-o molds
paper cups	nut shells
sea shells	

Sand Script.   Wet the sand surface and make it smooth by pulling a ruler over it. Encourage the children to draw designs, print their names, or write messages on it with sticks.

Sand Designs.   The children may wish to create original designs or patterns on a smooth, wet sand surface. Provide a variety of tools for this kind of activity, including combs, potato mashers, spatulas, forks, hand rakes, and sticks.

Sand Hands (or Feet).   Put wet sand into a small box and ask the child to press his hand into it so he makes a distinct impression. Fill the impression with a thick plaster of paris mixture (the consistency of a milkshake) and allow it to set for about forty-five minutes. It should feel cool and hard. When it is dry, the child should be able to lift a solid replica of his hand from the sand. The children may try to match the sand hands to the original owners.

This technique can also be used to make molds of shells, bones, keys, or any other interesting objects.

Sand Combs.   Help children make textures and patterns in the sand play area by constructing sand combs. Cut a 4″ × 8″ piece of ¼ -inch plywood. Draw a comb pattern on the wood and cut it out with a saw, as shown in Figure 52. The children can rake the combs through the sand to create pleasing textures and patterns.

Sand Timers.   Children not yet ready to read time on clocks may be introduced to the concept of keeping time by making a simple sand timer to measure how long they want to play a game or perform some activity.

Glue the tops of two identical jar lids together with a strong epoxy adhesive. Make sure it's dry, then punch holes in the lids with a hammer and a thin nail. (See Figure 53.) Alternate the sides into which you punch the holes. Add sand to one of the jars until it is nearly (but not totally) full. Screw the lids onto the jar and attach the other jar to the top. Then, turn the timer over and begin timing.

Sand Castle.   This fingerplay is a fun follow-up to sand play activities.

I dug in the sand
(Make digging motion)
And carefully made
Five sand castles
(Hold up five fingers)
With my pail and spade.
I felt like a king
(Stand up tall)
With a golden crown
(Form circle overhead)
Till a big blue jay
(Flutter hands)
Knocked my castles down.
(Hold five fingers up; knock them down with the other hand)

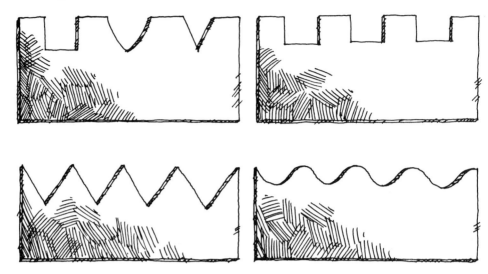

Figure 52

So I dug again
(Make digging motion)
In that sandy shore
Till I had ten sand castles
(Hold up ten fingers)
And was king once more.
(Stand up tall; make circle overhead)

Art

Sound early childhood programs offer daily opportunities for young children to use art materials freely. This means that once you have prepared the materials in the art center, the children should be allowed to explore, originate, and experiment—to do what they want to do. This way the children take pride in what they have created on their own, free of adult standards commonly associated with the use of patterns, coloring books, or dittoed drawings to fill in. The children must understand that only one person needs be pleased with what they create—the child him- or herself.

Even though your program will be geared to allowing the children to work on art materials in their own way, certain ground rules should be established to insure the safe functioning of the class.

1. Art materials must be handled with care.

2. Art materials must not be used to touch or hit others.

3. Art materials must be used in creating only; they must not be carelessly wasted or destroyed.

4. Art materials must be kept in the art center.

5. Children must not interfere with others; they work on their own creations.

By setting forth and maintaining these ground rules, you will actually be able to provide for greater degrees of self-expression and creativity than if there were no guidelines at all. Rules help children understand appropriate behaviors. Without them, children may abuse materials and interfere with the work of others.

Basic Preschool Art Supplies

Teachers of preschool children are able to choose from a wide variety of suitable art materials for their children. Basic art supplies found in early childhood settings include those on the following checklist.

☐ *Crayons*—assorted colors and sizes

☐ *Newsprint Paper*—12″ × 18″ or 18″ × 24″ for drawing or painting

☐ *Paint Brushes*—various sizes, 1/4-inch to 1-inch (round and flat bristle)

☐ *Poster Paint*—liquid or powder form

☐ *Tempera Paint*—liquid or powder form

☐ *Chalk*—assorted colors and sizes

☐ *Modeling Materials*—clay, Play-Doh, salt and flour mixes

☐ *Yarn*—assorted colors and sizes

☐ *Finger-paint Paper*—12″ × 18″ or 18″ × 24″

☐ *Pencils*—kindergarten size

☐ *Scrap Materials*—for collages or texture experiences

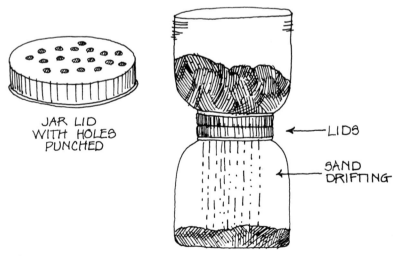

JAR LID
WITH HOLES
PUNCHED

←———LIDS

SAND
DRIFTING

Figure 53

- ☐ *Glue*—for collages and cut paper designs
- ☐ *Construction Paper*—assorted colors and sizes
- ☐ *Scissors*—5-inch blunt-nosed with rubber-coated finger holes
- ☐ *Paint Containers*—old cans or plastic jars
- ☐ *Sponges*—for clean-up jobs and prints
- ☐ *Smocks*—protective garments for children involved in messy activities

These materials may be used in a variety of creative ways, including those that follow.

Easel Painting

Perhaps the most popular of all preschool art activities, easel painting provides children with initial opportunities to discover and explore their growing artistic abilities. When first given an opportunity to paint at the easel, children often experiment with tempera or poster paints and a variety of brushes in a sense-pleasure, play-experiencing form, and color with little concern for the depiction of objects. By about age four or five, however, experimental circular motions turn into heads and treetops, while longer strokes become legs, arms, tree trunks, and horizon lines. Such figures will not actually look realistic, but remember that young children are progressing through *first* experiences in depicting reality— this is a giant step in the development of their thinking abilities.

The easel painting area should be in a quiet, uncluttered part of the room near a sink or toilet facilities (important in case of spills and other accidents). Newspaper or long sheets of butcher paper should be spread on the floor to catch drips and spills. Furnish small containers of creamy tempera paint that can be held within easel trays, and a variety of brushes for experimentation. The easels should be available each day, so each child knows that she can paint when she wants to.

In addition to preparing the easel area, your role includes helping the children prepare for their painting experiences. Help them into their protective smocks (usually old shirts or plastic aprons) and help them find brushes that feel comfortable in their hands. Encourage and assist the children during their efforts, making sure not to interfere unless a special need arises, such as cleaning a messy brush or answering a question.

Such informal instruction opens new possibilities for children and helps them develop creative skills. In the same way, children can be led to experiment with thick lines, thin lines, circles, swirls, and various color combinations.

After the children have begun to feel comfortable with easel painting, introduce other variations. Some ideas follow.

Finger Painting

You can buy finger paints from commercial sources or mix your own using the recipes provided later in this section. To use finger paints, first dip special finger-paint paper (freezer wrap or any paper with a shiny surface will also work) in water. Then have the children spread the paint with their fingers; they might also experiment with combs, yarn, forks, brushes, and other objects to make unique designs. And how about elbows, sides of hands, fingernails, or sides of fingers as design-makers? (To change the texture of the finger paint, add sand, cornstarch, salt, coffee grounds, or fine sawdust.)

A large work area is best for finger painting, as it allows children to make rhythmic movements with their arms. Let them try painting directly on the table rather than on finger-paint paper. Make a print by placing newsprint on top of the design, gently rubbing, then pulling off the paper. The table can be cleaned off quickly with a sponge.

Cornstarch Finger Paint

Mix 1½ tablespoons cornstarch to each cup of water desired. Blend cornstarch with water to a smooth consistency. Add food coloring. Cook until clear and the thickness of pudding.

Linit Starch and Soap Finger Paint

1 cup Linit starch
1½ cups boiling water
½ cup soap flakes
1 tablespoon glycerine

Mix starch with just enough water to make smooth paste. Add boiling water and cook until glossy. Stir in soap flakes while mixture is warm. When cool, add glycerine and coloring (powder paint, poster paint, or food coloring). Store in an airtight jar.

Flour-Salt Finger Paint

2 cups flour
2 teaspoons salt
3 cups cold water
2 cups hot water

Mix salt and flour. Pour in cold water gradually and beat mixture until smooth. Add hot water and boil until mixture becomes clear. Beat until smooth. Add food coloring.

Starch and Water Finger Paint

½ cup laundry starch
½ cup cold water
4 cups boiling water
2 tablespoons liquid or dry tempera

Mix starch and cold water until smooth. Stir in boiling water quickly. Add paint.

Paste and Water Finger Paint

commercial white paste
water
food coloring

Mix paste and cold water to a smooth, creamy consistency. Add food coloring and blend. A small amount of soap flakes may be added to cut down on stickiness.

Other Painting Experiences

Blow Painting.   Drip a small thin blob of tempera paint on the child's drawing paper. Have the child quickly blow through a drinking straw, spreading the paint in different directions. For variety, use contrasting colors of construction paper for the child to create designs on.

Blob Painting.   Drop a large blob of tempera paint or ink on a piece of drawing paper. Put another piece of paper on top and press firmly (or roll with a rolling pin) from the center outward to spread the paint. Remove the top paper and encourage the children to talk about what they "see."

Bubble Painting.   Use a hand mixer to blend one cup Ivory Snow and one cup water. Mix until thick. Spoon the mixture into small cups and add food coloring to make a variety of colors. The children can use brushes or their fingers to spread the bubble paint on their papers.

Screen Painting.   Hold a piece of screen over a sheet of drawing paper. Dip a toothbrush into some tempera paint and brush it onto the screen so that the paint splatters onto the paper. (See Figure 54, top left corner.)

As a variation, lay cutout shapes, leaves, or other objects on top of the drawing paper. The paper under the shape will stay free of paint as the child splatters. Remove the shape for an interesting design. (Note: Children younger than age five or six may not be able to spread the paint effectively.)

Watercolor Fun.   Soak a piece of drawing paper in water. Ask the children to paint on the wet paper immediately. Watch the watercolors blur and blend together as the children paint.

String Painting.   Soak 12- to 18-inch lengths of yarn in several cans of tempera paint. Leave about five inches outside the pan to be used later for holding the yarn. Have the children fold a sheet of construction paper in half, open it, and place a soaked string in a squiggly position on the right side of the fold, as illustrated in the top right corner of Figure 54. Then have the children fold the paper back over, press down on it, and, while pressing with one hand, pull the string out with the other. The process can be repeated on the same sheet with several colors and by wiggling the string to see what happens.

Note: If the child is unable to pull the string with one hand while pressing down with the other, ask another child to hold the paper down while the first pulls. They can take turns this way.

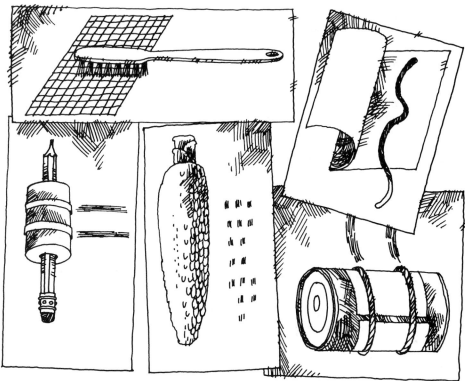

Figure 54

Sidewalk Artists.   Fill coffee cans with water and add food coloring until the colors are vivid. Give the children brushes and allow them to paint away on the sidewalk. Don't worry about a mess—the "paint" will easily wash away with a good rainfall or a hose. Be sure to emphasize that painting on the sidewalk with other paints at other times is not allowed.

Mirror Painting.   Have the children stand before a mirror with brushes and tempera paint. Encourage them to paint their mirror image with mustaches, glasses, freckles, and other features. The tempera paint will wash off easily for the next child.

Water Painting.   Give children large paint brushes and pails of clear water. They may "paint" fences, walks, tricycles, sides of buildings, and other indoor or outdoor equipment until content.

Printing.   Spread some thick tempera paint in a pan and furnish plenty of paper. Have the children dip an object into the paint and press it onto a piece of paper. Use objects such as buttons, keys, coins, forks, combs, screws, leaves, pine cones, sponges, Q-tips, corks, and so on.

Roller Printing.   Use a variety of common household materials as rollers—tin cans, toilet tissue rolls, spools, rolling pins, hair curlers, corn cobs, and so on. Put rubber bands, glue some yarn, cut notches, or paste cardboard shapes onto the rollers, as illustrated in the bottom half of Figure 54. Roll the rollers in thick tempera paint and then roll out the designs onto individual or class-size papers.

Foot Painting.   Spread large sheets of butcher paper on the floor. Pour a small amount of buttermilk onto the paper, and add about ½ teaspoon of liquid tempera paint. Seat a few children in chairs (the paint and paper will be very slippery), take off their shoes and socks, and encourage them to move their feet on the paper to make creative designs.

Creamy Finger Painting.   For the ultimate in sensory experience, collect a variety of liquid or creamy ingredients (such as shaving cream, paste, liquid starch, vegetable oil, hand cream), and place them on a table. Provide sheets of finger-paint paper and allow the children to use the materials as they wish (within reason, of course).

Ice Cube Artists.   To cool children down on a hot day, give them ice cubes to draw on the cement or other warm hard surface outside.

Magic Color Bag.   Pour ¼ cup liquid starch and 3 tablespoons powdered tempera paint into a large Ziplock bag. Squeeze out all the air and close the bag tightly, taping the top to prevent leaks. Blend the starch and powdered paint by squeezing the bag gently. Place the bag on the table, inviting the children to move their hands and fingers to create design after design.

Spray Art.   Direct the children to sprinkle small amounts of powdered tempera paint from salt shakers onto tagboard or other heavy paper. Then they can squirt water from spray bottles lightly over the powdered paint. Allow the paint to dry and shake off any excess powder. The effect will be marvelous, and this activity will help children in learning color names, color concepts, and mixing colors to create new ones.

Magic Pictures.   Encourage the children to draw a picture or design on white paper with a white crayon or chalk. Then they can paint over the paper with watercolors and watch their original drawing emerge.

Plastic Materials

These materials may be rolled, pounded, pinched, patted, molded, shaped, and broken. Children first enjoy plastic materials such as clay or playdough for their sensory appeal, but eventually they become interested in making recognizable objects. Recipes for plastic materials follow. Store them in airtight containers or plastic bags; adding a teaspoon of alum will increase longevity.

Uncooked Dough

3 parts flour
1 part salt

1 part water
small amount of vegetable oil (for smooth texture)

Mix all the ingredients thoroughly and knead until the mixture takes on the appropriate consistency. Add one tablespoon of alum for every 3 cups of flour if you want the mixture to last longer. Otherwise, the mixture should last for up to two weeks. Adding food coloring is an interesting variation.

Cornstarch Dough

1 part cornstarch
3 parts salt
1 part water

Heat the water, slowly adding the cornstarch. Stir until well mixed. Knead the dough, adding more water if necessary. The dough will dry without cracking.

Cooked Dough

½ cup flour
¼ cup cornstarch blended with cold water
2 cups boiling water
½ cup salt
food coloring (optional)

Add salt to boiling water. Combine flour with cornstarch and water to make paste. Pour hot mixture into cold. Cook in a double boiler until glossy. Refrigerate overnight. Knead in flour until right consistency, adding color with flour.

Flour and Salt—Cooked

2 cups flour
2 teaspoons salt
3 cups cold water
2 cups hot water
food coloring (optional)

Add salt to flour, then pour in cold water gradually and beat mixture with eggbeater until smooth. Add hot water and boil until it becomes glossy. Beat until smooth, then mix in coloring.

Quick Playdough

¾ cup flour
½ cup salt
1½ teaspoons alum
1½ teaspoons vegetable oil
½ cup boiling water
food coloring (optional)

Mix flour, salt, and alum. Add oil and boiling water, and stir until well blended. Add food color, if you wish, and knead it in. Refrigerate in an airtight container. (This is a good reusable clay, though it is not so good if you want to dry out pieces, as it tends to be a little crumbly.)

Crayons

Crayons should be available in a special place along with other essential early childhood materials such as puzzles, blocks, and manipulative toys. Young children spend a lot of time with crayons, although not always drawing in the adult sense. Children simply like to scribble, and the larger the scribbling surface the better. Young children should not be given an impression that they must represent something as they experiment with crayons. But some youngsters (especially five-year-olds) will begin to gain enough control of their movements to draw representations of animals, people, or objects. These children should be encouraged, but at the same time, be allowed to experiment and explore the medium.

Crayons can be used in a variety of ways; the following section offers just a few possibilities.

Textured Surfaces.   Provide several different kinds of textures on which to draw or scribble:

sandpaper	wallpaper
wood	old window shades
fabrics	cardboard
newsprint	discarded screening
oilcloth (the back side)	

Rubbings.   Simplest things are made by placing some type of flat textured material under a sheet of paper (such as newsprint) and asking the children to rub over it lightly with a crayon. Furnish a variety of objects with interesting textured surfaces: keys, coins, doilies, combs, paper clips, and so on. Geometric shapes cut out of construction paper, popsicle sticks, yarn, rubber bands, pipe cleaners, or leaves are more examples of textured materials suitable for rubbings.

Crayon Melt.   Grate a number of crayons and keep the shavings in piles of separate colors. The child selects the colors of his choice and arranges them between two sheets of waxed paper. The teacher presses the waxed paper with a warm iron.

Lazy Crayons.   Encourage the children to lay the crayon on its side and experiment with different designs by dragging the crayon, twisting it, and so on.

Arts and Crafts Ideas

Although an early childhood program should mainly focus on creative expression and sensory pleasure, you may wish to offer special art projects occasionally, especially around holidays. This does not mean displaying fifteen identically colored dittoed turkeys at Thanksgiving time, but rather providing activities that give children something to share with family members at home. Some possibilities are described in the following pages and are illustrated in Figure 55.

Spooky Pictures.   Give the children orange and white crayons and ask them to draw a Halloween design or picture with them. Encourage the children to press hard because a thick layer of crayon is necessary. Then brush one coat of thin black tempera paint over the picture.

Hairy Pumpkin.   Scoop the seeds and meat from a medium-sized pumpkin. Place a styrofoam block or cylinder into the pumpkin so that it extends about two or three inches above the top. (See Figure 55, top left.) Encourage children to bring in colorful leaves from the playground or fall flowers (such as mums) from home. Stick the leaves and flowers into the styrofoam until a pleasant arrangement results.

Variation: You may wish to have each of your children make an individual hairy pumpkin to take home as a centerpiece gift. In this case, organize a field trip to a pumpkin farm and encourage children to search for small pumpkins for the project.

Figure 55

Fall Trees.   Draw a large skeleton of a tree on a bulletin board display. Take the children on a walk to collect fall leaves. (Acorns, pine cones, and chestnuts can also be collected.) Ask the children to observe the leaves and look for likenesses and differences in them. Ask each child to affix a piece of tape or glue to the leaves, seeds, or nuts. Finally, have the children place their leaves on the branches or around the base of the tree.

Turkey Ties.   At Thanksgiving time, solicit some old neckties from parents. Make the basic turkey shape from construction paper and staple it to a bulletin board or mount it on heavy tagboard. Have the children staple or glue the old neckties onto the paper turkey to make the tail, as shown in Figure 55, bottom right. The ties can then be used to discuss concepts related to size, shape, color, and so on.

Snowman.   Beat equal amounts of Ivory Snow and water until the mixture is very stiff, let the children take turns mixing. Have the children spoon the mixture onto a cardboard snowman shape and spread it evenly. Allow the snowman to set overnight.
     The next day the children can decorate their snowman by painting on facial features and buttons with black tempera paint. They may wish to tie a fabric strip around the neck to serve as a scarf and add a construction paper top hat.

Easter Chicks.   Cut apart cups from styrofoam egg containers so that each child has one. Have the children cut two eyes from black construction paper and one orange triangle for the beak. Then have them dip a cotton ball in glue and set it into the cup. Brush the eyes and beak with glue and set them in place on the cotton ball.

Easter Egg.   Fill a large jar three-quarters full of liquid starch. Punch a hole in the lid. Place a ball of twine in the starch, thread one end through the lid, and place the lid back on the jar. Pull the string through the hole while a child wraps it around an inflated balloon. Encourage the child to wrap the balloon in several directions with phrases such as "around and around," "up and down," and so on. Once the balloon has been wrapped several times, have the child finish her wrapping at the top so the string can later be used as a hanger (see Figure 55, upper right). Allow the balloon to dry overnight.
     The next day, if the balloon has not popped by itself prick it with a pin. The children can then push Easter basket grass through the openings in the yarn until the egg is full.

Tub Turtles.   Collect a number of empty plastic margarine tubs. Have the children use tempera paint to decorate pieces of styrofoam packing material for the legs, tail, and head of a turtle. Glue the styrofoam pieces to the tub as illustrated in Figure 55, middle row, left side.

Caterpillars.   Cut apart enough cardboard egg cartons so that each child can have one three-cup section. Punch two holes in the first section. Supply pipe cleaners and three or four different colors of tempera paint; have the children make caterpillars by painting the egg-carton sections and putting pipe cleaner antennae through the punched holes.

Paperweight.   Take the children on a nature walk and ask them to find a medium-sized stone. Bring the stones back to the classroom and wash them off. Supply tissue paper in a variety of colors; have the children cut or tear the tissue paper into small pieces. First, the children brush a mixture of one-half water and one-half white glue on a small part of the stone. They cover this area with tissue paper then cover the paper with the glue and water mixture. They repeat this procedure until the entire top of the stone is covered, overlapping the pieces to make it more attractive. Wait until the top is dry before covering the bottom in the same way.

Peek-a-Boo Eggs.   Give each of the children a 9″ × 12″ piece of construction paper and an egg-shaped template. Ask them to trace the template and draw a zigzag line across the width of the shape. The children decorate the egg and cut it out along the outside border as well as along the zigzag line. The children choose a small chick precut from construction paper and glue it to the inside half of the bottom shell. Then, help the children staple two rubber bands that have been cut, so that each is a straight line to both halves of the shell. When the child pulls apart the egg, he can see the chick appear. (See Figure 56.)

Bunny Ears.   First the children decorate the bottom of paper plates with crayons, paint, colored paper, or material. Tell them to cut two slits at opposite ends near the edge of the plate. (You may have to do this.) Next, have the children place an unblown balloon through each slit with the expandable part of the balloon on the bottom side of the plate. Tell the children to blow up the balloons. Tie them closed with a piece of string. Then help the children staple two lengths of string or ribbon to the plate to use as an under-the-chin tie. (See Figure 56.)

Flower Buds.   Ask the children to draw four or five lines vertically with brown crayon on a sheet of colorful construction paper. Dab small dots of white glue along the lines. The children should crinkle pieces of yellow tissue paper and place them on the glue. Set aside until dry.

Fuzzy Animals.   Either give the children templates of farm animals to trace around or a number of precut animal shapes to choose from. Have the children glue pussy willow buds inside the outline.

Tree Blossoms.   Have the children draw or cut out a tree trunk with branches. They should put dabs of glue on the branches and attach popped popcorn on the branches for blossoms. Additional spring features such as small green leaves, birds, or butterflies can be drawn in with crayons.

Wiggly Creatures.   Gather enough pine cones so that each child has one. Be sure they are dry so that the sticky resin won't cause a problem. Give each child four rubber bands large enough to encircle the pine cone without needing to be stretched. Have the children put the rubber bands on the pine cones, pulling them down into the ridges until they are firmly attached. Cut the hanging part of the rubber band with scissors, so the rubber bands dangle like legs. Eyes may be cut from construction paper and pasted onto the wiggly creatures. (See Figure 57.)

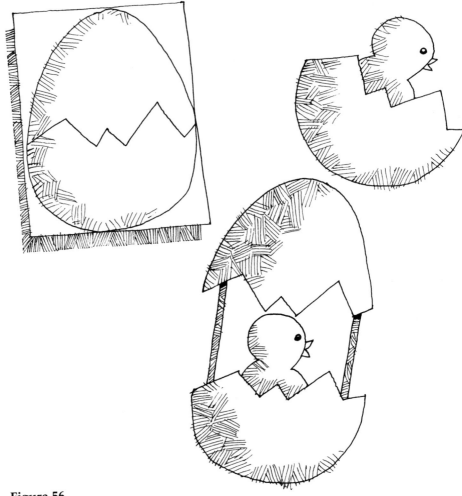

Figure 56

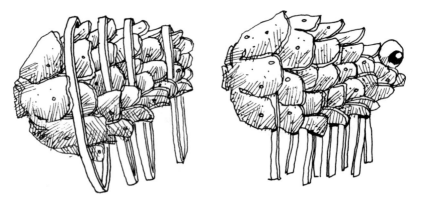

Figure 57

Music

Nearly everyone who has ever worked with young children will agree that young-sters seem to possess a natural interest in and love for music. This natural pleasure should be used and turned into experiences that prolong the child's original enjoyment. The types of musical experiences most appropriate for preschool settings are those in which the children freely and openly get to sing or play instruments. If, instead, we teach music by demanding regimentation and causing pressure, we have a good chance of damaging the special joy that children natu-rally bring to any musical setting.

A Musical Environment

You can serve as an example for the children by the interesting music you use throughout the day. Why not play soft music on the record player during free play or snack time? Also try singing a pleasant tune when it's time for certain activities. These tunes can be improvised or based on a song familiar to the children. For example, one teacher used the tune of "Here We Go Round the Mulberry Bush" for helping children during the cleanup period:

This is the way we wash our hands,
Wash our hands, wash our hands.
This is the way we wash our hands,
And clean up for our snack.

Use musical signals to remind the children that it is time to change activities. One teacher, for example, used this piano signal to gather her children at the story carpet. This series of three notes signalled the children to stand (notice how the last note is raised in tone).

These notes signalled the children to sit.

Singing in the Preschool Setting

Begin group singing activities when you sense that the children are ready for it. Such sessions should not be made part of a rigid schedule, but should occur whenever children seem to be in the mood. First songs should be action songs—relatively fast-paced songs that involve some types of body movements. The standard action songs, "Eency Weency Spider" and "Where Is Thumbkin?" (described in Part One) are two such favorites.

Sing the song all the way through and invite the children to join in the actions. If the children wish to hear the song a second time, sing it again. However, do not ask if they want to hear it a third time—someone will say no. Some children will learn the words quickly and will soon join in, but do not insist that everyone sing. Especially avoid making comments such as, "Everyone sing now" (a sure way to quiet the children), or "Buddy knows the words already—everyone listen to him sing" (a sure way to discourage anyone from learning the words). *Stay away from* the practice of singing a line over and over again until the children learn it and then moving from line to line until the entire song is learned. This type of dissection leads to certain boredom and eventual loss of interest.

Pick up the song again the next day and repeat the same procedure. By this time the children should be fairly familiar with the lyrics and many of them will join you in words and actions. If the children have not willingly begun to join you by about the third day, there is no point in continuing to push it. Find another song that has a strong possibility of attracting the children. Some excellent songbooks are listed at the end of this section. Or try some of the following popular action songs.

"Did You Ever See a Lassie (Laddie)?"   Form a circle with one child in the center. The child in the center should name a body movement before the class begins to sing. Then while the class is singing they should follow the leader and mimic the movement (jumping jacks, hip twists, touching toes, windmill, etc.) announced by the center child.

"London Bridge."   Divide the children into two groups. Two-thirds of them make London bridges by standing face to face and joining hands over their heads. The rest of the group moves about the floor, trying not to get caught on "my fair lady," when the bridge comes down. Those caught choose new walkers.

1. Lon - don bridge is fall - ing down,   fall - ing down,   fall - ing down;

Lon - don bridge is   fall - ing down,   my   fair   la - dy.

2. Build it up with iron bars, iron bars, iron bars; build it up with iron bars, my fair lady.
3. Iron bars will bend and break . . .
4. Build it up with solid gold . . .
5. Suppose someone should steal the gold? . . .
6. Get a man to watch all night . . .
7. Suppose the man should fall asleep? . . .
8. Get a dog to bark all night . . .
9. Suppose the dog should run away? . . .
10. You can watch the bridge yourself . . .

"Old King Glory of the Mountain."   Arrange the children in a circle and designate one child to be "king" or "queen." The king parades around the outside of the circle as the others stand and sing. As the words *first, second,* and *third* are sung, the monarch taps the shoulder of the child she is passing at the time. Only the *third* person, however, leaves the circle to follow the queen on her parade. The song then begins again with the queen choosing additional children for the parade. The song is repeated until all children are in the parade except one, who then becomes the king for a new game.

Old king glo - ry of the   moun   - tain.   The moun-tain was so high, it

near - ly reached the sky.   The   first one, the sec-ond one, the third fol - low me.

"Mary Wore a Red Dress." Gather the children into a circle, everyone sitting on the floor. Describe one of the children's clothing, using the name "Mary" to describe a girl and "Johnny" to describe a boy. The chosen child moves to the center of the circle and improvises a dance when indicated in the second verse of the song. (You may wish to substitute the child's actual name as well as the color and type of clothing.)

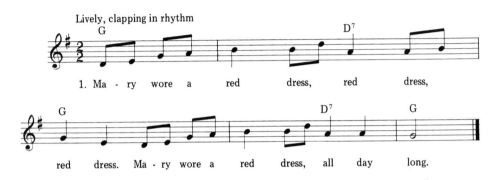

Lively, clapping in rhythm

1. Ma - ry wore a red dress, red dress, red dress. Ma - ry wore a red dress, all day long.

2. Mary did a little dance . . .
3. We'll all clap for Mary . . .

"The Noble Duke of York." Form a circle and designate one child to be the "duke." The duke leads the other children during the first verse as they march in a circle. During the second verse, the children stand in the circle and stand straight during the words "when they were up, they were up"; sit down during the words "when they were down, they were down"; and squat or kneel during the words "when they were only halfway up, they were neither up nor down."

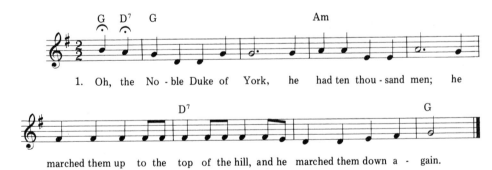

1. Oh, the No - ble Duke of York, he had ten thou - sand men; he marched them up to the top of the hill, and he marched them down a - gain.

2. And when they were up, they were up,
   And when they were down, they were down,
   And when they were only halfway up,
   They were neither up nor down.

"The Bus."   Encourage children to make additional verses and motions for this action song.

1. The peo-ple on the bus go up and down, up and down, up and down.
   (Stand up, then sit or squat down.)

The   peo - ple on the bus go   up and down,   all   through the   town.

2. The wheels on the bus go round and round. *(Move arms in circles.)*
3. The horn on the bus goes toot, toot, toot. *(Make beeping motion with hands.)*
4. The money in the box goes ding, ding, ding.
5. The wipers on the glass go swish, swish, swish. *(Move arms back and forth, together.)*
6. The driver on the bus says, "Move on back." *(Turn head to side, put hand to side of mouth, imitate bus driver's voice.)*
7. The baby on the bus cries "Wah, wah, wah." *(Rub eyes with fists.)*

"Pawpaw Patch."   For the first verse, the children look around and try to find Susie. For the second verse, they pretend to pick pawpaws and put them in their pockets. Finally, they use their arms to motion "come on!"

1. Where, oh where is   dear lit-tle Su - sie? Where, oh where is   dear lit - tle Su - sie?

Where, oh where is   dear lit - tle Su - sie? Way down yon-der in the   paw - paw patch.

2. Picking up pawpaws, puts them in her pocket . . .
   Way down yonder in the pawpaw patch.
3. Come on boys, let's go find her . . .
   Way down yonder in the pawpaw patch.

"Farmer in the Dell."   The children form a circle with one child in the center as the "Farmer." The circle moves to the left as the children sing. On the second stanza, the "farmer" chooses a "wife," and for each subsequent stanza, the newcomer chooses the next character. Those chosen stay inside the circle until

the end, when all but the "cheese" return to the circle. The "cheese" becomes the "farmer," and the game starts again.

The farmer in the dell, the farmer in the dell.
Heigh ho, the derry oh, the farmer in the dell.
The farmer takes a wife . . .
The wife takes the child . . .
The child takes the nurse . . .
The nurse takes the dog . . .
The dog takes the cat . . .
The cat takes the rat . . .
The rat takes the cheese . . .
The cheese stands alone . . .

"Hokey Pokey." The group forms a circle and acts out the words of the song, holding up both hands and shaking them as they turn around slowly, doing the "hokey pokey." At the end, the children clap once, then they can repeat the verse, using other body parts.

You put your right hand in.
You put your right hand out.
You put your right hand in,
And you shake it all about.
You do the hokey pokey,
And you turn yourself about—
That's what it's all about!

"Looby Loo." The children first walk around in a circle, then stop and act out the words. The verse can be repeated with various other body parts.

Here we go Looby Loo, here we go Looby Light.
Here we go Looby Loo, all on a Saturday night.
I put my right hand in, I put my right hand out.
I give my hand a shake, shake, shake,
And turn myself about.

"Mulberry Bush." For the first verse, the children hold hands and walk in a circle. For subsequent verses, they stop walking and act out the words to the song.

Here we go 'round the mulberry bush,
The mulberry bush, the mulberry bush.
Here we go 'round the mulberry bush,
So early on Monday morning.
This is the way we wash our clothes,
Wash our clothes, wash our clothes,
This is the way we wash our clothes,
So early Monday morning.

Other verses:

. . . iron our clothes . . . Tuesday
. . . scrub the floors . . . Wednesday
. . . sew our clothes . . . Thursday
. . . sweep the house . . . Friday
. . . bake our bread . . . Saturday
. . . go to church . . . Sunday

"Ring Around the Rosie."   The children walk around in a circle, holding hands. On the last line they all drop to the floor.

Ring around the rosie
A pocket full of posies,
Ashes, ashes,
We all fall down!

Other Popular Songs

"A Tisket, A Tasket"

"Bluebird"

"Hush, Little Baby"

"I Know an Old Lady"

"I'm a Little Teapot"

"Jacob's Ladder"

"Jennie Jenkins"

"Jingle Bells"

"Kookaburra"

"Kumbaya"

"Little Peter Rabbit"

"Oh Where, Oh Where Has My
   Little Dog Gone?"

"Pop Goes the Weasel"

"Punchinello"

"Sally Go Round the Sun"

"Skip to My Lou"

"Ten Little Indians"

"The Bear Went Over the
   Mountain"

"This Old Man"

Songbooks for Preschool Programs

Kathleen M. Bayless and Marjorie E. Ramsey. *Music: A Way of Life for the Young Child,* 3 ed. Columbus: Merrill Publishing, 1987.

Tom Glazer. *Eye Winker Tom Tinker Chin Chopper: Fifty Musical Fingerplays.* Garden City, N.Y.: Doubleday, 1973.

Marvin Greenberg. *Your Children Need Music.* Englewood Cliffs, N.J.: Prentice Hall, 1979.

B. Joan E. Haines and Linda L. Gerber. *Leading Young Children to Music,* 3 ed. Columbus: Merrill Publishing, 1988.

Ella Jenkins. *This Is Rhythm.* New York: Oak Publications, 1962.

Ella Jenkins. *The Ella Jenkins Song Book for Children.* New York: Oak Publications, 1966.

Dorothy T. McDonald. *Music in Our Lives: The Early Years.* Washington: National Association for the Education of Young Children, 1979.

Robert Nye and Meg Peterson. *Teaching Music with the Autoharp*. Northbrook, IL: Music Education Group, 1982.

Raffi. *The Raffi Singable Songbook*. Toronto: Chappell.

Ruth Crawford Seeger. *American Folk Songs for Children in Home, School, and Nursery School*. New York: Doubleday, 1980.

Maureen Timmerman and Celeste Griffith. *Guitar in the Classroom*. Dubuque, Iowa: Brown Publishing, 1976.

Katherine Tyler Wessell. *The Golden Songbook*. New York: Golden Press, 1981.

Joy Wilt and Terre Watson. *Rhythm and Movement*. Waco, Texas: Creative Resources, 1977.

Musical Instruments and Rhythm

Like singing, rhythmic expression should at first be encouraged through spontaneous activity. Allow the children opportunities to move rhythmically in their own way for short periods of time during the day. Often, children will do so if different kinds of music are played on the record player. You will find them clapping or tapping as they attempt to "keep time to a regular beat." Other children will be content to twirl and move to the music. Still others will enjoy holding colorful scarves in their hands and allowing them to glide smoothly to the beat of the music. Such random body movements eventually become more controlled as children are exposed to planned rhythm experiences.

The initial experiences should involve steady rhythmic patterns, not necessarily from songs. For example, the teacher may steadily beat on a drum or tambourine as the children walk in a circle. He may ask the children to alter their gait as the beating is either speeded up or slowed down. Other initial activities include:

- □ Play the high-pitched piano keys in a spirited way as children prance like elves or fairies around the circle. Then play some low keys in a deliberate way and ask the children to march like giants around the circle. Other such contrasting combinations include hopping like grasshoppers and plodding like bears; flitting like bees and lumbering like elephants; cavorting like ponies and trudging like rhinos.

- □ Use even rhythms on the drum or tambourine during patterns of walking, marching, galloping, and skipping. (Skipping is a very difficult skill for four- and five-year-olds to acquire. Don't force a child to skip if he has difficulty doing so—offer to help, while allowing him the satisfaction of choosing his own rhythmic movement.)

- □ Use some of the many excellent records of rhythmic tunes that encourage creative movement to music. (Hap Palmer records are especially good for such activities.) Encourage the use of chants for children's actions, including jump rope chants. One popular jump rope chant is:

Teddy Bear, Teddy Bear, go upstairs;
Teddy Bear, Teddy Bear, say your prayers;

Teddy Bear, Teddy Bear, turn out the light;
Teddy Bear, Teddy Bear, say good-night.

As the children gain opportunities to experience such creative rhythmic activities, they will begin to anticipate the prospect of using rhythm instruments. If you bring all the instruments out at one time, however, the children are liable to become too excited about them. It is best to simply place multiples of one or two instruments at a time (drum and triangle, for instance) in the preschool setting so the children will have opportunities to experiment with them freely. Of course, there will be some "noise" at first, but if you alternate their use between the outdoors and indoors, most problems can be overcome. At this point, you should talk informally with the children about their instruments, focusing on the sounds they make. Identify the instruments for the children by using the appropriate terms; say "triangle," for example, instead of "clang-clang." As the children explore the instruments, you may want to help them discover the proper way to hold them. For example, have the child tap a triangle while holding it by one side (as she has been doing) and then tap it while holding it by the string. Don't say, "See, you were holding it wrong," but keep your comment open-ended. "Which way sounds better?" As the children get used to playing an instrument properly, you may ask them to furnish the rhythmic pattern in rhythm activities. In the same way, you can add new instruments as the children become familiar with the old ones.

As such informal, creative experiences are provided for young children, they will slowly learn to manipulate the instruments properly and gain sufficient control for group experiences. If you choose to group your children as a "rhythm band," you will first need to develop sections of instruments. Those instruments most popularly used in preschool settings include *triangles, drums, rhythm sticks, cymbals,* and *bells.* Give each section enough time to work together so they are able to coordinate their efforts. Don't expect all sections to play in unison—the responsibility of each section playing together is demanding for preschool youngsters. Only at the end, for one or two beats, should you expect all the children to play in unison. A suggested procedure for organizing a rhythm band experience follows.

☐ Choose a record with an appropriate beat or select a suitable song to be played on a musical instrument.

☐ Decide on the sequence in which each instrument will be played. For example, one teacher developed this plan for "Jingle Bells":

Jingle bells, jingle bells   *(Bells only)*
Jingle all the way   *(Triangles only)*
Oh, what fun   *(Cymbals only)*
It is to ride   *(Drums only)*
In a one horse open sleigh   *(Rhythm sticks only)*
(Repeat first verse)

☐ Develop cues with which to signal each group to enter the song. You may choose to hold up the instrument to be played, show the children a picture of the instrument, use a cue word such as "cymbals," or simply point to the next group to play.

The suggested rhythm instruments can be purchased from school supply outfits. However, many teachers have found that teacher- or child-made instruments are often just as effective. Some of the many instruments that can be handmade include the following.

Wind Chimes.   Hang pieces of various materials from a straight bar, a triangular wooden frame or a circular band of metal stripping so they will strike each other when the wind moves them. (See Figure 58.) For variety of sounds, use different sizes of materials. Some suggested materials include:

nails	dowels	pieces of ceramic tile
metal scraps	pieces of bamboo	
strips of wood	pieces of pipe	

Woodblock Tambourine.   Collect some bottle caps. Remove any cork or plastic, then hammer a nail through the bottle caps and partway into a wood block. Make sure the hole is wide enough so the cap will slide freely along the nail. Use as many nails and as many caps on each nail as desired. (You may wish to make the hole in the cap first with a larger-sized nail than the ones used to attach the cap to the wood.)

Nail Scraper.   Hammer a few nails into a block of wood so they are all the same height. Leave a space and repeat with different sized nails as illustrated in Figure 59, or hammer the new set in deeper. To play, run a large nail along the separate rows of nails.

String Guitar.   Insert a screw eye near each end of an 8-inch wood strip. About 1-½ inches from each end of the wood strip, saw a ¼-inch-deep groove across the strip. Insert popsicle sticks sideways into the grooves and tie a length of fishline between the two screw eyes. Tighten the fishline with a large nail by turning one of the screw eyes. (See Figure 60.)

Figure 58

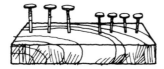

Figure 59

Drums. Use old coffee cans or large vegetable cans that can be obtained from school cafeterias. Cover the open end with inner tube rubber stretched as tightly as possible and secure the rubber with heavy cord or wire, as shown in the upper left corner of Figure 61. A drumstick can be made from a dowel rod with a piece of foam rubber glued on the end.

Tube Kazoos. Collect a number of toilet paper tubes or paper towel tubes cut in half. Cover one end of the tube with waxed paper and secure it with a rubber band. (See Figure 61.) Punch a hole in the tube about two or three inches from the waxed paper end. The children will enjoy humming a tune into their kazoos.

Washtub Bass. Drill a hole through one end of a 30-inch dowel, about an inch from the end. In the other end, cut a ¼-inch groove, perpendicular to the direction of the hole. The groove will be hooked over the rim of a washtub to hold the dowel securely in place. (See Figure 61.)

Punch a hole in the center of the washtub. Tie a 3-inch dowel to one end of a 3- or 4-foot string and run the string through the hole from the inside to the outside. The 3-inch dowel will prevent the string from coming all the way through. Thread the free end of the string through the hole in the 30-inch dowel and tie a large knot to keep it from coming out. Hook the notch of the dowel over the rim of the washtub and brace the tub by putting one foot on the rim. As you pull the stick toward or away from you, the string is either lengthened or shortened, resulting in different pitches.

Rattles. Fill plastic bottles or boxes, wooden match boxes, or cans with a variety of materials that make unique sounds when shaken. Examples of such materials include marbles, pebbles, dried beans, salt, sand, and so on.

Shoe Box Guitar. Cut a hole in the lid of a shoe box and secure the lid tightly to the box. Cut a hole in one end of the box large enough to attach a cardboard tube to resemble the neck of a guitar as shown in Figure 61. Stretch three or four rubber bands of varying widths around the box and across the hole in the lid. Add a bridge by sliding a dowel rod under the rubber bands. The children pluck the rubber bands and make different musical sounds.

Figure 60

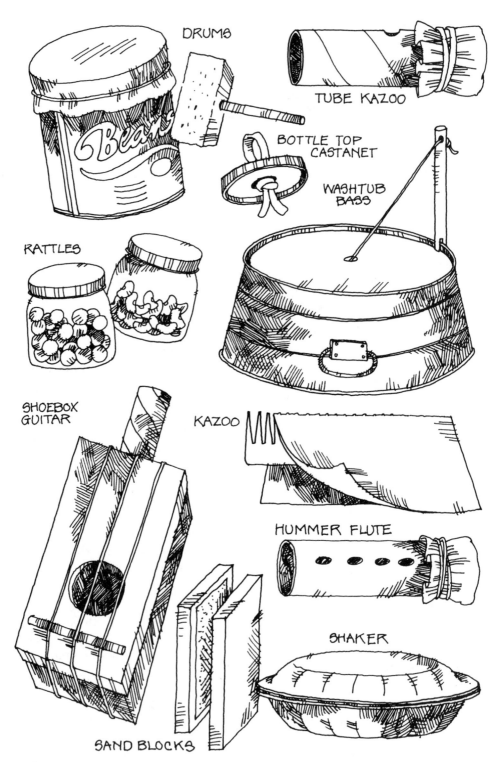

DRUMS

TUBE KAZOO

BOTTLE TOP
CASTANET

WASHTUB
BASS

RATTLES

SHOEBOX
GUITAR

KAZOO

HUMMER FLUTE

SHAKER

SAND BLOCKS

Figure 61

Bottle Cap Castanets.   Get some bottle caps or small jar lids. Punch a hole in the center of the caps with a hammer and thin nail. Push a rubber band through the hole, leaving a small loop in the band on the outside of the cap, and tie a knot on the inside so that the band cannot slip out. Put one castanet on the child's thumb and one on the middle finger, making sure the rubber-band loop is not cutting off the child's circulation. Then have the children bang the castanets together.

Kazoo.   Fold a piece of wax paper and place the teeth of a comb in the fold. Have the children place their lips softly on the fold and hum a tune while moving the comb from side to side.

Sand Blocks.   Cover one side of two blocks of wood with coarse sandpaper. Have the children hold the blocks in their hands with the sandpaper sides facing. They can rub the blocks together while keeping the musical tempo.

Hummer Flute.   Get several paper towel tubes and punch about four holes on the top. Cover one end of the tube with waxed paper and attach it firmly with a rubber band. The child hums into the open end, fingering the holes to obtain musical sounds.

Shaker.   Put a number of bells, seeds, or pebbles on a paper plate. Cover that paper plate with another and staple or tape the edges closed. The children shake the plate and use it as a rhythm instrument, much like a tambourine.

Records

Appropriate records of good quality should be available for use in the preschool setting. Such records can benefit your program in several ways: they can be listened to for pure enjoyment, they can guide marching, dancing, or singing activities, and they can be used to teach basic concepts. There are many popular records made especially for children. Among the most popular are those of Hap Palmer, Raffi, Ella Jenkins, Steve Millang and Greg Scelsa, Miss Jackie, and Sharon, Lois, and Bram of television's *Elephant Show.* Look for them at your favorite record or educational supply store.

PHYSICAL ACTIVITY

The first six years of a child's life involve an incredible amount of physical activity. Children are learning to develop strength and control of their bodies through self-initiated activity. This activity normally enhances two major areas of physical development: large muscle growth and small muscle growth. Good programs for young children furnish many opportunities for exercising these growing muscles through organized programs of physical activity. Some suggestions for such programs follow.

Body Image

Young children begin to develop body awareness during infancy, and this awareness must be extended through their early years. The following developmental classroom activities can help youngsters become aware of the different body parts, as well as of the ways in which their bodies move.

Body Parts Identification

Touch the different parts of your body as you say, for example, "I'm touching my nose. Touch your nose." Continue with ears, chin, eyes, mouth, shoulders, neck, arms, elbows, knees, stomach, and so on. Then try the following variations:

□ Touch the parts with your eyes closed.

□ Touch the parts with two hands.

□ Touch the parts only after hearing "Simon Says . . . "

□ Touch body parts with parts other than the hand or finger; for example, "Touch your knee with your toes," or "Touch your elbow with your knee."

□ Invite the children to take turns offering the verbal command.

□ Touch the body part with an object in the environment, such as, "Touch your knees to the floor," or "Touch your fingers to the wall."

□ Use songs such as "Hokey Pokey" to encourage the children to move specific body parts.

Basic Body Movements

After children are aware of the basic body parts and gain further control of them, they are ready to pursue additional activities that refine rudimentary movement skills and encourage creative movement.

   Note: Most of these activities may be accompanied by music. They are illustrated in Figure 62.

Walking.   Walk fast; walk slow; walk backwards; walk on tiptoes; walk on heels; walk sideways; walk with hands on head; walk with hands on hips; and so on.

Standing.   Stand on tiptoes for a count of five; stand on right foot for a count of five; stand on left foot for a count of five; stand in each of the previous ways with eyes shut.

Balancing.   Get a 2" × 4" × 8' board for these activities. First, the children are asked to stand on the board to see if they can control their bodies. This ability to balance is basic to other activities. When the child displays good balance, ask him to walk with one foot on the board and one foot on the floor. Then encourage the child to take a short series of steps with both feet on the balance board. Gradually, children will learn to walk forward on the balance board. Then, they can be asked to:

Figure 62

- ☐ Walk slowly forward.
- ☐ Walk sideways (first the dominant side leads and then the other leads).
- ☐ Walk with a beanbag on their heads.
- ☐ Walk slowly backward.
- ☐ Walk slowly backward with a beanbag on their heads.

Running. Run fast; run slowly; run on tiptoes; run with hands behind their backs; and so on.

Jumping. Jump up and down in place; use only one foot while jumping; jump forward; jump backward; jump into the air and make a quarterturn; jump with eyes closed; and so on.

Galloping. Help children learn this skill by showing them the correct procedure. Play some background music appropriate for galloping and invite the children to become galloping ponies or reindeer. Then show them how to gallop—by stepping forward on one foot and bringing the other foot up beside it; then stepping forward on the first foot and again bringing the second beside it. Gradually encourage the children to repeat the process to the music until they achieve a smooth galloping gait.

Skipping.   Skipping is perhaps the most difficult body movement for young children to master; it cannot be done by some until age five or six. Thus, you must offer a good deal of direct instruction in this skill. Tell the children to step forward on one foot while holding the second foot in the air (you may want to hold it up for the child). The first foot then makes a hop, and the second foot steps forward. In this way, the children are led tc step and hop on the first foot, step and hop on the second, and so on until the step-up sequence becomes smooth and natural.

Creative Movement Activities

Once the children have mastered the preceding basic large muscle skills, you may wish to capitalize on their imaginations in order to further refine their capabilities. Some suggested activities follow.

Mountain Train.   Place a "mountain" in a large, open space. A beanbag chair will do, as will any other item that children can crawl over safely. To form the train, the children are asked to line up on their hands and knees and hold the child's ankles in front of them. Have two children practice crawling in this fashion, coordinating the efforts as they attempt to move their "train." Some rhythmic "choo-choo" sounds from the teacher adds to the fun. Gradually link one more child at a time until there is a five to six car train moving in unison. Form two or more trains. The conductor (teacher) leads one train at a time over the mountain and down the other side.

Footsies.   Ask two children to lie down on the floor, feet touching feet. On signal, they try to roll across a defined area keeping their feet touching all the time.

Simon Says.   The leader gives commands to players, some prefaced by the words "Simon says" and some not prefaced by those words. The players must listen carefully and do only those actions prefaced by "*Simon says.*" The leader tries to see how many times she can catch players who respond to a command not prefaced by "Simon says." (See Figure 63.) Two-, three-, and four-year-olds love to play this game, but often have difficulty responding to the "Simon says" preface. They just enjoy the movements. To keep this spirit, allow the children to stay in the game whether or not they are "caught."

My Little Gray Pony.   Arrange the children in a straight line and read them the following poem:

My little gray pony is locked in the barn
And wants to go out to play.
    (*Imitate the actions of a pony locked in*)
Just see him come out and go over the fence
    (*Pony comes out and jumps over the fence*)

And gallop and gallop away,
And gallop and gallop away,
And gallop and gallop away,
Just see him come out and go over the fence
And gallop and gallop away.

At the start of the rhyme, the children should paw and prance as if anxious at being restrained. Then, two or three at a time, the children should jump over a rope strung between two chairs and finish acting out the galloping actions.

Little Red Caboose.   One child (or the teacher) is chosen to be the engineer and calls all the cars of a train together (each child is a car). The engine is called first, followed by the tender, flat car, tank car, boxcar, cattle car, passenger car, etc., ending with the caboose. As each child's car is called, she hooks onto the cars in front of her. After the train is completed, the "whistle" blows and the train rhythmically chugs off to the following song:

Little Red Caboose—chug, chug, chug.
Little Red Caboose—chug, chug, chug.
Little Red Caboose behind the train, train, train.
Smokestacks on his back, back, back, back.
Coming down the track, track, track, track.
Little red caboose behind the train—toot, toot.

Catch the Beanbag.   Sit in a circle with the children and start passing around a beanbag, saying a nonsensical sound that must be repeated by each child as it makes its trip (for example, "beep"). Do this as many times as the children need in order to coordinate their actions.

As they get used to the process, introduce a new element. Assign a sound to a ball (example: "zap") and start passing it around the circle a few seconds after the beanbag started. Keeping both objects moving as fast as they can, the children attempt to catch the beanbag with the ball.

Figure 63

A second variation of this passing game involves passing both objects as in the activity described earlier, but the teacher starts the ball out in an opposite direction to the beanbag. The children try to see who gets "caught" with saying "beep" and "zap" at the same time.

Around the World.   Divide your class into two equal groups, each group in a circle. Assign each child a number. Child number one in each group starts to pass the beanbag around the circle. As the bag completes one trip, child number one drops out. As it completes two trips, child number two drops out, and so on until the last child drops out. See which group completes its trip the quickest.

Dogs Fly.   Play this game as a variation of Simon Says. Explain to the children that you are going to describe how animals move. If the form of locomotion is natural to that animal, the children are to act it out. If it is not, the children are not to move. See who gets caught!

Example: "Elephants fly . . . fish swim . . . bugs crawl . . . horses gallop . . . caterpillars swim . . . cats walk . . . whales run."

Jack-in-the-Box.   Have the children pretend they are jack-in-the-boxes, squatting low and making themselves as small as possible. When you finish your command, "Jack-in-the-box, jack-in-the-box, where are you? Please pop up!" the children should jump high into the air and clap their hands above their heads. Repeat several times.

Elephant Walk.   Play a song on your record player that has a slow, lumbering rhythm. Have children bend forward at the waist, clasp their hands, and allow their arms to swing loosely back and forth to simulate an elephant's trunk as they walk slowly to the music.

Melting Snowmen.   Ask the children to gather into an informal group and stand tall and erect as snowmen. Choose a "sun" who tiptoes or skips around the snowmen five times. Count the number of times the "sun" makes a circuit, encouraging the children to continually melt by further relaxing their bodies each time. By the fifth circuit, the children should be in a "melted" position on the floor.

Froggie's Meal.   Have the children pretend they are frogs by squatting down with their hands on the floor. Make a sound like an approaching insect and tell the children they must make a high leap upward to catch the insect and then land in the same squatting position. For added fun, the children should imitate the sound of a frog as they jump. When squatting, they should look around and blink their eyes. Repeat several times.

Musical Rugs.   Place enough rug squares (or any other small, flat item) randomly on the floor so that there is one more player then rug squares. While lively music is being played, the children move (march, hop, skip, or whatever the music suggests) around the area without stepping on the rugs. Stop the music quickly; the children try to stand on a rug square. See who gets caught!

Bell Ringer. Suspend a bell from a tree branch or ceiling. Line up the children a few yards from the bell. Taking turns, each child tosses a beanbag at the bell, attempting to ring it.

Balloon Partners. Two children are partners. Each pair must take an inflated balloon to a finish line without using their hands. They can use any other part of their bodies.

Freeze. Play lively music on the radio or tape recorder. Invite the children to move freely as the music is playing. Every so often, quickly turn off the sound and ask the children to "freeze." See if they can hold the position for about two or three seconds; then, start up the music again.

Shadows. Two children work together as a pair. One child performs a basic body movement and the other child must imitate what was done. They take turns being the leader.

Songs

Several songs lend themselves to practicing basic body movements. The following song is sung to the tune of "There Is a Tavern in the Town." The children place their hands on the part of the body mentioned in the song.

Head, shoulders, knees, and toes,
Knees and toes.
Head, shoulders, knees, and toes,
Knees and toes and—
Eyes and ears
And mouth and chin and nose.
Head, shoulders, knees, and toes,
Knees and toes.

To the tune "Hokey Pokey," encourage the following movements:

Put your right hand in.
    (Toward center of circle)
Take your right hand out.
Put your right hand in,
And shake it all about.
We'll shake it in the morning or we'll shake it after noon.
That's what it's all about.

Other verses:

. . . left hand . . .
. . . right foot . . .
. . . left foot . . .
. . . head . . .
. . . whole body . . .

Create new words to familiar tunes while encouraging children to exercise. For example, this is one of many possible variations of the tune "Jingle Bells."

Clap your hands,
Clap your hands,
Clap them just like me,
Oh, what fun it is to clap,
And sing so joyfully.

Other verses:

. . . touch your toes . . .
. . . stretch up tall . . .
. . . walk in line . . .
. . . row your boat . . .
. . . throw a ball . . .

Running Activities

In the classroom or outside, organize the children in well-spaced formation. Ask them to run in the following ways:

☐ Run in a large circle.
☐ Run with long strides.
☐ Run with short strides.
☐ Run quickly or slowly.
☐ Run toward or away from the teacher.

For variety, ask the children to:

☐ March like a toy soldier.
☐ Jiggle like jelly.
☐ Flop like a rag doll.
☐ Bounce like a rubber ball.
☐ Flitter like a snowflake.

Rope Activities

A long length of rope can be placed on the floor or ground and then used in the following ways:

☐ Have the children who are able walk a straight line along the rope forward and backward (as shown in the left of Figure 64).
☐ Make the rope into a circle and ask the children to walk the circle forward or backward.
☐ With the rope in a straight line, have the children hop over it and then hop back again.

Figure 64

☐ Make curves in the rope and have the children run or hop so each step will be taken in a new curve.

☐ Ask the children to invent a new way of moving with the rope.

Tightrope Walker.   Establish a straight line about ten feet long on the floor of your classroom. Invite the children to walk along the line as far as they can without ringing a small bell held in their hand (see Figure 64). For variety, try making a curved line, a circle, and other shapes used previously.

Animal Games

Animal Imitations.   Invite the class to walk like animals. It is fun to have the children choose the animal they would like to portray and ask the others to guess what they are. At times, you may suggest certain animals. Or a special "zoo parade" involves all the children without a guessing format. (For ideas see Figure 65.)

Going to the Zoo.   To encourage creative movements of many kinds, gather the children in a group and invite them to go with you on an imaginary trip to the zoo. On this special trip, the children must choose an animal to imitate as their means of getting there. Lead them by saying, "We're going to the zoo. How is Diana going to get there?" "I'm going to fly like a bird," says Diana. Encourage the rest of the children to follow the first child's lead and perform the actions described in the previous activity—flying like birds, hopping like frogs, waddling like ducks, swimming like fish, crawling like snakes, and so on.

Circus Time.   Arrange the children in a circle, seated on the floor. Select one child to stand in the center to act as a "ringmaster." The ringmaster passes out one slip of paper to each child, each slip picturing an animal with a distinctive movement, such as a horse, elephant, bird, and so on (or hang the picture around

WALK LIKE A SPIDER
(ON ALL FOURS)

PULL YOURSELF
LIKE A SEAL
(THE LEGS
DRAGGING
BEHIND)

SPRING LIKE A KANGAROO
(SQUAT AND JUMP)

SWIM LIKE A FISH
(PADDLING ARMS AND LEGS)

PLOD LIKE AN ELEPHANT
(WITH ARMS AS THE TRUNK)

WADDLE LIKE A DUCK
(BENDING KNEES AND
RAISING ARMS SLIGHTLY)

KICK LIKE A MULE
(HANDS AND FEET ON THE
FLOOR – FEET KICKING
BACKWARDS INTO THE AIR)

CRAWL LIKE A SNAKE

Figure 65

the child's neck). When signalled by the ringmaster, the child steps to the center of the circle and pantomimes the animal on his slip. After the ringmaster has given each child a chance, she organizes a parade in which the children move in a circle, pantomiming their respective animals.

Games with Rules

Games should be chosen to help children define and master specific physical skills rather than to establish a winner or loser. If excessive competition results from the game, constant failure can kill a child's motivation. Therefore, games with rules that involve winners and losers should be chosen carefully and used only with children who are emotionally prepared to play them. Some four-year-olds may be capable of this, but it is not normal until well into the kindergarten year.

Obstacle Course. Use movable playground equipment, cardboard boxes, barrels, ropes, chairs, and so forth to plan an obstacle course on the playground. Once ready, encourage the children to jump over, run around, or crawl under the various obstacles and get through the course as quickly as possible without upsetting the objects.

Red Light/Green Light. Children line up alongside each other at one end of the playground. A leader stands at the opposite end of the playground with his back to the rest of the children. The leader yells so that all can hear, "1–2–3–green light!" and the players run toward the leader as fast as they can. The leader then calls "1–2–3–red light!" which is a signal for all children to stop running. The leader turns around quickly to see if all the players have stopped. Any player caught still moving by the leader must return to the starting point. The first player to reach the leader is the winner.

Cross the River. Use 8½" × 11" construction paper of various colors and paste different geometric figures on them. Arrange them on the floor and explain to the children that they are going to try to cross a river by stepping on stones (the geometric shapes). The teacher guides the children across the river by saying, "Hop to the green square, hop to the red circle, hop to the blue rectangle," and so on.

Red Rover. Mark off two end boundary lines with lengths of rope. Children stand in back of one line while the leader stands facing them between the two lines. The leader calls out, "Red Rover, Red Rover, let (a child's name) come over." The child called must cross the space and the opposite boundary line before she is caught by the leader. Any child caught must stay in the center to help the leader. The last one caught is the new leader.

Duck, Duck, Goose. Arrange the children in a large circle and designate one child to be "It." "It" walks around the circle and touches certain children and says "Duck" with each touch. When he touches a child and says "Goose," however, that child must get up and run around the circle. She becomes "It," and the players switch places.

Cross the Stream.   Draw two lines on the playground or on the classroom floor. The space between the two lines represents a stream. The children attempt to jump over the stream without getting "wet."

Dog and Bones.   One child is chosen to be the dog. He sits with his back to the group with a beanbag (the bone) on the floor behind him. Taking turns, the other children try to sneak up and steal the bone without being heard. If the dog hears a child, he says "Bark, bark!" and that child must go back. If that child is able to steal the bone without getting caught, however, she returns to the group who chants, "Dog, oh dog, where is your bone?" The "dog" then has three chances to guess who has his bone. The one who stole the bone then becomes the "dog," whether or not her name is guessed.

Catch-Ups.   Remove the bottom from a large plastic container such as a bleach bottle. Attach a large cork to one end of a piece of yarn and slip the other end into the neck of the bottle and attach it there by screwing the lid on tight. (See Figure 66.) The children hold onto the handle and try to catch the cork in the bottle. This is an adaptation of a traditional Mexican game and should be described as such, especially if Latin-American children are in your care.

Race Track.   Mark out a curvy path on the floor or playground with masking tape, rope, or chalk. The children run from the start of the track to the finish as quickly as they can without touching or going beyond the sides of the track.

Wings.   Especially on days when winds are brisk and steady, invite the children to don a variety of wings and run about as imaginary butterflies, birds, super-

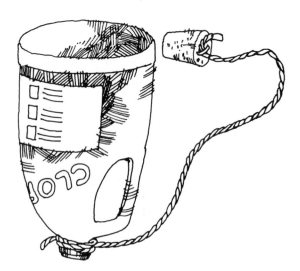

Figure 66

heroes, or anything else that jogs their creativity. Some effective wings are illustrated in Figure 67. They include an old sheet; crepe paper streamers stapled onto a cloth strip; and a plastic garbage bag slit to form a large sheet. (Plastic bags can be dangerous, so children playing with them should be closely supervised.)

Walking Cans.   Get some large cans with one end removed. Punch a hole with a nail in two opposite sides of each can near the closed ends. Cut pieces of heavy twine and string one piece through each can as shown in Figure 68. Tie the ends together on the inside with a good, secure knot to form a large loop. Encourage children to stand with one foot on one can and one foot on another remaining steady by holding onto the twine. They may want to walk a short distance on a hard-surfaced play area.

Balloon Bat.   Give each child in your group an inflated balloon. Give the children a signal to start, whereupon they throw their balloons into the air. The children see how long they can keep the balloons in the air by tapping them back when they begin to come down.

Jack, Be Nimble.   Construct several "candlesticks" out of potato chip canisters by making a slit in the plastic top and pulling a red kerchief through it (see Figure 69). Say the nursery rhyme, "Jack, Be Nimble," and have the children take turns jumping with both feet over the candlesticks as the last line is recited. (You may wish to encourage the children to jump one by one over their candlesticks by substituting their names for *Jack.*)

Jack, be nimble
Jack, be quick
Jack, *jump* over the candlestick.

GARBAGE BAG

CREPE PAPER STREAMERS

OLD SHEET

Figure 67

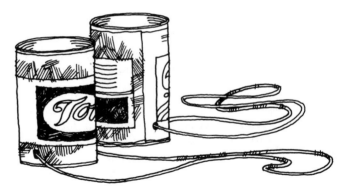

Figure 68

Say the rhyme again, this time asking the children to jump backward over the candlestick. Continue with variation such as jumping sideways or with arms stretched in front.

Action Verses.   Compose a set of verses by which you can encourage various body movements. For example, while playing outdoors, these rhymes can be used:

Little frogs, little frogs,
Hop to the wall;
Little frogs, little frogs,
Please come back, I call.

Little lions, little lions,
Run to the door;
Little lions, little lions,
Give a great big roar.

Little ducks, little ducks,
Waddle to the gate;
Little ducks, little ducks,
Hurry—don't be late.

Little birds, little birds,
Fly to the swings;
Little birds, little birds,
Flap and flap your wings.

Popular Group or Individual Exercises

Squat Bends.   The children stand straight with their arms extended to the front. They bend their knees halfway down as if they were going to sit on a chair, trying to keep their backs straight. Then, they stand up straight again. Repeat as many times as appropriate.

Toe Touches.   The children stand straight, putting their hands on their waists and spreading their legs slightly. On a count of one, they bend from their waists, attempting to touch their left toes with their right hands. Then, on a count of two, they stand up straight again with hands on waist. On a count of three, the children bend from the waist and touch their right toes with their left hands, and on a count of four, they move back to the original hands-on-waist position. Repeat as many times as needed.

Leg Pushes.   The children each choose a partner. Then each pair sits on the floor with the partners facing each other, putting the soles of their feet together with knees bent at about a 60-degree angle. (See Figure 70, bottom left.) On signal, the children both push their feet, trying to push the partner away.

Arm Rotations.   The children extend their arms straight out from the sides of their bodies. Keeping their arms rigid, the children move them so their hands make small circles.

Stretches.   The children stand straight with their arms at their sides. When they are asked to reach high toward the sky, they raise their arms. After a short period, they lower their arms and repeat the exercise.

Sit-Ups.   The children lie flat on their backs with their arms stretched back over their heads. On signal, they sit up by using their stomach and back muscles, and move their arms over their heads and forward to touch their toes.

Scissors.   The children lie flat on their backs with their arms at their sides and their legs straight. Keeping their legs straight, the children cross the right leg over the left by rotating the lower trunk, and place the right foot on the floor. Keep alternating legs.

Figure 69

Figure 70

Wheelbarrow.   The children choose partners. One child lies on his stomach with legs spread; the second child stands between the first child's legs and grasps his ankles, trying to lift him up. The first child tries to walk by using only his hands.

Elastic Exercises.   Buy some lengths of ¼-inch-wide elastic at a variety store. This elastic is often very inexpensive. Tie together the ends of a 12-foot length, and encourage a group of children to get inside and make a round shape. Ask other children to make squares, rectangles, or triangles. The shapes can move as the children move. Shorter lengths can be used by individual children for the same purpose.

"Junk" Playground Equipment

You can equip an entire playground with what could be considered "junk." Tractor tire sandboxes are practical and inexpensive (but be sure to cover any sandbox at night to keep cats out). A tire slit in half along the tread can be used as a boating channel, and tires half-buried in the ground form climbing archways or crawling tunnels. Old concrete sewer pipes and barrels supported by wooden mounts make good crawling tunnels, as well. A painted telephone cable spool can be used as a table, as can a piece of plywood screwed securely to a tree stump. (Plain tree stumps are fun to play on, too.) Inner tubes are great for children to bounce on (they also enjoy rolling and trotting along behind them), and straw bales are fun for jumping and climbing. Railroad or landscaping ties become balancing boards, a small tire attached to a knotted rope becomes a swing, and orange crates or cartons become a variety of vehicles for dramatic play. Have the children paint a bright mural on a blank wall or fence and your playground is complete. (See Figure 71 for ideas.)

Small Muscle Development

The young child needs to experience many activities that lead to control of the finger and hand muscles and the ability to coordinate hands and eyes. (See Figure 72 for a few possibilities.) Children learn to develop skill and coordination by engaging in many school-related activities such as:

painting a pattern	placing a peg in a pegboard
drawing a picture	eating with a fork or spoon
cutting paper	hammering nails into wood
pasting cutout papers	completing a puzzle
writing the alphabet	holding a cup
doing a fingerplay	rolling clay or Play-Doh

Also allow plenty of time for the children to practice dressing skills: lacing, buttoning, zipping, and snapping. Use either commercially produced dressing frames or the children's own clothes.

All of these activities are accomplished by using the small muscles of the hand and fingers. Although parents don't get as excited about these accomplishments as they do over advancements in such large motor skills as walking or catching a ball, small muscle development is nevertheless an impressive area of growth. Children must have opportunities to exercise and coordinate the control of their small muscles through activities that encourage grasping, releasing, and manipulating objects. Here are some activities to consider.

Small Muscle Activities

Shape Toys.   Children put three-dimensional plastic shapes into appropriate openings in a special box. (One kind of shape sorter is illustrated in Figure 73.)

Beads.   Children can pick up *wooden beads* with large holes and either string them onto a sturdy cord with a knot at one end or plop them back into a can. Colorful *pop-lock beads* are fun for children to snap together and pull apart. Or you can make *"junk" beads* out of empty thread spools, straws cut in pieces, macaroni, and other common objects suitable for stringing. Encourage the child to duplicate or create patterns of color or shape.

Stacking Rings.   Children stack the colorful plastic rings in order according to size.

SEWER PIPES

CABLE SPOOLS

TIRES

BARRELS

STRAW BALES

TREE TRUNKS

Figure 71

152

Figure 72

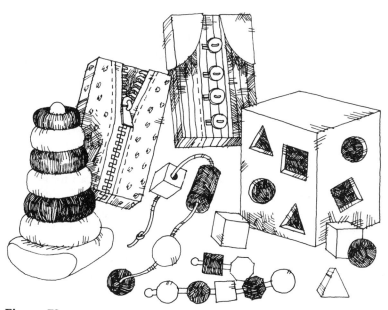

Figure 73

Using Scissors.   Supply blunt-nosed, 5-inch scissors with rubber-coated finger holes; be sure to have some left-handed as well as right-handed varieties. Poster paper, butcher paper, or construction paper are good for first cutting efforts; be sure not to use paper that is either too thin or too thick. Then, you will want to help the children cut by using these suggestions:

☐   Allow them to cut the paper freely. Offer some scraps of paper and invite the children to cut them into smaller pieces. They will enjoy pasting their cut paper onto a sheet of construction paper to create a collage.

☐   Provide pages torn out from old magazines. Ask the children to cut out the pictures they like. Some may cut right through the picture but will gradually get the idea of cutting around an object.

☐   For variety, offer other objects to cut up: drinking straws, thin styrofoam, yarn scraps, broom straws.

☐   Cutting along lines involves an ability to coordinate the movement of both hands with the eyes. By about four to four and a half years of age, most children will have advanced to the point where they are able to cut along patterns or shapes. Repeated practice with a variety of patterns should be provided.

Train Ride.   Draw two parallel lines across a long sheet of paper. Give a child a small toy train and have him move the train along the lines from left to right. Over the next few weeks the child can progress to a one-dimensional drawn train and eventually to a crayon, to trace a line parallel to the ones you drew.

Clothespin Clutch.   Give each child a clip-type clothespin and then have the class sit in a circle on the floor. Wad up a piece of paper and put it on the floor in front of one child, who must pick it up using the clothespin. The child then passes it to a child sitting next to her, who must receive it with his clothespin. Try to continue moving the paper around the circle without dropping it.

Special Tracers.   Set out a variety of seasonal or holiday tracing patterns. Encourage the children to trace and color those that appeal to them. Some possibilities are illustrated in Figure 74.

Puzzles

Puzzles are frequently used in early childhood settings, both for enjoyment and for the many physical and conceptual skills derived from putting a puzzle together. It is possible to use puzzles with children as young as one and a half or two, but to take full advantage of them, it is advisable to consider the following procedure.

First puzzles should be *whole-object puzzles*. These are the type which illustrate a familiar object with only a single puzzle piece. These puzzles are sold commercially, or you can make them yourself. Follow this procedure in making your own puzzles.

Figure 74

1. Find a picture of a single, large, eye-catching object such as a bell, piece of fruit, or a house. Mount the picture on cardboard: then carefully cut its shape out of the cardboard by cutting along the edge of the picture.

2. Remove the picture and cutout shape from the frame, and paste the frame on a separate piece of cardboard. Then reinsert the puzzle piece.

3. Show the child the puzzle with the puzzle piece intact. Talk about the picture—name the object, describe its color, relate it to the child's past experiences.

4. Remove the puzzle piece and encourage the child to handle the object. Continue talking about it.

5. Show the child how to put the puzzle piece back in the frame. Say, for example, "Now I'm going to put the banana back in its hole. Watch carefully. Plop—there it goes. You try it."

6. Encourage the child to try to replace the piece on her own. You may need to provide some assistance at first, but the child eventually will master the skill on her own.

Adaptations of these steps can introduce the child to two- or three-piece puzzles. Two- or three-piece puzzles should also be of large, familiar objects, such as mushrooms, butterflies, a cup and saucer, and so on (objects that can be divided). The puzzles can be made in the same way as one-piece puzzles.

After the child masters the skills associated with completing two- or three-piece puzzles, move her to more complex types—four to eight pieces at first, then on to eight- to twelve-piece puzzles. These puzzles are too difficult to construct yourself, so search for those offered by commercial producers. In searching for these puzzles, remember that the puzzle picture should appeal to youngsters and be simply and brightly portrayed.

Cooperative Puzzle.   To help children work together toward achieving a common goal, display an unfinished puzzle at an independent work center where small groups of children may gather together. Challenge them to complete the large puzzle. It may take several days to complete, but they will be learning valuable lessons about cooperation and teamwork.

BASIC CONCEPTUAL SKILLS

The ability to form mental images of objects or events (concepts) is an important part of learning. Basic to this conceptualization process is the ability to recognize similarities and differences among things and to order them into groups or classes according to some common characteristic. This process can be effectively stimulated only if we provide the child with appropriate experiences and with the verbal capability necessary for accurate communication. Such experiences must be made as concrete as possible. For example, it is not difficult for youngsters to develop a mental image of a cat. They can experience cats directly, and their senses are involved in investigating the various characteristics of cats. However, the concept "cat" cannot stand by itself in the child's mind, especially when she is introduced to dogs, rabbits, and other furry, four-legged creatures. How does the child perceive which is a dog, a cat, or a rabbit? She must look for certain distinguishing characteristics—features that set one thing apart from another. Otherwise, all furry, four-legged creatures become "cat" to the child.

Firsthand experiences provide the children with the opportunity to distinguish among objects in order to form accurate mental images. Such distinguishing criteria normally within the preschool child's grasp are: color, size, shape, and other physical qualities such as hard/soft, rough/smooth, and big/little. Related activities normally fall into two basic categories: *classification* (grouping objects according to some common characteristic) and *seriation* (arranging objects in some kind of pattern). Suggested classification and seriation activities follow shortly, but first we'll look at a technique for presenting them to youngsters.

1. Introduce the characteristic's name. For example, in working with colors, the teacher may show the child a red crayon and say, "This is a *red* crayon." Then, showing the child a red flower, say, "This is a *red* flower." After a few additional red objects are introduced in a similar manner, the teacher may point to a separate object and ask, "What color is this pencil? What color is this ball?"

2. As the child becomes skillful at identifying the characteristic by name, he is ready to be introduced to a contrasting characteristic. In this case, it might be the color blue. Follow the same procedure as used with the original color.

3. Once the child has indicated the ability to identify contrasting characteristics by name, you may wish to provide concrete reinforcement activities to enhance his development. For example, collect a number of red and blue buttons and mix them together. Ask the child to put all the blue buttons in one jar and all the red buttons in another.

Concept Games

The following activities will help reinforce the child's understanding of a concept once it has been introduced.

Sorting Pairs.   Collect pairs of objects, one big and one little. Encourage the children to sort the objects according to size, putting the big objects into one box and the little objects into another. Sample objects include balls, pencils, crayons, cans, marbles, buttons, or toy people and animals.

   The same basic technique can be used to reinforce qualities other than size, such as shape, color, temporal sequence (first, next, last), texture (soft, hard, rough, or smooth), function (things we work with, things we play with), and so on. For example, provide a variety of buttons or bottle caps. Ask the children to sort them (in an egg carton or in separate containers) according to size, shape, or color.

Day and Night.   From catalogs, magazines, coloring books, or dictionaries, cut out pictures of things that normally happen during the day and things that normally happen at night. Have the children sort the daytime pictures into a box illustrated with a drawing of the bright sun and the nighttime pictures into a box illustrated with a drawing of the moon and stars.

Position Game.   Use a box with a lid and a variety of objects for this learning activity to reinforce relative terms. Ask the child to "Put the dog *inside* the box," "Put the cow *near* the box," "Put the horse *under* the box," "Hold the truck *above* the box," and so on.

Food Sort.   Put a mixture of dried foods into a shoe box. Have the children sort these foods according to whatever characteristic they choose— size, shape, color, type of food, and so on. Egg cartons, cups, or plastic glasses work well as sorting containers. The following dried foods are appropriate: macaroni of various shapes, split peas, lima beans, dried corn, pinto beans, kidney beans, rice, and navy beans.

Food Textures.   Arrange pineapples, cucumbers, coconuts, apples, oranges, and other rough or smooth foods on a table. Encourage the children to handle the foods and to talk about the differences in texture. You may ask them to separate the foods according to texture. Afterward, invite them to taste samples of each.

Weight Cans.   Fill three cans of the same size with sand to different levels—for example, one-third full, two-thirds full, and completely full— and cover the cans so that the children cannot see what is inside. See if the children are able to order the cans from heavy to light. A fourth can (empty) can be added to encourage finer distinctions. Once the children are able to order in this manner, add four more cans containing equal amounts of sand as the first set, and ask the children to match equal pairs.

Sniffing Bottles.   Collect ten baby food jars with lids. Choose ten items with distinctive odors, and wrap a little of each item in a gauze square to prevent it from spilling, or soak the gauze in the item. Insert one gauze square into each jar and invite the children to open one jar at a time and guess what is in each by its odor. Try to find a picture of each item so the children can match the picture to the smell. Some common items that work well for this activity include:

peanut butter	perfume
lemon wedge	cocoa
coffee	orange wedge
pickle	onion salt
after-shave lotion	Vicks VapoRub

After the children gain confidence in this activity, you may wish to make a second set of matched smells. The children will find it interesting to try to match jars from one set with those from the other according to odor.

Feely Box.   Get an old packing box and decorate it with bright colors and designs. Cut two holes in opposite sides and stitch old socks (with toes removed) to the holes (see Figure 75) through which the children will reach their arms. Each day, put a surprise object into the box and ask the children to feel it and guess what it is. Paintbrushes, sponges, drinking cups, combs, balls of string or yarn, and feathers are but a few of the objects appropriate for this activity.

Nesting Cans.   Save various sizes of cans ranging from small tomato paste cans to large institutional cans. Cover the cans with colorful contact paper and encourage the children to stack them so they make a tall tower. When they are finished, the children may turn over the cans and nest them all inside the largest can.

Nuts and Bolts.   Gather an assortment of different sizes and shapes of nuts and bolts and place them in a box. Encourage the children to match the appropriate nuts and bolts to make a complete set.

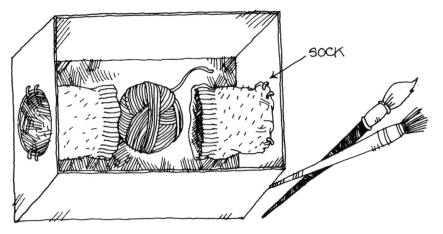

SOCK

Figure 75

Lids and Containers. Collect an assortment of containers and lids and place them on a table. Ask the children to match the lids to the appropriate containers.

Where Do I Belong? Divide a large piece of tagboard into sections as shown in Figure 76. Cut out pictures of items that you wish to have the children put into categories—for example, trees, carpenter's tools, food, and animals. Paste one picture of each item in each square in the left column. Then have the children put all the pictures of trees in the row that begins with a tree, all the tools in the row that begins with a tool, and so on until all the squares are filled.

A Row of Tubes. Cut a number of paper towel tubes so that you have five to ten tubes of varying sizes. Have the children arrange the tubes in sequence.

Mouse Tails. Cut out the shapes of ten tagboard mice. Attach a yarn tail to each mouse, starting with a 1-inch length for the first mouse and progressing to a 10-inch tail for the last. (See Figure 77.) Ask the children to put the mice in order on the basis of tail length.

Lock Board. Cover a large board with a number of latches and locks commonly used on doors. Have the children try to unlatch each type.

Touchy Walk. Fill separate plastic dishpans with different textured materials—sand, beans, buttons, bits of sponge, styrofoam bits, and the like. Have the children take off their shoes and socks to step into each dishpan. Discuss the sensory experiences with the children. Ask, for example, "Which was rough? smooth?" and "How did it feel?"

Sand Hide-and-Seek. When you are sure that your children can work with small objects without being tempted to swallow them, hide buttons, pennies, or little

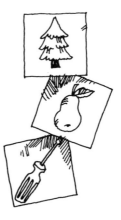

Figure 76

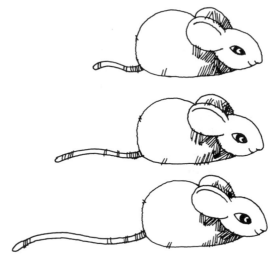

Figure 77

toys in a bowl of sand. Then have each child find the hidden objects in the grainy sand by using his or her fingers. When this loses appeal, give the child a strainer to sift out the treasures.

Color Games

The following activities will help children learn to identify and match colors.

Fill 'er Up.   Paint four egg cartons, one orange, one yellow, one blue, and one green. Buy forty-eight small plastic eggs, twelve each of the colors of the egg cartons. Cut two holes in a box large enough for the children to fit their hands into and place all the eggs in the box. Have four children each choose an egg carton, and then take turns putting their hands through each hole and pulling out two eggs. If either or both of the eggs match the child's carton, she keeps the eggs. Any eggs that do not match go back into the box, and the next child tries. Continue the game until all the egg cartons are filled.

Matching Colors.   Select two or three colors that the children are learning. Cut a square of each color from construction paper and paste those squares on white tagboard. Have the children search through a shoe box of plastic chips, buttons, or farm animals and sort each object by color onto the appropriate piece of tagboard.

Color Sort.   Collect a number of colored beads or buttons and place them in a shoe box. Cover several tin cans with construction paper of corresponding colors, and encourage the children to put the objects into the can of the matching color.

Treasure Hunt.   Paint six boxes with tempera paint—one red, one blue, one green, one yellow, one orange, and one purple. Have the children search the room for objects with these colors (or bring things from home) and put the objects into the appropriate boxes.

When all the materials are collected you may wish to dump them on the floor and invite the children to put them back into the corresponding boxes.

Color Clown.   Draw a large clown and place him in the room where he can be easily reached by the children. Extend colorful construction paper balloons from the clown's hand with pieces of bright yarn. Glue a small magnet strip to each balloon, as shown in Figure 78. Cut a corresponding set of colorful balloons from construction paper, print the color name on each, and attach magnet strips to their backs. Have the children match the colors of the clown's balloons to the color-word balloons.

Color Clothespins.   Collect several pieces of fabric in various solid colors. Buy a bag of plastic clothespins whose colors match the fabric colors (or paint some wooden clothespins the appropriate colors). String up a short clothesline in the corner of the room. Ask the children to hang the red fabric with the red clothespins, the yellow fabric with the yellow clothespins, the blue fabric with the blue clothespins, and so on.

Figure 78

The Color House.   Make six envelopes from construction paper, one envelope for each of the following colors: red, white, blue, green, yellow, black (or any other combination of six colors). Attach them with glue or staples (leaving the tops open) to a sturdy tagboard house like the one illustrated in Figure 79, where they become windows.

Cut several pieces of construction paper of the same colors, making sure the pieces can be inserted into the envelopes and yet stick out about one inch above the top. Mix these papers together in a shoe box and invite the children to sort the colored papers into the appropriate windows.

Shape Games

The following activities will help children learn to identify and match shapes.

Shape Sort.   Make a set of four 5″ × 5″ cards. On each card draw or paste one of the four basic shapes (circle, square, rectangle, triangle). Collect objects of various sizes that conform to each shape, such as circular toy dishes and bottle caps; square blocks and toys; rectangular dominoes and books; triangular hangers and musical instruments. Ask the children to sort through the various objects and place them on the card with the appropriate shape.

Beanbag Toss.   Make three beanbags from old fabric pieces and some dried navy or pinto beans. Make one beanbag a red square, another a green circle, and the third a yellow triangle. Cut a large hole of the same shapes in the tops of three cardboard cartons and paint the cartons the corresponding colors. (See Figure 80.) Have the children stand back from the boxes and try to throw the beanbags into the corresponding holes.

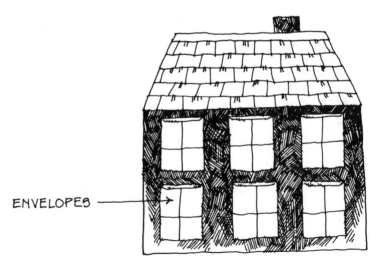

ENVELOPES ⟶

Figure 79

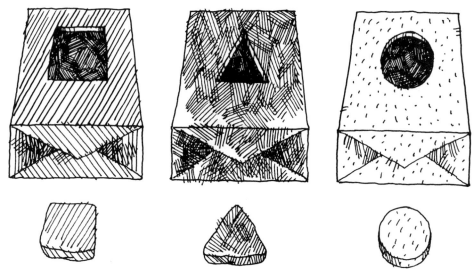

Figure 80

Shape Tape.   Cut as many strips of 1½-inch masking tape as needed to provide each child in a group with one 12-inch strip. Place one strip on the table with the sticky side up and fasten it to the table with two smaller pieces of tape (as shown in Figure 81). Cut out a series of 1-inch geometric shapes of various colors. Make a pattern of geometric figures on your tape and ask the children to make a pattern just like yours.

   Hint: Flannel strips may be cheaper than masking tape in the long run (they're reusable). And if you leave a section at the end, some children may welcome the challenge to guess what the next shape might be.

Puzzle Box.   Reinforce the lid of a large shoe box by gluing extra cardboard to the inside. Cut pieces of sponge into a variety of shapes. Place each shape on the inside of the shoe box top and trace around them with a pencil, making sure that your lines are slightly larger than the pieces of sponge. Use a sharp cutting edge to cut each shape from the box top. Encourage the children to insert the shapes into the shoe box by matching them to the appropriate holes.

Cross the Stream.   Tape a series of geometric shapes to the floor in patterns. Invite the children to join you on an imaginary walk in the woods. Pantomime a series of actions to encourage the children's active imaginations—actions such as watching a butterfly, or slapping the mosquito that just bit your arm. After a few minutes, announce to the children that they have approached a wide stream and the only way to cross it is to step on the colorful construction paper shapes. Give each child specific directions, such as: "Martha, cross on any of the circles," "Will, cross on any of the red squares," "Pam, cross on the biggest green triangles." The directions can be individualized to account for specific differences in the children's abilities.

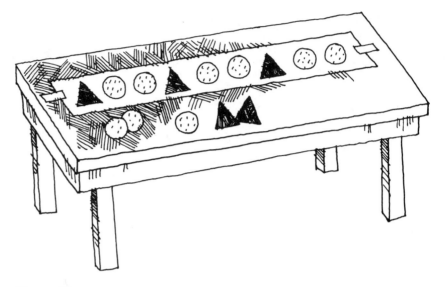

Figure 81

Shape Tree.   Draw a large tree on a sheet of heavy tagboard. Cut shapes from various colors of construction paper and glue them to the tree. Glue a small magnetic strip to each shape on the tree. Cut out a corresponding set of construction paper shapes and glue a magnetic strip to the back of each of these also. Have the children then match each shape to the corresponding shape on the tree.

Sailboats.   Construct a complete sailboat from colorful construction paper as shown in Figure 82(A) and mount it on heavy tagboard. On another sheet of tagboard draw only the parts shown in Figure 82(B). In an envelope, provide the missing parts, with each part made of the same construction paper as the original. Have the children take out the missing parts one at a time and place each on the appropriate area of the incomplete boat.

Objects and Shapes.   Gather a number of everyday objects found at home or at school—items such as a pencil, hammer, screwdriver, doll, cup, fork, and so on. Trace around the objects on dark construction paper and cut out the silhouette. Mount the silhouettes on heavy white tagboard. Have the children match the real object with its corresponding silhouette.

Concept Wheels.   Cut out one 18-inch tagboard circle and enough 12-inch tagboard circles so that each child in your group has one. Attach a spinner to each circle with a paper fastener. Paste or draw identical cutout shapes on all the wheels as shown in Figure 83. Turn your spinner to a shape. Have the children imitate your action and identify the shape and color pointed to.

Color-Shape Game.   When the children know (can match) at least four colors and at least three shapes, give them practice at discriminating among them. Use a

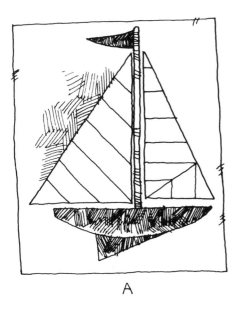

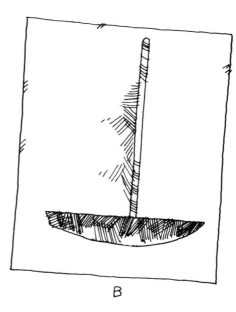

Figure 82

Figure 83

piece of butcher paper or plastic that is large enough for several children to stand on at the same time. Paint or paste the shapes on the paper which the children already know. Make the shapes using all four known colors. (See Figure 84.) Construct small, matching cards with one color-shape per card, as shown in Figure 85. Then have the children *pick* a card, *walk* to, and *stand* on the matching color-shape.

Also invent other ways to use this material. For instance, give some fun directions, such as, "Go over to this (color-shape) and roar like a lion."

Perceptual Games

The following activities will help children develop visual and patterning skills.

1. Have the child choose from three glasses of water the one that is not like the others. Food dye or a different level of water can account for the difference in one glass.

2. Place crayons of different colors in front of the child. Make sure that only two crayons match in color. Select one of the matching crayons and ask the child to find the other.

3. Place a number of geometric forms with at least one matching pair in front of the child. Point to one of the shapes for which there is a match and ask the child to find another just like the one you selected.

4. Collect a series of drawings, fabric squares, candy bar wrappers, soda pop cans, or whatever is handy. Place four or five of these items in front of the child in positions similar to those illustrated in Figure 86 (there should be

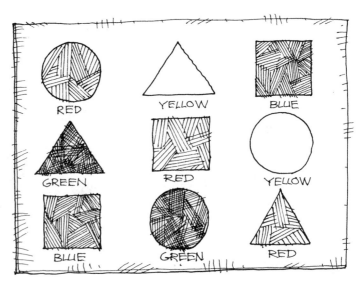

Figure 84

Figure 85

one match for the first object). Point to the first object and say to the child, "Look at this picture. Now look at the rest of the pictures and find one *just like* this one [point]. Make sure you look at all the pictures before you decide." As a variation, try a pattern where the child must find the one picture or object that is *different*.

5. Play "Search and Tell." Arrange some common items on a table and provide clues for the children. Encourage them to listen carefully and to select the object that is:

    fuzzy (a piece of fur)
    soft (a sponge)
    red (a ball)
    wet (a glass of water)

6. Collect a variety of seeds and mix them together in a box. Ask the children to group the seeds so that all those that look alike are placed in the same jar. Use a variety of seeds such as sunflower, beans, peas.

7. Fill a plastic dishpan with damp sand and provide four or five different cookie cutters. Ask one child to choose any cookie cutter he wishes and make tracks in the sand with it. The second child must not look. When the first child is done, the second child looks and tries to decide which cookie cutter was used to make the tracks.

8. Place a series of different objects, such as pine cones, leaves, and rocks, around the room. Give each child a matching object and signal the group to begin their "treasure hunt." Have the children move around the room and try to find as many objects as they can that are just like the one given them by the teacher.

Figure 86

9. Prepare a set of cards with two pictures on each card. Some pairs should be alike and some different. Have the children look at each card and put all those with matching pictures in one pile and all those with nonmatching pictures in another.

10. Cut out large magazine pictures and mount them on tagboard. Cover each with clear contact paper or laminate it. Cut the picture into strips, as shown in Figure 87. Have the child put one strip down at a time and try to guess what the picture is. To check her guess, the child puts all the strips together.

Lacing Boards #1.   Make lacing boards by tracing large cookie cutters or clear picture outlines onto heavy tagboard. Punch holes along the outline (you can also push paper fasteners into the holes). Have the children thread yarn in and out of the holes or around the paper fasteners to outline the shape.

Lacing Boards #2.   Cut out a 14″ × 24″ sheet of tagboard. Divide the board in half, lengthwise. Punch paper fasteners through the top and bottom halves as shown in Figure 88(A). Then, thread yarn in some pattern on the top half by turning it around the paper fasteners as shown in Figure 88(B). Have the children duplicate the top pattern on the paper fasteners in the bottom half.

Photo Match.   Take a front view and a back view photograph of each child in your room. Mount the photos on tagboard to make them sturdy. Put them all in a box and mix them up. Have the children examine the photos and match each front view with its appropriate back view.

Sticker Puzzles.   Get a variety of gummed picture stickers (seasonal or holiday stickers are especially good) from a variety or gift shop, or cut pictures from a children's magazine. Mount each picture on a square of tagboard, and cut each square in half—vertically, horizontally, or diagonally. Mix up all of the cards and put them in a box. Have the children match the two halves that fit together to make a complete picture, as shown in Figure 89.

Fabric Match.   Glue various fabric scraps onto pieces of square cardboard. Use a wide variety of interesting textures (corduroy, felt, satin, fur, etc.) and a wide variety of colors and patterns. Make two squares of each fabric. Put all the squares into a box. The children will enjoy finding the squares that match.

   Hint: Wallpaper samples will work just as well as fabric squares.

Figure 87

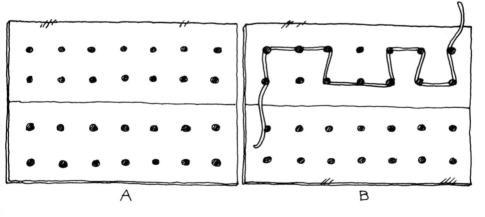

Figure 88

Figure 89

Opposites. Cut separate gameboards from tagboard (8″ × 16″). Divide each board into eight 4″ × 4″ sections. Cut out sets of contrasting pictures (such as summer/winter, happy/sad). Glue one set on the game boards and the other on a series of 4″ × 4″ playing cards. Provide each player with a gameboard. Turn the playing cards face down on the playing area. Then have the players take turns drawing one card from the pile. If it is the opposite of a picture on her gameboard (as in the example shown in Figure 90), the player places it over that picture. If it's not, the card is returned to the pile. The first player to cover her gameboard wins.

Sequence Sort. Tell the children you are going to show them some pictures. Then hold up three pictures similar to those shown in Figure 91: one of an apple, another of a person eating the apple, and the third of just the apple core. Ask the children to look at the pictures and tell you what happened first, what happened next, and so on. Choose other picture sets based on ideas your children are familiar with. For an example, see Table 1.

What's Missing? Stand in front of the children and tell them to look very closely at what you are wearing because you will soon step behind a screen where they cannot see you and change something. Remind the children to examine you carefully because they will have to guess what is missing. If the children are young, alter something obvious such as removing a shoe. If they are older try something like taking off your watch. Encourage children to guess what is different; offer clues if they experience some difficulty. Encourage the children to take turns changing something as you did.

LANGUAGE AND LITERACY

The process of language acquisition has fascinated parents, teachers, and re-searchers for years. Although many hours have been spent observing and ana-

Table 1

Picture 1	Picture 2	Picture 3
Hen on nest	Chick breaking through	Chick walking near hen
Planting seed in ground	Flower blooming	Flower in vase
Flat balloon	Person blowing up balloon	Balloon filled with air
Baby	Young child	Adult
Getting out of bed in morning	Playing outdoors	Going to bed at night

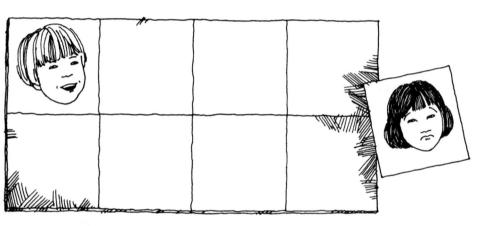

Figure 90

Figure 91

lyzing children's language learning, one common conviction surfaces consistently: *children who hear speech around them will learn to speak.* They do not need direct instruction from parents or caregivers; they only need to *listen* to the language *spoken* around them and try to make sense out of what they hear as they attempt to duplicate it. Because their imitative efforts delight people who surround them, they receive motivation through an adult's warm responses.

The same innate interest and curiosity that motivate children as they acquire oral and listening skills also drive young children as they strive to develop *literacy skills.* Preschoolers gain considerable insight into reading and writing long before they are "taught" those skills in formalized school settings. Youngsters realize that certain marks are called letters, that these letters are combined together in special ways to communicate information, and that certain rules or principles guide these formations.

Language-related experiences during the early childhood years should be characterized by active and interactive experiences. Children should be offered opportunities to continue learning oral and listening skills in a "natural" way. Their innate interests and need to communicate in an "adult" fashion should also be capitalized upon as the real impetus for literacy learning; basal readers, workbooks, and dittos have no place in a supportive early childhood language arts program.

Speaking

An ideal language environment includes provision for a great deal of natural speech. Children normally have much to say and speak eagerly if given a chance. Here are some examples of how you can capitalize on the natural inclination of children to speak to adults and with each other.

☐ *Provide a wealth of direct experiences.* When children touch the cool nose of a cow, feel the softness of grass under their bare feet, or smell the pungent odor of a freshly peeled orange, they are building a rich storehouse of things to talk about. A child can add a great number of words to his vocabulary if there is someone around to listen and respond to his verbal reactions.

☐ *Allow much spontaneous talking.* Language grows most rapidly when children engage in conversations that mean something special. Oftentimes children will want to talk with each other, but they also value the time spent in conversations with adults. One way you help children's language grow during these conversations is to use the technique of expansion. This involves responding to a child's verbal expression with elaborations of her statement. At two years, for example, a child commonly says, "Doggie bark," and the teacher responds, "Yes, the doggie is barking." The teacher has extended the immature sentence by adding words to it according to the child's ability to understand.

☐ *Really listen when a child talks to you.* Look directly at the child and offer sincere responses to what he has said. Smile, nod, or pat the child to indicate your satisfaction with his efforts. Paraphrasing the child's comment or asking an open-ended question ("How did that make you feel?") informs the child that you not only listened, but that you care about what was said.

☐ *Ask good questions.* Try to get the children to talk in ways that go beyond a yes or no response. "Do you like the red paint?" is a closed ended question that results in a yes or no answer. "Please tell me about all that red paint on your paper," leads the child to think more deeply and express her ideas in a more complex way.

☐ *Be patient.* Some children hesitate, stammer, repeat themselves, or even "trip over" themselves in eagerness when trying to talk. If a child struggles, do not take over and complete his thought. You might say something like: "Please take your time and try to tell me again."

☐ *Plan group-oriented conversations.* Allow opportunities for children to talk to the whole group when they are all together.

☐ *Encourage word play.* Children love to make up nonsense syllables, words, or phrases as they play. They go beyond the limits imposed by adult speech as they invent their own rhythmic and melodious languages: "Daggies, doggles, goo-goo geeze. Too, too, too, too, tykle geeze," or "Kachinka, chinka, chinka. Kachinka, chinka, choo. Kachinka, chinka, chinka. Moo, moo, moo, moo, moo!" These were two separate creative productions of four-year-olds in one preschool program. Young children love to experiment and play with everything; language should be no exception.

Group Conversation Activities

Children's speaking skills develop when they are given many opportunities to talk informally during the day. Youngsters will talk about their experiences with little or no prodding; last night's favorite TV show or how their neighbor cut down a tree can be hot topics of conversation as they enter the room. Taking off coats and boots as well as play in the special centers stimulates other talk. Cleaning up the room, playing outdoors, or going on a field trip are events that encourage children to gush forth with even more free-flowing verbal expression. In addition to these many informal opportunities to speak, teachers and caregivers offer opportunities for group-oriented conversation. Some examples of group-oriented possibilities are given next.

Interest Table.   In order to encourage conversation and questioning, arrange a special nook of your classroom with an attractive small table display. Behind a small table, draw a character looking down at the table in apparent awe of what is there. (See Figure 92.) Each day or so, put something new on the table to arouse the children's interest. Encourage them to ask questions or make comments. Among the objects that capture the children's attention are: feathers, pine cones, fresh or dried flowers, fruit pits, seeds, tree bark, brushes, leaves, sea shells, bottles, and rocks.

Figure 92

Classroom Treasures.   To spice up the traditional "show-and-tell" routine where a number of children bring in toys or objects on the same day and the group is required to sit and listen as each is described, try establishing a thematic approach to supervised sharing. Decorate a box to look like a treasure chest and place it next to a colorful parrot puppet and a large illustrated pirate as shown in Figure 93. Each day, the parrot "secretly" approaches a child and makes a different oral request, i.e., "Ahoy there, Matey. Please bring something *blue* for our treasure chest tomorrow." The child also receives a note to be taken home and shared with a parent describing the special treasure he is responsible for bringing to school the next day. When the child arrives at school the next day, the object to be shared is "secretly" placed into the treasure chest until sharing time. At that time, the parrot puppet invites the child to tell about his treasure and encourages the other children to ask questions about the object.

Other special treasures that might be requested by the parrot include objects that rhyme with a key word ("Bring something that rhymes with *boy* for our treasure chest tomorrow"); things that can be found in the environment (some colorful fall leaves); items reflecting a special hobby or interest; a photograph, such as a baby picture; favorite books or stories; a favorite game; a souvenir from a special trip; a favorite song; and so on.

For those children who will sometimes forget their responsibility, you may want to invite them to look around the room and choose an object to share. Or, you may have a box of "extra treasures" of your own that the children might look through for their object to be shared.

Treasure Hunt Show-and-Tell.   Before the children arrive for the day, tie a special "treasure" to the end of a ball of yarn. Hide the object and walk away from it, unwinding the yarn as you move around the room. Go over, under, around, and through as many classroom features as practical. Hide two or three such treasures, each connected to a different colored ball of yarn. The children unwind the yarn until they discover hidden treasures. Allow them to talk or ask questions about their objects as the other children listen and watch. Repeat the game daily so that each child gets a chance to unravel the yarn.

An Original Masterpiece.   Each week a different child is featured on the original masterpiece bulletin board. On Wednesday, a child is asked to be next week's masterpiece. She is asked to bring in photos, hobbies, crafts, mementos, or other objects that can be displayed on the bulletin board. These items are brought to school on Thursday or Friday so that the teacher can arrange the entire bulletin board for the first day of school the following week. The "masterpiece" child is given time to explain the significance of the items on display and to answer any questions from the group. The bulletin board then remains intact throughout the week. (See Figure 94.)

Listening Skills Games

Many types of games can strengthen listening skills. These activities must be offered as games, not "lessons," where children are to concentrate and listen attentively.

Figure 93

Figure 94

Sound Jars. Fill several pairs of plastic containers with different materials: sand, water, pebbles, small styrofoam packing "popcorn," and grains of rice. Replace the lids, then ask the children to shake each container near their ears and match up the pairs that produce the same sounds. Color code the bottoms as a self-checking device.

Guess the Source. Select a glass jar, a metal pie tin, and a piece of wood and place them on a table. Tap them with a pencil so the children are familiar with their respective sounds. Then, taking turns, the children close their eyes as you tap an object. The child opens her eyes and guesses which object was tapped.

Sound Crowd. Collect objects that have distinctive sounds, such as a bell, paper (when being crumpled), a horn, a whistle, and so on. Seat the children about you, ask them to cover their eyes, and encourage them to listen carefully as you make each sound. As you go through your collection of objects, give each child an opportunity to guess the source of at least one sound. Use each object several times if your children are especially motivated by the activity.

Sound Match-Ups. Tape-record several sounds heard in unique places or made by unique things within the home or community—for example, dogs barking, cats meowing, birds chirping, alarm clock ringing, automobile starting, door opening and closing, toilet flushing, fire siren screeching, feet stomping, and the like. Have pictures of the source of each sound (i.e., dog, cat, bird, etc.) available at the table. Give each child two pictures. Ask the children to listen carefully and to raise the correct picture when the corresponding sound is heard. Be sure to space the sounds so that the children will not have difficulty keeping pace.

Sounds of the Day.   Furnish your children with many opportunities to listen to and distinguish among sounds in their own environment. Ask the children to close their eyes and try to identify the sounds you make:

knock on table	snap rubber bands
shuffle feet	bounce a ball
clap hands	snap on lights
ring a bell	splash water
crumple paper	shut the door
rattle keys	run water in the sink
cough	cut heavy paper with scissors

Matching Sounds.   Ask the children to close their eyes while you make two separate sounds. The sound pairs may be the same or they may be different. Ask the children to tell you whether the sounds were the same or different.

This same activity can be done using different musical instruments or playing different notes on a single musical instrument such as a xylophone.

Guess Who I Am.   Ask all the children to shut or cover their eyes while you tap someone on the shoulder. Have that child then recite a simple phrase while the others listen—for example, "One, two, buckle my shoe, three, four, shut the door." Ask the children to guess, while their eyes are closed, who is doing the speaking.

The Sound Game.   Have the children form a circle. Choose one child to be "It." Give "It" a cloth bag filled with a variety of objects having distinctive sounds, such as an eggbeater, box of rice, bell, musical triangle. The children join hands and circle clockwise while "It" remains stationary outside the circle holding the cloth bag. The children continue until they hear the call, "Stop." "It" chooses something from his bag and makes a sound with it. The player who has stopped directly in front of "It" must guess what is making the sound. If she guesses correctly, she then trades places and becomes "It."

Who Has the Bell?   Ask the children to sit in a circle while one child leaves the room. Give a small bell to one child in the circle and ask him to close it in his fist. Direct all the other children to make fists with their hands, too. When the first child returns to the room, all the other children stand up and shake their fists above their heads. The first child must try to identify the one with the bell. Once your children gain skill with one bell, try more than one!

Rhymes and Poems

Nursery rhymes and poems are effective listening and speaking skill-builders. Children naturally love to play with words so the captivating rhythm, rhyme, and mirth of these sources become effective learning motivators. Begin a sequence of rhyming activities by first asking the children to identify rhyming words in a familiar context. For example, read a popular nursery rhyme such as:

Jack be nimble,
Jack be *quick,*
Jack jump over the candle*stick.*

Then say, "*Quick* and *stick* rhymed. They sounded the same at the end. Listen to this nursery rhyme and tell me which words rhyme."

Little Jack *Horner*
Sat in the *corner.*

Hickory, Dickory, *dock!*
The mouse ran up the *clock.*

Little Miss *Muffet*
Sat on a *tuffet.*

I know a little *girl*
Who had a little *curl.*

Little Boy Blue come blow your *horn;*
The sheep's in the meadow, the cow's in the *corn.*

Ding, dong *bell,*
The pussy's in the *well!*

Mary, *Mary,*
Quite *contrary.*

One, *two,*
Buckle my *shoe.*

Humpty-Dumpty sat on a *wall;*
Humpty-Dumpty had a great *fall.*

A dillar, a *dollar,*
A ten-o'clock *scholar.*

Provide a variety of these experiences. As a variation, give the children four words and ask them to tell you which ones rhyme. For instance:

☐   broke, round, found, pencil
☐   wagon, bed, word, red

Then, move to activities where the children need to supply their own rhyming words in a familiar context.

I am thinking of a word.
It rhymes with *floor.*
It is kept closed in the winter.
What is it? (door)

It rhymes with *thing.*
It is worn on the finger.
What is it? (ring)

It rhymes with *dandy.*
It is good to eat.
What is it? (candy)

It rhymes with *sweater.*
It is something we write.
What is it? (letter)

I rhyme with *how.*
I am an animal that likes to eat.
What am I? (cow)

I rhyme with *silk.*
I'm good to drink.
What am I? (milk)

It rhymes with *pop.*
A rabbit can do this.
What is it? (hop)

It rhymes with *far.*
You can ride in it.
What is it? (car)

I rhyme with *rest.*
A bird lives in me.
What am I? (nest)

I rhyme with *rain.*
I'm a girl's name.
What am I? (Jane)

I rhyme with *farm.*
You put me in a sleeve.
What am I? (arm)

I rhyme with *goat.*
You sail me.
What am I? (boat)

I rhyme with *bed.*
I am a color.
What am I? (red)

I rhyme with *"hi."*
I am a little animal.
Who am I? (fly)

I rhyme with *hop.*
You clean spills with me.
What am I? (mop)

I rhyme with *locket.*
You put things in me.
What am I? (pocket)

I rhyme with *mail.*
Most animals have one.
What am I? (tail)

I rhyme with *white.*
You like to fly me.
What am I? (kite)

I rhyme with *rain.*
I can fly.
What am I? (plane)

I rhyme with *do.*
I am a color.
What am I? (blue)

Next, ask the children to supply the rhyming word to complete your sentences. For example

❑   An animal that rhymes with *hat* is _____ .

(cat)

❑   A little *mouse* ran into the _____ .

(house)

❑   My new *bed* was painted _____ .

(red)

❑   That *bean* was the color _____ .

(green)

❑   Touch your *nose,* then wiggle your _____ .

(toes)

Finally, have the children generate the word that rhymes. Ask them to:

▪ Name a vegetable that rhymes with *born.*

▪ Name a word that rhymes with *night.*

Offer the following group or independent activities for reinforcement of rhyming skills.

Rhyming Pictures. Present the child with three pictures, two of which go together because they rhyme—for example, *mouse* and *house*. Have the child say the picture names and set apart the two pictures that go together.

Feed the Dog. Construct a large dog puppet from an old sock (see puppetry section, pages 94–95). Make a slit at the back of his mouth and attach a cloth bag behind the slit (see Figure 95). From a group of pictures, have a child select two that rhyme and say the words aloud. If she is correct, the child may "feed" the words to the dog.

Rhyming Box. Fill a box with a variety of objects for which it is easy to find rhyming words. Have a child close his eyes, reach into the box, and pull out one item. Ask him to look at the object and give a word or two that rhymes with it. Allow the child to keep all the objects that he has rhymed in front of him.

Fish Aquariums. Collect a group of small boxes that will serve as aquariums. Glue a picture onto each that will serve as the rhyming stimulus. Cut out a number of fish and glue a rhyming picture to each. Have the children choose a fish, name the picture on it, and place it into the aquarium with the corresponding rhyming word. An example is illustrated in Figure 96.

More Fun with Rhymes

When the teacher or caregiver reads a selection in exaggerated, funny ways, the children often become interested in playing with the language to create their own variations of the original rhyme. Just imagine the fun young children would have, for example, adding their own lines to the following rhyme.

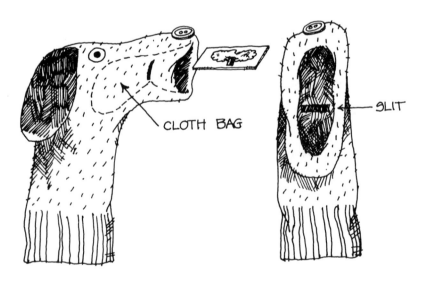

CLOTH BAG

SLIT

Figure 95

Figure 96

Bow-wow, Says the Dog

Bow-wow, says the dog;
Mew, mew, says the cat;
Grunt, grunt, goes the hog;
And squeak, says the rat.
Who-o-o-o, says the owl;
Caw, caw, says the crow;
Quack, Quack, goes the duck;
And moo, says the cow.

Ding, Dong Bell

Ding, dong bell,
The pussy's in the well!
Who put her in?
Little Johnny Green.
Who pulled her out?
Little Tommy Stout.
What a naughty boy was that,
To drown poor little pussy cat,
Who never did any harm,
And killed the mice in his father's barn.

Humpty-Dumpty

Humpty-Dumpty sat on a wall;
Humpty-Dumpty had a great fall.
All the king's horses,
And all the king's men,
Couldn't put Humpty together again.

Fiddle-De-Dee

Fiddle-de-dee, fiddle-de-dee,
The fly shall marry the bumblebee.
They went to church, and married was she;
The fly has married the bumblebee.

Baa Baa Black Sheep

Baa baa black sheep
Have you any wool?
Yes sir, yes sir,
Three bags full.
One for my master,
One for my dame,
One for the little boy who lives down the lane.

Sneeze on Monday

Sneeze on Monday, sneeze for danger;
Sneeze on Tuesday, kiss a stranger;
Sneeze on Wednesday, get a letter;
Sneeze on Thursday, something better;
Sneeze on Friday, sneeze for sorrow;
Sneeze on Saturday, see your sweetheart tomorrow.

A Red Sky in the Morning

A red sky in the morning
Is the sailor's warning.
A red sky at night
Is the sailor's delight.

To Market, to Market

To market, to market, to buy a fat pig;
Home again, home again, jiggety jig.
To market, to market, to buy a fat hog;
Home again, home again, jiggety jog.

The following books are among many that contain strong elements of humorous language play:

Dr. Seuss's many books.
The limericks of Edward Lear.
Paul Galdone, *Henny Penny.*
Fred Gwynne, *The King Who Rained.*
Fred Gwynne, *A Chocolate Moose for Dinner.*
Mercer Mayer, *What Do You Do with A Kangaroo?*
Bill Morrison, *Squeeze a Sneeze.*
Beatrice de Reniers, *May I Bring a Friend?*
Harve Zemach, *The Judge: An Untrue Tale.*

Fingerplays

Fingerplays are important activities for promoting physical growth, but they also assume a vital role in fostering overall language development. Their child-oriented verses, rhymes, or short stories appeal to young children and encourage pleasurable repetition of words and free use of voices. Fingerplays may be enjoyed by the entire group at once or by only a few children, but remember that any fingerplay should be matched to the coordination level of your children. For example, the popular fingerplay "Here is the church and here is the steeple" is much too complex for four-year-olds—they usually feel defeated as they try to lock their fingers into the positions suggested within the verse. The fingerplay time should be one of confidence building and fun-filled wordplay, so situations that frustrate or defeat the children should be avoided.

Children enjoy these rhythmic jingles and are easily captivated by their words and accompanying motions. They can be used for many purposes, including the following:

1. They help relax children and direct excess energy.

2. They help children develop memory skills.

3. They help children develop the skills of listening and following directions.

4. They help children grow in language, number, and other cognitive skills.

5. They provide small and large motor activity.

When using fingerplays for any reason, remember to follow these basic guidelines:

1. Use motivating facial and verbal expressions.

2. Say the rhyme and show the accompanying action.

3. Repeat the rhyme, if necessary.

4. Say to the children: "Please help me say it while I do the motions."

5. Repeat the rhyme again with the children and invite them to join you in the finger action. They should now be ready to do so.

6. Never force a child to join you during the fingerplay. She may not have learned it as quickly as the others, or her level of small motor development may cause her difficulty in mastering the accompanying movements. To force her to join would shame her in front of the others and cause great harm to a fragile self-concept.

7. Know the rhymes yourself. Do not read them when you teach them—this can be distracting for the children. Show that you are interested in the fingerplay and enjoy sharing it. The best way to get children interested is for you to show you enjoy it first.

Mr. Turkey

Mr. Turkey's tail is big and wide.
    (Spread fingers)
He swings it when he walks.
    (Swing hands)
His neck is long,
    (Stretch neck)
His chin is red,
    (Stroke chin)
He gobbles when he talks.
    (Open and close hands—make gobbling sounds)

Rest

I know it's best
To take a rest
So I take my little key.
I'll lock the door,
    (Children lock lips)
Pull down the shades,
    (Children close eyes)
So I cannot talk or see.

Five Bunnies

"My baby bunnies go to bed,"
The little mother rabbit said.
"I'll have to count them first to see
If they have all come back to me.
One bunny, two bunny,
    (Raise one finger for each bunny)
Three bunny dear,
Four bunny, five bunny,
Yes, they're all here.
They're the sweetest things alive
My bunnies 1,2,3,4,5."

The Red Balloon

I had a little red balloon,
So then I blew and blew
    (Blow up imaginary balloon)
Till it became all big and fat
    (Hold large balloon)
And grew and grew and grew.
I tossed it up into the air
    (Make tossing motion)
And never let it drop;
    (Catch the balloon)
But once it bumped upon the ground
    (Tossing motion)
And suddenly went POP!
    (Jump back)

Ten Fingers

I have ten little fingers.
    (Hold up hands)
They all belong to me.
    (Point to self)
I can make them do things.
Would you like to see?
    (Point to eyes)
I can open them up wide,
    (Spread fingers)
Shut them up tight,
    (Make tight fist)
Put them together,
    (Fold fingers together)
Jump them up high,
    (Reach above heads)
Jump them down low,
    (Touch floor)
Fold them quietly,
    (Fold fingers together)
And sit (or stand) just so.

Five Little Chickadees

Five little chickadees sitting on a door,
One flew away, then there were four.
    (Hold five fingers up and fold one down as indicated in the rhyme.)

Four little chickadees sitting in a tree,
One flew away, then there were three.

Three little chickadees looking at you,
One flew away, then there were two.

Two little chickadees sitting in the sun,
One flew away, then there was one.

One little chickadee having no fun,
He flew away, then there was none.

My Hands

My hands upon my head I place,
            (Follow actions as rhyme indicates)
Upon my shoulders, upon my face.
At my waist and by my side,
And then behind me they will hide.

Then I raise them way up high,
And let my fingers swiftly fly.
Then clap one, two, three,
And see how quiet they can be.

Listening Time

Sometimes my hands are at my side,
            (Follow actions indicated by rhyme)
Then behind my back they hide.
Sometimes I wiggle fingers to,
Shake them fast, shake them slow.
Sometimes my hands go clap, clap, clap,
Then I rest them in my lap.
Now they're quiet as can be,
Because it's listening time, you see!

Clap With Me

Clap with me, one, two, three,
            (Follow actions indicated by rhyme)
Clap, clap, clap, just like me.
Shake with me, one, two, three,
Shake, shake, shake, just like me.
Roll with me, one, two, three,
Roll, roll, roll, just like me.
Snap with me, one, two, three,
Snap, snap, snap, just like me.
Fold with me, one, two, three,
Now let them rest quietly.

The Robot

There is a robot
Big and strong;
Watch him stiffly
Walk along.
(Move arms and legs like a robot)
His head turns left,
(Turn head to left)
His head turns right,
(Turn head to right)
And both his eyes
Shine wide and bright.
(Open eyes widely)
Press this button
(Press nose)
And he will say,
"How are all my friends today?"
(Say in low voice)
Pull this handle
(Put left index finger with right hand)
And he will say,
"I am feeling quite okay."

The Beehive

Here is a beehive
(Close fingers together, thumbs inside)
But where are the bees?
Hidden someplace where nobody sees.
Soon they'll come out of their hive.
One, two, three, four, and five.
(Open one finger as you say each number)

One, Two, Buckle My Shoe

One, two, buckle my shoe.
Three, four, shut the door.
Five, six, pick up sticks.
Seven, eight, lay them straight.
Nine, ten, a big fat hen.
Nine, ten, say it again.

Snowflakes

We are ten little snowflakes
(Move hands and fingers in sprinkling motion)

Floating to the ground.
>   *(Point to the ground)*

"Sh," said the fairy,
>   *(Put finger to lips)*

"Do not make a sound."

Children are sleeping
>   *(Put hands together at side of head)*

But when they open their eyes
>   *(Point to eyes)*

The lovely white snow
Will be a big surprise.
>   *(Spread hands as if surprised)*

One Little Body

Two little feet go stamp, stamp, stamp,
>   *(Stamp)*

Two little hands go clap, clap, clap,
>   *(Clap)*

One little body stands up straight,
>   *(Stand straight)*

One little body sits quietly down.
>   *(Sit)*

Follow Me

Hands on shoulders, hands on knees,
>   *(Follow action as rhyme indicates)*

Hands behind you, if you please;
Touch your shoulders, now your nose,
Now your hair, now your toes,
Hands up high in the air,
Down at your sides and touch your hair;
Hands up high as before,
Now clap your hands, one, two, three, four.

Clap Your Hands

Clap your hands, clap your hands,
Clap them just like me.
Touch your shoulders, touch your shoulders,
Touch them just like me.

Shake your head, shake your head,
Shake it just like me.
Clap your hands, clap your hands,
Now let them quiet be.

Let's Make a Ball

A little ball,
   (Make a circle with pointer finger and thumb)
A bigger ball,
   (Make a circle with both pointer fingers and thumbs)
A great big ball I see;
   (Make large circle with arms)
Now, let's count the balls we've made;
One, two, three.
   (Repeat action of first three lines)

The Apple Tree

Away up high in an apple tree,
   (Point up)
Two red apples smiled at me.
   (Form circles with fingers)
I shook that tree as hard as I could;
   (Pretend to shake tree)
Down came those apples,
And mmmmmm, were they good!
   (Rub tummy)

Open, Shut Them

Open, shut them; open, shut them;
Give them a clap.
Open, shut them; open, shut them;
Lay them in your lap.

Creep them, creep them,
Right up to your chin.
Open up your little mouth
But do not let them in.

   (Repeat first verse)

*There Was a Little Turtle**

There was a little turtle,
   (Make circle with hands)
He lived in a box.
   (Form box with hands)
He swam in a puddle,
   (Make swimming motions)

*Poem by Vachel Lindsay.

He climbed on the rocks.
(Make climbing motions with hands)

He snapped at a mosquito,
(Make grabbing motion)
He snapped at a flea,
(Make grabbing motion)
He snapped at a minnow,
(Make grabbing motion)
And he snapped at me.
(Make grabbing motion)

He caught the mosquito,
(Clap hands)
He caught the flea,
(Clap hands)
He caught the minnow,
(Clap hands)
But he didn't catch me.
(Start to clap, but stop short)

Choo-Choo Train

This is a choo-choo train
(Bend arms at elbow)
Puffing down the track.
(Rotate forearms in rhythm)
Now it's going forward,
(Push arms forward; continue rotating motion)
Now it's going back.
(Pull arms back; continue rotating motion)
Now the bell is ringing,
(Pull bell cord with closed fist)
Now the whistle blows.
(Hold fist near mouth and blow)
What a lot of noise it makes
(Cover ears with hands)
Everywhere it goes.
(Stretch out arms)

Bear Hunt

Leader: Let's go on a bear hunt.
Children: Let's go on a bear hunt.
Leader: All right?
Children: All right.
Leader: O.K.?
Children: O.K.

Leader: Let's go!
>   *(Make walking sounds by clapping hands on knees; children repeat words and follow all motions of leader)*

Oh look!
What's that?
A big tree!
Can't go under it.
Can't go round it.
Can't go through it.
Have to climb it.
All right? O.K.? Let's go!
>   *(Make climbing motions; resume walking motions)*

Oh look!
What's that?
A big field!
Can't go under it.
Can't go round it.
Can't go over it.
Have to go through it.
All right? O.K.? Let's go!
>   *(Swish palms together; resume walking motions)*

Oh look!
What's that?
A big river!
Can't go under it.
Can't go round it.
Can't go through it.
Have to swim it.
All right? O.K.? Let's go!
>   *(Swimming motions; resume walking motions)*

Oh look!
What's that?
A dark cave!
Let's go in it.
All right? O.K.? Let's go!
Ooh—it's dark in here.
The walls are wet.
>   *(Make feeling motions)*
Oops—my toe bumped something!
What could it be?
It feels furry!
It has a tail!
A large back!
Two ears!

A big nose!
Two eyes!
Ooh—big teeth!
It's a bear!!
Let's run!
    (Clap hands faster on knees; go through activities backward—swim river, swish
    through field, climb tree, walk home)

Rabbit Song

In a cabin in a wood,
    (Draw cabin with hands)
A little man by the window stood.
    (Shade eyes and look around)
Saw a rabbit running by,
    (Make rabbit hopping with hands)
Knocking at my door.
    (Knock on chest)
"Help me! Help me!" the rabbit said,
    (Throw hands in air)
"Or that farmer will shoot me dead."
    (Point fingers like gun)
"Little rabbit, come inside:
Safely you'll abide."
    (Wave imaginary rabbit in, and stroke him in your arm)
(At end of each verse, leave out the words for one motion and do the motion in silence, until
whole song is pantomimed)

Jack-in-the-Box

Jack-in-the-box
Sits so still.
"Won't you come out?"
"Yes, I will!"
    (Hand closed, thumb inside; then thumb jumps out)

Ten Little Firemen

Ten little firemen
Sleeping in a row:
    (Extend both hands, fingers curled, to represent sleeping men)
Ding, dong goes the bell,
    (Pull bell cord with one hand)
And down the pole they go.
    (Close both fists, put one on top of other, slide them down pole)
Off on the engine, oh, oh, oh,
    (Steer engine with hands)

Using the big hose, so, so, so.
    (Make nozzle with fist)
When all the fire's out, home so-o slow.
    (Steer engine with hands)
Back to bed, all in a row.
    (Extend both hands, fingers curled)

Who Feels Happy?

Who feels happy, who feels gay?
All who do, clap their hands this way.
    (Follow action as rhyme indicates)
Who feels happy, who feels gay?
All who do, nod their heads this way.
Who feels happy, who feels gay?
All who do, tap their shoulders this way.
    (Encourage the children to suggest additional things to do.)

Hickory, Dickory, Dock

Hickory, dickory, dock
    (Swing one arm to represent a pendulum)
The mouse ran up the clock.
    (Wiggle fingers and have them climb above the head)
The clock struck one,
    (Clap hands once.)
The mouse ran down,
    (Wiggle fingers downward.)
Hickory, dickory, dock.
    (Swing arm like a pendulum.)

Five Frogs

Five little frogs sitting on a stump,
The first one said, "Oh, let's jump."
The second one said, "Are you all in a row?"
The third one said, "Here's a line to toe."
The fourth one said, "Oh, you're slow."
The fifth one said, "1–2–3–go!"
And splash they all went into the water below.

Five Kittens

Five little kittens sat under a tree
As happy as five little kittens could be,
This one is laughing, he is jolly and fat.
This one is crying, he is a big boo cat,

This one is purring, he is a sweet little dear.
This one is growling, he is naughty I fear.
This one had lapped up a saucer of milk
And was stroking his fur
Till it looked like silk.
Along came a dog, with loud bow-wow-wow.
And they scampered up a tree, and they're up there now.

Ten Chicks

Said chick number one, "Why, where can I be?"
Said chick number two, "What queer things I see."
Said chick number three, "I'm ready to dine."
Said chick number four, "This corn meal is fine."
Said chick number five, "This brown bread is better."
Said chick number six, "It ought to be wetter."
Said chick number seven, "I'm off for a walk."
Said chick number eight, "I'm tired don't talk."
Said chick number nine, "Guess I'll go to sleep."
Said chick number ten, "Good-night then, peep, peep."
So each little chick tucked his round yellow head,
Right into his mother's soft warm feather bed.

Reading Stories

Someone must read to children at least once a day. Children listen attentively to stories as their imaginations are stretched and their ability to visualize people, objects, and events is enhanced. There is no one special way to share stories with young children; readers differ in style. There are some who choose to use cultural or period dress as a focus; others use puppets, chalkboards, storyboards (felt, flannel, or magnetic), or other props to present a story. Each has its own special way of bringing a story to life for young children, but, as I have heard someone once say, those various props may entertain but they do not "speak to the inner child." It is more through the careful use of one's voice that the true value of storytelling as a listening experience can be fully explored. The following suggestions may help you weave the special magic that makes a good story a permanent part of the memories of all children.

Prepare Yourself

☐ Read the story silently at least twice.

☐ Read it into a tape recorder and listen for sections that need to be improved.

☐ Sit or stand in front of a mirror as you make adjustments in intonation, stress, and pacing.

☐ Time the story. A good rule of thumb is to keep the story between five and fifteen minutes long.

☐ Don't worry about the time you'll take to prepare a story well. Good story-tellers can prepare only up to about five stories a year. A well-prepared story will fascinate children and will become even more loved if it is repeated.

Prepare the Environment

☐ Seat the children in a semicircle in front of you to allow for maximum eye contact.

☐ Sit on the floor with the children or sit on a low chair. (Some teachers prefer rocking chairs for a "homey" feeling.)

☐ Make sure the children are comfortable and able to see well.

Present the Story

☐ *Plan a good introduction so children get an idea of what the story is going to be about.* Be careful not to get too involved with highly detailed descriptions of characters or events but give the children an idea of the main characters and what their major situation will be.

☐ *Use your voice effectively.* Speak naturally, but be aware of the ways in which loudness or softness and fastness or slowness can affect the mood of a story. For example, suspenseful parts may call for a soft, slow, mysterious tone while happy parts may call for livelier, louder, joyous tones. Your voice can be used to add surprise, sadness, question, or fear to the story, but remember not to get overly dramatic. If you do, you will shift the focus from the plot to the storyteller and interrupt the children's interest and concentration.

☐ *Maintain eye contact with the children.* A good reader of children's stories must concentrate on the words in a book, but at the same time know the story well enough to glance regularly at the audience. Look at your children as you read. A few well-timed gestures will also add to the vividness of the story.

☐ *Anticipate questions and minor interruptions during the reading or storytelling period.* Handle children's questions or comments tactfully, so the flow of the story is not interrupted. For example, one child became so absorbed in a story that he blurted out just before the climax, "Oh, I wonder how the kitten will be saved." Another child insightfully offered the actual solution: "I know—the mama cat will save her." Although the storyteller could have become flustered at the revelation of the story's ending, she remained composed and simply commented, "Your idea was very good, Robin, but let's all listen and see if you were right." The children in this case were drawn right back into the story. Often teachers themselves cause unnecessary interruptions by throwing out questions or explaining new words along the way. Such digressions add nothing to the story and mainly serve to lessen interest or interrupt plot continuity. Never interrupt a story yourself except in extreme necessity, as for instance when a child is being disruptive and you must ask him to stop. But don't think that stories should be exclusively receptive in nature. Welcome the children's comments and questions, keeping in mind that stories should encourage expressive as well as receptive language skills.

☐ *Share pictures throughout the story if they help clarify or illustrate the evolving sequence of events.* By sitting on a low chair or on the floor, you will be in perfect position to hold up the book for the children to see. Hold the book all the way open in a steady position. Some teachers, when reading a story, prefer to hold books at either side; others find it more comfortable to hold them in front. Whatever the position, be sure that all children can see the picture without having to crane their necks or move unnecessarily. If the children are seated in a semi-circle, you may have to move the picture so they all can see. In these cases, it is important to hold the book and pause so the group seated to your left can focus their eyes on the picture; hold and pause at the center; and hold and pause to your right. Some teachers share poorly by holding the pictures so the children on the left are able to focus and then slowly sweeping to the right without stopping the picture along the way. It is difficult for the children in the center to focus on the moving picture, and they may not be able to see it properly. Short sweeps and pauses are necessary so the focal point can remain fixed for a short period of time.

Discuss the Story

After the story is over, the children may enjoy discussing the main characters or plot for a short period. This will not always be the case, but if you find that interest is high, guide the discussion with questions like the following:

☐ Tell us what you liked (or didn't like) about the story.

☐ If you had been (story character) how would you have felt when _____ happened?

☐ In what other way could (character) have solved this problem?

☐ Which character from the story would you most like to meet? Why?

☐ How do you think (character) felt when _____ happened?

☐ What story character would you most like to be? Why?

☐ Why do you think (character) did what he did?

☐ Did someone in the story change his mind about something? What was it? Why did he do it?

☐ What do you think happens to (character) now after the story ended?

☐ Have you ever had a problem like (character)? What did you do about it?

☐ Did you like the story? Why? Why not?

☐ Which picture did you like the most? Why?

☐ What things happened in the story that could really happen? That could not really happen?

❑ What would you change about the story?

❑ Did you know another story like this one? What is it? How are the stories alike?

Supplement Your Style

Storyboards are good aids for sharing stories with your children. They help focus attention on the story and add interest and enjoyment. "I Know an Old Lady" by Rose Bonne is an example of an ideal storyboard story. (See example in Figure 97.) The teacher can attach silhouettes of everything the lady swallows to a cutout of the lady. *Hint:* Whatever your choice of story, be sure the figures attach easily to the storyboard.

   Story aprons are another type of visual aid that encourages children's listening enjoyment. They are made by sewing a number of colorful pockets onto a chef's apron. The pockets contain objects or pictures that illustrate major characters or events in a story. Children enjoy the intrigue of finding out what will be taken out of each pocket as the story progresses.

Literacy

Recent research in the acquisition of literacy skills indicates that reading and writing develop much like oral language and listening—through self-driven motivation within a natural, developmentally appropriate environment. Early childhood expert Terry Salinger describes that environment in the following section.

Figure 97

Making the Literate Environment Work*

A classroom alive with print and a teacher committed to children's natural acquisition of literacy skills—these are a start. Making a positive, supportive environment work for young children takes skill, planning, and willingness to move beyond traditional curricular approaches. Making it work also takes patience, for children will progress at individual speeds and with personal needs. Teachers in preschool centers often miss opportunities to integrate, demonstrate, or exploit opportunities for literacy events. Highlights of an ordinary day in a preschool follow and are accompanied by suggestions for capitalizing on children's emerging literacy.

Arrival.   When children arrive, they sign in in the attendance book and put their belongings in a cubbyhole marked with their own names. Children are encouraged to select a book for browsing while waiting for circle time.

Circle Time.   The teacher displays a chart containing the pledge to the flag and points to each word as children recite; a teacher-made calendar is also displayed, and words for the month and day of the week, yesterday and tomorrow are discussed. A chart tablet is again used for visual reinforcement as children learn a new song. The teacher knows that the children cannot read these texts but wants them to become familiar with print directionality and sight words and with the idea of having a visual equivalent to what they say.

Center Time.   Centers are labeled with signs, occupancy quotas, and rules. The class includes a literacy center where the teacher helps children write a caption book entitled "A Book About Me." The top of the first page reads "This is a picture of me . . . "; at the bottom is written, "My name is _____ ." The teacher reads each page to the children and shows them where to write and draw. Children in the art center are encouraged to write on their work or at least to dictate a sentence to be transcribed. The library center is used for quiet browsing and listening to tapes of stories. The housekeeping center includes ample writing material so that children can take phone messages, write letters, pay bills, and make shopping lists. An assistant teacher and several children make pudding for a snack. The teacher begins asking children to "read" the package label, which they do as "pudding," "Jell-O," and "chocolate." They follow a recipe, written on a chart tablet, that uses words, pictures of cups and measuring spoons, and an actual pudding package; it displays a "What-you-need" and "What-you-do" format familiar to the children.

Free Time.   Browsing through books, playing with junk mail, working in the literacy center (for example, with a typewriter) are all encouraged during free time. Children may request transcription of stories developed as part of dramatic or block play or art work.

Storytime.   Storytime includes a new story and an old, favorite, predictable book that has been rewritten as a big book. The teacher points to the words in the big

*Salinger, Terry (1988). *Language arts and literacy* (pp. 81–82). Columbus: Merrill Publishing.

book, and children read along with parts they know by heart. The teacher calls on individuals to read specific parts, and the children read with confidence, sometimes not reading the text exactly but always keeping to the main ideas. During the new story, the teacher asks for responses to simple questions and discusses the book after reading.

Letters Home.   Mimeographed letters about a trip are to be sent home, but children are given time to "write" their own messages at the bottom of the letter. Parents, accustomed to this process, will spend a few minutes reading the whole letter with their children and discussing plans for the outing.

Throughout the day in this preschool, children see print being used and even participate in producing written messages. Their efforts are respected and welcomed, and they begin to get the feel of using reading and writing purposefully. These strategies could be used as effectively in kindergarten classrooms.

Labeling Activities

1. Name tags worn by the children on the first day of school offer opportunities to observe, compare, and contrast the printed words with the greatest meaning for the children—their names. Children take great pride in their name tags and enjoy looking for likenesses and differences between their own tags and those of their friends.

2. Label each child's storage box, locker, or coat hook with his name. On the first day of school, you may want to take each child's photograph with an instant camera, mount it on durable tagboard, print the child's name on it, and then scatter all the labeled pictures on the floor. Ask the children, one at a time, to find their tags and take them to their lockers where an aide can hang them. This procedure can be extended by informally including other reading skills— for example, "Jana did a wonderful job finding her name. Now, let's have someone whose name begins just like Jana . . . J . . . find it. That's just great, Jimmy, you really did fine."

3. Write the child's name and date on a piece of artwork when it is finished. This repeated exposure is sure to help the child recall her name, and she will take pride in seeing her name on something she created. When labeling, though, try to put the name in the upper left-hand corner so the child will become used to looking at that part of a page whenever she begins to read.

4. Label objects in the classroom when they will have most meaning. For example, if a pair of gerbils is brought into the classroom and the children's interest in the new additions is high, you may wish to print the word *gerbils* clearly on a bright piece of paper and attach it to the gerbil cage. Discuss the word with the children. If the children decide to name their gerbils, you may want to construct a name label. Similarly, labels can be made for a flower, fish, the book center, and so on.

Periodically, invite the children to play a naming game. First, take down the special labels and then ask for volunteers to name each special thing in the room. As they do so, print the word on a 3" × 5" card. The child should say the word and tape it to the object. Continue until each child has had at least one turn. Later, take the cards down, place them on the floor, and ask which of the words the children know. As they read the words, the children may place the cards back on the objects. Review the words often with your children. Make a duplicate set of cards for children to use alone in matching words and objects.

5. At times, children in a dramatic play area may ask you to provide certain labels for them as they try to make their play a bit more realistic. For example, one group of children set up an ice-cream store and were about to open for business when they realized that they needed a name for their store and a listing of the available flavors. The teacher wrote down on a sheet of paper the name the children selected as well as the flavors. The words served as a model for the children as they made their own signs with marking pens and tagboard.

6. For snack time, use placemats made from wallpaper samples and label each mat with your children's names. Change the location of the placemats daily and encourage the children to find their own. As the children begin to recognize each others' names, they may (one or two at a time) take turns arranging the placemats for the entire group.

Experience Stories

The language experience approach is often initiated with four- and five-year-olds. The teacher, capitalizing on a direct experience, writes about it as dictated by a child or group of children. The experience chart becomes the children's first reading experience as they begin to recognize their spoken words in print. The basic reading skills of word recognition and comprehension can be taught through use of an experience story and follow-up activities. The following sequence is recommended for use in the preschool or kindergarten classroom:

1. Provide a direct experience that will interest your children and stimulate them to talk informally. Children eagerly express their thoughts when recounting such experiences as making cookies, visiting the zoo, watching someone shear a sheep, planting a seed, or feeding a pet.

2. Children dictate their ideas and feelings, and you write them on chart paper (18" × 36") exactly as they are spoken. (See Figure 98.)

3. As you record each child's words, read them back to the group, emphasizing left-to-right progression.

4. After each child has had an opportunity to contribute, read the entire story back to the group.

5. You may ask the children to read from the chart. Some may read only the title or a word. Others may be able to read their entire sentence as you point to each word.

6. Possible follow-up activities:

   □ Check to see if the children can recognize words and sentences; for example, ask if anyone can "find the sentence that Sharon told us."

   □ Hold up a card containing a key word in the story and see if anyone can recognize it on the chart.

   □ Ask questions to check on comprehension; for example, "What color are the hamster's eyes?"

7. Some children may like to illustrate the story once it is complete. Write the story title and the child's name at the top of the drawing paper.

8. Often a child will have a story to accompany an art experience, which you can use as an extension of the experience chart. Write down the words as the child speaks them and follow the suggestions given previously for group experience stories.

OUR HAMSTER

James said, "We have a pet hamster. His name is Fluffy."

Joan said "He has brown fur and big brown eyes."

Carmen said, "Fluffy is a funny hamster."

Jackson said, "He always scratches and digs."

Faith said, "We love Fluffy."

Figure 98

9. Illustrated individual experience stories make attractive and interesting "library books" when several children contribute to the project.

Word Games

Word Computer.   Construct a triangular stand, approximately 12″ × 5″, as illustrated in Figure 99. Prepare two sets of cards: one set with pictures and one set with the corresponding written words. Using large notebook rings, attach the cards to the stand so that each card may be flipped over.

The child flips a card from the first set and flips cards from the second set until he gets a match.

Feed the Dog a Bone.   Draw a dog's face on a heavy sheet of tagboard and make a slit in its mouth, as shown in Figure 100. Cut a number of bones from tagboard and write words that have been previously introduced to the children (shapes, numerals, colors, and other concepts are appropriate, also). The children feed the dog a bone by reading the word and dropping the bone through the slit.

Word Puzzles.   Glue a large 3″ × 4″ picture on a heavy piece of 4″ × 4″ tagboard. Print the name of the picture across the top of the tagboard and cut the card apart so that a part of the picture and some letters are on each part. Make several cards of this type. Mix all of the parts in a shoe box and have the children sort the pieces and put each picture together like a puzzle.

Ice Cream.   Give each child in a group a cardboard cone on which he will tack scoops of ice cream. Cut several scoops of ice cream from colorful construction paper and print a word on each scoop (add a picture if you desire). One child spins a spinner and gets to try to identify the words on as many scoops as the

Figure 99

Figure 100

spinner indicates. (See Figure 101.) If he says the words correctly, he may add as many as he identifies to his cone. The object is for each child to build as high an ice-cream cone as he can by identifying sight words (or numerals, shapes, etc.).

Treasure Walk. Place objects around the room and print the word for each on a piece of paper. Give one or two words to each child and invite them to go on a treasure walk to find the objects identified on their pieces of paper.

Hunting Game. One child covers her eyes while the rest of the group places two familiar word cards face up on the table and chooses one word to be "It." When the others say, "Ready," the child opens her eyes and sees whether she can guess the "It" word. The children rotate until each has had about three or four turns.

Pack Race. Give three or four children each a shuffled stack of identical cards on which familiar words have been printed. One child turns up the top card on his pack and calls the word. Each of the other children tries to see who can find that word first in his or her deck. The caller and the one who finds the word place it face up in front of them on the table. The other children place their cards face down in front of them. Rotate to a new caller each time. The children see who can end up with the most cards turned face up.

Railroad Game. Have the children sit in a semicircle in front of you. One child, the "conductor," stands behind the chair of the first child in the group. The teacher flashes a card on which is printed a familiar word. If the conductor says the word first, she continues to be conductor and moves to the back of the next child. If the child who is seated says the word correctly, that child gets to be the conductor and changes places with the original one. Continue in this manner until interest wanes.

Figure 101

Personal Word Books.   Invite the children to cut out and paste magazine pictures to illustrate words they know. Print the word on the paper for the child if he cannot do it himself. The child collects these sheets and designs a cover with crayons and construction paper; then you staple the cover and papers together to create a personalized word book.

Match Game.   Construct two-piece matching puzzle games out of tagboard where the children must fit together a word and its picture, as illustrated in Figure 102.

Writing to Read

Reading and writing are part of the same process. As children exercise their strong developmental interest in writing, they are using a trial-and-error approach to unlocking the written language. For instance, once you have offered repeated labeling experiences, where they see words used as labels or captions in the classroom, young children will attempt to imitate your lead by using pictures *and* words to share information. Their first efforts may appear as scribbles, but you can be assured that each mark has some special meaning.

Set up a *writing center:* an area in your room where pencils, crayons, marking pens, and plenty of paper are stored. Children can practice writing their names, names of friends, or the labels found around the room. Again, you will find children approaching this task with varied levels of expertise, but this practice will help them make many new discoveries.

When youngsters begin to show an interest in handwriting and are sufficiently mature in other areas of development, they are probably ready to try some reinforcement games. Initial experiences should be informal, mainly just getting the child to experiment with writing. Later, as small muscles grow and mature, the children will be led to make increasingly accurate reproductions of model letters or words.

Writing Practice Games

Clay Letters.   Encourage the children to mold letters or words from modeling clay or Play-Doh.

Finger-Paint Slide.   Children love the medium of finger paint, primarily because of its sensory quality. Encourage the children to use sweeping motions while making letters or words in the finger paint.

Touchy Letters.   Cut letters out of sandpaper and glue them to cardboard or blocks of wood. Have the children run their fingers over the letter outline as they say the letter name aloud. This activity helps children remember the shapes once they begin to write the letters.

Sandy Writing.   Spread colorful terrarium sand on the bottom of a shoe box lid. Encourage the children to make letters by running their index fingers through the sand.

Letter Puzzles.   Make a variety of letter puzzles for the children. For instance, cut letters comprising a child's name into two separate pieces. Have the child try to put the pieces together.

Secret Message.   Lay waxed paper over plain drawing paper. Draw a geometric shape, a numeral, a letter, a word, a child's name, or a simple message on the waxed paper, being sure to press hard as you do so. Give the drawing paper to a

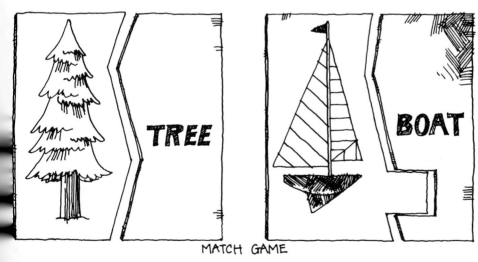

MATCH GAME

Figure 102

child, who then brushes watercolor over the paper. The watercolor will not stick to the clear wax, and the child will be able to guess the geometric shape, numeral, or whatever. (This activity is especially good at Halloween.)

Name Game.   Cut a number of 1-inch squares from heavy cardboard. Print each child's name on the squares (one letter to a square). Draw squares on an envelope and print the child's name on the squares (again, one letter to a square). Put the cutout squares inside the envelope. Have the child pour the letters from the envelope and match them to the name on the outside of the envelope.

Palm Trace.   Provide a paintbrush and water-soluble paint. Have children work in pairs. One child shuts her eyes as the other child paints a letter or numeral on her palm with the brush. The first child calls out the name of the letter or number and then looks to see if she was right.

Name Cookies.   Cut out enough 3-inch letter shapes for each child in your group to have his or her first initial. Cover each letter with aluminum foil and give them to the children. Have the children mold cookie dough over the aluminum letters and put them into the oven. The children can paint their cookies with frosting when they come out of the oven.

   Hint: Baking supply shops or variety shops often have letter or numeral cookie cutters.

Feel the Letter (or Numeral).   Get a carton with partitions (such as a wine case). Stand it on its side, with the open partitions facing you.

   Attach a piece of fabric to the top of each section of the carton, so that the fabric covers the open front of that section. (See Figure 103.) On separate index cards, paste letters made from various materials, such as an A from sandpaper, a B from aluminum foil, and so on. Put one card on the bottom of each section of the carton.

   Have a child reach into one of the sections and try to determine through his sense of touch which letter of the alphabet is on the card. Place a worksheet with corresponding partitions at the learning area so that the children can write down the letter they chose for each section.

Letter Bags.   Prepare eight drawstring bags and number them one through eight. Make or buy sturdy cardboard letters (or numerals). Place one letter in each bag. Have a child place her hand into one of the bags and try to identify the letter by touch.

Letter Carrots.   Cut carrot and leaf forms from orange and green tagboard, respectively. On the leaf form, print each of the lowercase letters; on the carrot form, print each of the uppercase letters. Put the carrots in one box and the leaves in another. Have the children take a carrot form from one box and choose from the other a leaf form to match it.

Mitten Match.   Using wallpaper samples or wrapping paper mounted on heavy tagboard, cut out many pairs of mittens, each pair with one uppercase and one

CHILDREN WRITE IN
EACH GUESSED LETTER
ON THE CORRESPONDING
PARTITION OF THE
WORKSHEET

Figure 103

lowercase form of a letter. Put the mittens in a box and have the children match left and right mitten pairs.

Puzzle-Picture Letters.   Cut a piece of 12" × 12" tagboard. Divide it into sixteen 3-inch squares. Print a capital letter on each square. Cut another piece of 12" × 12" tagboard exactly like the first and divide it the same way. Put the two pieces face-to-face and identify which boxes on the second square match the boxes on the first square. Then, turning the second tagboard back toward you, print a corresponding small letter in each box. Draw or paste a large, colorful picture on the back of this second tagboard, and cut it into sixteen 3-inch squares. (See Figure 104.) Mix up the squares. Have the children pick up a square, match it to the appropriate capital letter, and place it face down on the capital letter. They continue in this way until a puzzle picture appears.

Guess the Letter.   Pin a letter to the back of a child's shirt. Then have the rest of the group offer clues to help the designated child guess the letter. Familiar words that begin with the letter sound are often the best clues.

Human Letters.   Challenge your children, alone or in pairs, to create letters of the alphabet with their bodies.

Figure 104

MATHEMATICS

A sure understanding of mathematics develops slowly because children need much time to understand these inherently abstract ideas. So, although some children may enrapture their parents by counting, "One, two, three, four . . ." or adding, "One and one is two," they may be simply parroting phrases heard over and over again and are not really counting or adding with understanding. When this happens, our children recite with as much comprehension as trick ponies who pound their hoofs at a trainer's signal. To prevent such situations from developing, you face a key challenge. You must provide many experiences in an organized way to help the child grasp basic mathematical concepts. This challenge can be initially met by examining developmentally appropriate activities designed to build and reinforce the following mathematics skills:

1. *Number* (recognizing how many objects are in a set)
2. *Numeral* (recognizing the number names)
3. *Sequence* (recognizing the proper ordering of the numerals)

Incidental Learning

Some of the first mathematical concepts that children acquire are what I refer to as *nebulous concepts*. They are not precise, but only vague notions of something. Consider young toddlers, for example. Their teachers are very good at helping children enlarge upon nebulous concepts. Mrs. Bryan, for example, rarely says anything like, "You may have some cookies if you wish." Instead, she wants her children's everyday experiences to enrich and strengthen their vague mathematical concepts, so she might instead say, "You have *two* cookies today—would you like *round* ones or *square* ones?" She realizes that mathematics is not just a process of memorizing correct answers. It is a study of the relationships between different things. For that reason, Mrs. Bryan is extremely careful: if a toddler picks four cookies instead of two she does not say, "I told you to take only two. Here, I'll take two back." Doing that does not allow the child to think about the situation. Instead she says, "You took *four* cookies, but you may have only two." The child may then ponder the situation and put one cookie back. Instead of now telling him he is wrong, Mrs. Bryan chooses to focus on his correct mathematical idea and praises him for it: "That's very good, Stanley. You knew some cookies had to be put back, didn't you? You knew you had to take some cookies away from four to make two. Put one more back and you'll have two." Mrs. Bryan, knowing such situations should be kept as open-ended as possible, decided that accurate mathematical facts and processes were not as important at this age as the child's ability to sense relationships among sets of objects.

Children must be able to play and use numbers whenever opportunities present themselves or are created by imaginative teachers. Good teachers give children those chances by offering a multitude of experiences involving numbers—cooking, water play, sand play, blocks, dramatic play, puzzles, and table toys. This has often been referred to as *incidental learning*.

Through incidental learning, one teaches mathematics skills in the context of the child's play activities, instead of structuring specific mathematics lessons. At the snack table, for example, the teacher may say, "There are four chairs, one for each of you." She may singly count the cups or cookies as they are passed out to each child. Children at the sandbox or water table may fill containers, empty them, and experiment with how much more sand or water is needed to fill a larger container than it takes to fill a smaller one. Cooking activities give the children practice in measuring ingredients with cups and measuring spoons. Size relationships are begun as the teacher asks the children to cut the pieces of celery "just as big as this one." During an informal tea party in the kitchen play area, the children match the number of cups and saucers to the number of children participating. Boys or girls at the woodworking area plan to "measure" a piece of wood and saw it so that it is the same length as another piece. Block construction leads other children to choose the biggest block for the base of a building and the smallest for the top. Separate shelves are provided for blocks of different shapes, so the children practice shape recognition as they remove and replace blocks used for construction projects.

Number Rhymes

Fingerplays and action rhymes make a young child's school day very exciting. Wise teachers use these same activities to teach beginning number concepts informally. A pair of white canvas painter's gloves decorated with appropriate figures, or fingers decorated with suitable finger puppet characters, help children learn basic concepts through imaginative play activity. (Note: In addition to the fingerplays included here, others such as "Two Little Blackbirds," "Five Little Squirrels," and "Ten Fingers," found elsewhere in this book, are also appropriate.)

Silly Willy

Ten jolly pennies
Happy all the time
Taken all together
They make a silver *dime*.

Ten little pennies,
I wish they were mine;
Silly Willy spent one,
Then there were *nine*.

Nine little pennies
Jingling on a plate;
Silly Willy lost one,
Leaving only *eight*.

Eight little pennies,
Bright as stars in heaven;
Silly Willy spent another,
Leaving only *seven*.

Seven little pennies
Saw some candy sticks;
Silly Willy bought one,
Leaving only *six*.

Six little pennies
Happy and alive;
Silly Willy wasted one,
Then there were *five*.

Five little pennies
Taken to the store;
Away went another one,
Then there were but *four*.

Four little pennies!
Oh, deary me!
Willy lost one in the sand,
Then there were but *three*.

Three little pennies,
Lonesome, sad, and blue;
Willy bought a candy cat,
Then there were *two*.

Two little pennies
Wishing for some fun;
Silly Willy spent another,
Then there was but *one*.

One lonely penny!
Sticky raisin bun!
Willy bought it with his penny
Leaving pennies *none*!

Five Pets

I have five pets that I'd like you to meet,
They all live with me on Mulberry Street.
    (*Hold up one hand*)
This is my chicken, the smallest of all,
He comes a-running whenever I call.
    (*Point to little finger*)
This is my duckling. He says, "Quack, quack, quack!"
As he shakes the water from off his back.
    (*Point to next finger*)

Here is my rabbit. He runs from his pen
Then I must put him back in it again.
    (Point to middle finger)
This is my kitten. Her coat's black and white.
She loves to sleep on a pillow at night.
    (Point to index finger)
Here is my puppy, who has lots of fun!
    (Point to thumb)
He chases the others and makes them run!
    (Move thumb slowly and fingers rapidly)

Ten Little Cowboys

Ten little cowboys looking very fine;
One tripped on his spurs, and then there were nine.
Nine little cowboys sat up very late;
One overslept, and then there were eight.
Eight little cowboys riding off to heaven;
One stayed in Texas, and then there were seven.
Seven little cowboys chopping up sticks;
One cut himself in half, and then there were six.
Six little cowboys very much alive;
One stole a rancher's cow, and then there were five.
Five little cowboys running through the door.
One couldn't turn the knob, and then there were four.
Four little cowboys riding knee to knee;
One lost his stirrups, and then there were three.
Three little cowboys wearing chaps quite new;
One found a rattlesnake, and then there were two.
Two little cowboys resting in the sun;
One got all sunburned, and then there was one.
One little cowboy hadn't any gun,
Galloped home to find it, and then there was none.

Five Little Froggies

Five little froggies sat on the shore,
One swam after a minnow,
Then there were four.
    (Move arms in swimming motion)
Four little froggies looking out to sea,
One snapped at a fly,
Then there were three.
    (Hand snaps as if to catch a fly)

Three little froggies said,
"What will we do?"
One hopped to a toadstool
And then there were two.
(Hopping motion with hand)
Two little froggies sat in the sun,
One went to sleep and then there was one.
(Hands beside face, close eyes)
One lonely froggy said, "This is no fun."
He dived into the water,
And then there was none.
(Dive hand under arm)

Five Strong Police Officers

Five strong police officers standing by a store.
One became a traffic cop, and then there were four.
Four strong police officers watching over me.
One took home a lost boy, then there were three.
Three strong police officers dressed all in blue.
One stopped a speeding car, and now there are two.
Two strong police officers—how fast they can run!
One caught a bad man, and now there is one.
One strong police officer saw some smoke one day.
He called the firefighters, who put the fire out right away.

Ten Little Chicks

Two little chicks looking for some more.
(Hold up two fingers)
Along came another two and they made four.
(Hold up two more fingers)
Four little chicks getting in a fix,
Along came another two and they made six.
(Continue to add more fingers as indicated)
Six little chicks perching on a gate,
Along came another two and they made eight.
Eight little chicks ran to the pen,
Along came another two and they made ten.
Run to the haystack,
Run to the pen,
Run little chicks,
Back to mother hen!
(Move all ten fingers back and forth and end by crossing arms and hiding hands under arms)

Four Little Monkeys

Two little monkeys sitting in a tree,
   (Hold up appropriate number of fingers throughout)
Were joined by another and that made three.
Three little monkeys in the tree did play,
They chattered and chattered in a happy way.
Three little monkeys wishing for one more,
Another came to join them and that made four.
Monkeys, monkeys, how many do I see?
Four little monkeys sitting in a tree.

Five Little Bears

Five little cubby bears,
Tumbling on the ground.
   (Roll hands over)
The first one said,
"Let's look around."
   (Hold up thumb)
The second one said,
"See the little bunny."
   (Hold up index finger)
The third one said,
"I smell honey."
   (Hold up middle finger and sniff)
The fourth one said,
"It's over in the trees."
   (Hold up ring finger)
The fifth one said,
"Look out! Here come the bees!"
   (Hold up little finger, as fingers of other hand pretend to buzz about)

Five Enormous Dinosaurs

Five enormous dinosaurs,
Letting out a roar!
One went away,
And then there were four.
   (Start with five fingers held up, then fold them down one at a time)
Four enormous dinosaurs,
Crashing down a tree,
One went away,
And then there were three.

Three enormous dinosaurs,
Eating tiger stew,
One went away,
And then there were two.

Two enormous dinosaurs,
Having lots of fun,
One went away,
And then there was one.

One enormous dinosaur,
Afraid to be a hero,
He went away,
And then there was zero.

Teacher Planned Instruction

A suggested procedure for teaching basic math skills follows; you may want to create visuals such as those shown in Figure 105 to carry out each step of this six-step procedure.

1. Start with *visual* recognition/matching. Ask the child to place the same number of objects in front of him as you have in front of you.

2. Next move to *visual* and *verbal* stimuli. Give the child a card containing three squares. Ask him to place *three* counters on the card—one in each square.

3. Introduce the numerical symbol by giving the child a card containing three squares and the numeral. Ask him to place *three* counters on the card.

4. Finally, work with the numerical symbol only. Present the child with the symbol only and ask him to place as many counters on the table as indicated by the number.

5. After each numeral is introduced, give the child some cards, each of which has a single numeral cut from sandpaper. You and the child use the sandpaper numerals in three ways:

   □ Show the card to the child, ask him to move his fingers over the numeral, and tell the child what number it is.

   □ Place the cards in front of the child and ask him to give you the three, the four, and so on.

   □ Still with the sandpaper numerals in front of the child, ask him what number each one is. The child generates the number name.

6. For reinforcement, arrange the classroom with several centers that offer follow up activities. For example, give the children pictures of groups of things, and ask them to count the number of objects in each picture and match the picture to the appropriate numeral strip.

As a final step in the counting procedure, we move to the *ordering of numbers.* As we establish the names for the numbers, we stimulate exploration of size

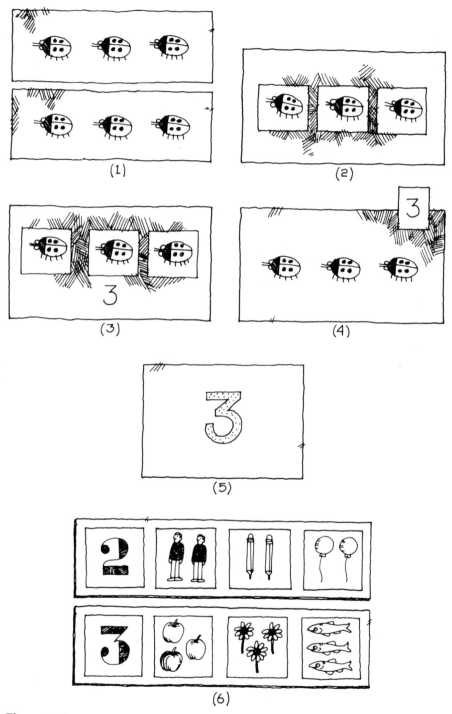

Figure 105

relationships between numbers (more than, less than, etc.). Now we seek to encourage finer discriminations among sets by developing the concept of "one more than." Begin by asking the children to stack blocks. Start with one block and ask the children to make a stack that has *one more* block than that. (See Figure 106.) Then ask them to look at the stack of two blocks and make another stack with *one* block *more than* two. Once the children order the objects in sequence, ask them to place a numeral card below each set. A number of creative, individual reinforcement activities can be organized into learning stations following this initial introduction.

Math Practice Games

Bean Drop. Number ten cups 1 to 10. Have the child count the number of dry beans that goes into each cup, drop them in, and arrange the cups in numerical order. (See Figure 107.)

Number Train. Have the child hook each railroad car (made from half-pint milk cartons) in numerical order from 1 through 10 and place the appropriate number of counters into each car. (See Figure 108.)

Number Balance. Ask the children to place a specified number of blocks into one pie tin on a balance scale and an equal number in the other. (See Figure 109.) Then have them take a number of blocks away from one tin and ask them to count the number of blocks in each. Establish which tin has *more than* and which tin has *fewer than.* Basic operations of addition and subtraction can be reinforced when children are asked to determine the number of blocks needed to add or subtract in order to achieve a balance.

Chips. Sit on the floor with a group of children. Have the children take turns rolling a die and counting the number of dots on the top. Each child takes the same number of chips for her collection as shown by the dots on the die. When

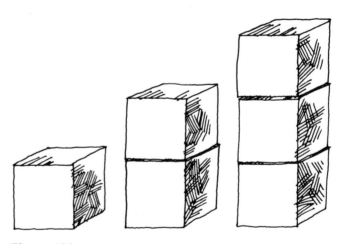

Figure 106

Figure 107

Figure 108

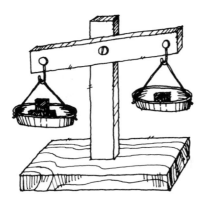

Figure 109

all the chips are gone, the children stack them up and match columns. Because counting is the object of the game and not accumulating the most chips, compare and contrast the size of the columns by asking, "Who has the tallest? the shortest?"

Marbles and Jars. Collect ten small plastic containers and label them with the numerals 1 through 10. Provide a box with lots of marbles. Two children work together. One child examines the numeral printed on each container, drops in the appropriate number of marbles, and puts the lid back on. A classmate then opens each container and counts the marbles to see if the correct number was put there. The marbles then go back into the box.

Junk Box Count. Collect a different number of various familiar objects, such as one building block, two pencils, three paper clips, and so on. Place all of the

objects in a large box, labeled "Junk Box." Prepare 3" × 3" tagboard cards, each
with a numeral from 1 to 10 on it.

Have the children take the objects out of the junk box and group identical
objects in sets. Then ask them to take a tagboard numeral and place it under the
set with which it corresponds, as shown in Figure 110.

Be near the child when the groupings are completed and ask questions such
as, "How many rubber bands did you count?" "Do you have more paper clips or
more pencils?" "Are there fewer pencils or fewer blocks?"

Birthday Cakes.   Prepare a round styrofoam (5-inch diameter) "birthday cake"
for each numeral from 1 to 10, and glue each to a heavy sheet of tagboard. (See
Figure 111.) Make ten nail holes around the perimeter of each cake. Have the
children look at the numeral on the side of each cake and put the corresponding
number of candles into the holes. You may then wish to have them place the cakes
in numerical order.

Marble Drop.   Provide ten paper cups, each labeled with a numeral from 1 to 10.
Put a corresponding number of marbles into each cup. Also provide a metal pie
tin.

Two children play this game. One child turns his back on the second child
(or an adult). The second child randomly selects a cup, takes the marbles out
and slowly drops them into the pan one at a time so that they can be easily heard.
The first child listens carefully, counting to himself the number of marbles that
were dropped. He then identifies which cup the marbles were from. The marbles
then go back into the cup. The children can take turns dropping the marbles and
guessing.

Egg Count.   Collect ten egg-shaped pantyhose containers and print a numeral
from 1 to 10 on each. Collect a number of small objects that can be easily placed
into the containers and put them together in a large box. Have the children take

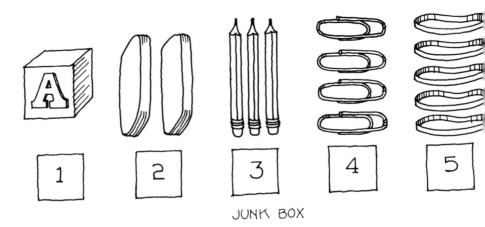

JUNK BOX

Figure 110

an egg-shaped container, examine the numeral, and place the appropriate number of objects in each.

Variation: You may wish to cut out a number of baby chicks for the children to count and place into the containers.

Number Airplanes.   Make airplane hangars by cutting oatmeal boxes down the center and gluing each half onto heavy tagboard. (See Figure 112.) Cover the hangars with colorful construction paper or paint them. Punch a hole in the top of each hangar and insert a wind sock (construction paper glued to a thin dowel) into each. Print a numeral on each wind sock. Supply plastic airplanes with from one to ten dots painted on their sides, and have the children place them into the proper hangars.

Numeral Kite.   Cut out ten kite shapes from colorful construction paper and write a numeral from 1 to 10 on each. Then cut ten lengths of yarn and tie one small piece of ribbon onto one piece of yarn, two pieces of ribbon onto another, and so on until ten pieces of ribbon are tied to a piece of yarn. Place the kites in front of the children and have them choose the appropriate tail for each. (See Figure 113.)

Number Steps.   Make a number path by outlining ten footsteps on durable laminated paper or oilcloth. Number each of the footsteps as shown in Figure 114. Cut out ten duplicate footsteps and place from one to ten dots on each. Have the children walk the path by starting at one and then matching the footsteps in order through ten.

Bears and Caves.   Get ten empty pint milk cartons, cut off the tops, and cover each with colorful construction paper to make them look like caves. Put from one

Figure 111

to ten dots on top of each container. (See Figure 115.) Buy ten rubber bears and place a numeral from 1 to 10 on each. Have the child match the numeral on the bear to the cave with the corresponding number of dots and put the bear into the cave.

Who's My Partner?   Split the children into two teams (up to twenty may play). Give one team secret papers that have from one to ten dots. Give the other team secret papers that have the numerals from 1 to 10. Have the children with the dots each knock that number of times on a table and ask, "Who is my partner?" The child with the matching numeral responds, "I am number (one)."

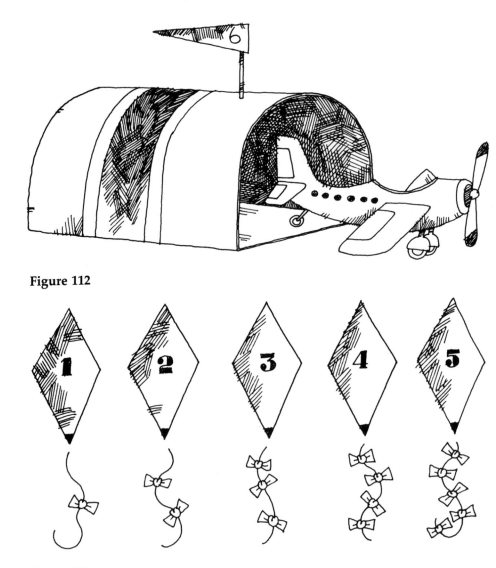

Figure 112

Figure 113

Number Line.   Buy ten colorful plastic hangers and number each from 1 to 10. Collect a number of colorful plastic clothespins, or paint wooden ones a variety of colors. Have the children attach the appropriate number of clothespins to each hanger.

The children's beginning understanding of addition and subtraction can be stimulated if you then say: "Take two clothespins away from the five hanger. How many are left?" or "Put one more clothespin on the three hanger. How many do you now have?"

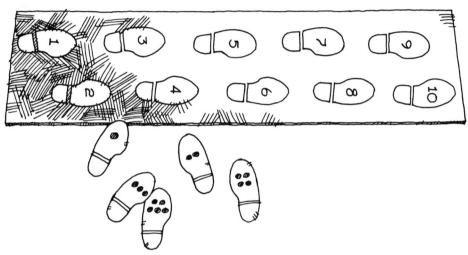

Figure 114

Figure 115

House Numbers.   Make house fronts approximately twelve inches tall out of heavy tagboard. Make one front for each of the numerals 1 to 10. Above each door, put a numeral representing the house's number. Cut off the top half of ten pint milk cartons and glue them to the back of each house to serve as a "mailbox." Then cut a slit in the front, as shown in Figure 116. Give the children envelopes containing "letters" that are only a series of dots. They are to count the dots and deposit the "letters" in the mailboxes of the appropriate houses.

Mushroom Match.   Cut mushroom shapes from colorful construction paper. Color from one to ten dots on the mushroom caps; write the corresponding numerals 1 to 10 on the stems. Cut apart the caps and the stems. Place all the caps in one box and all the stems in another. Have the children match the caps to the stems.

Snail Trail.   Using tagboard or heavy construction paper, make ten snails and label each shell with from one to ten dots. Now make two snail trails, randomly placing numerals (from 1 to 10) along the trails. (See Figure 117.) The child puts a snail trail on the floor or table, finds the snails that go on each part of the trail, and places them at their appropriate spots.

Zoo Animals.   Collect a set of ten plastic strawberry containers and place a numeral from 1 to 10 on the bottom of each. These will serve as the zoo cages when turned upside down. (See Figure 118.) Buy a set of plastic or rubber animals and ask the children to place the appropriate number of animals beneath the cages. Some children will place the same kind of animals under a cage (if there are enough to do so), others will make random collections for each cage. Either plan of attack is fine.

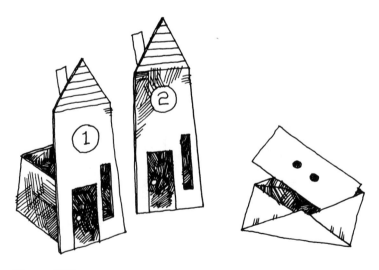

Figure 116

Number-Numeral Match.   Cut out twenty 3-inch square tagboard cards. Put the numerals 1 to 10 on ten of the cards and the corresponding number of stick figures on the remaining cards. Put sets of two matching cards (numeral and same number of stick figures) together and punch a hole through both. Then, take two other matching cards and do the same, making sure that the hole is punched in a different location from that of the previous pair(s). Mix up all the cards and put them into a decorated box. Have the children find the pairs that match. They can tell they are correct if the punched holes match. (See Figure 119.)

The King or Queen.   Select one child to be "The King" or "The Queen." Give her a stack of cards on which the numerals 1 to 10 (or 20) have been printed. Give other children a stack of cards on which pictures of from one to ten (or twenty) objects have been drawn.

     "The Queen" ("King") sits on the throne (chair) in the center of the circle as other children try to dethrone her by holding up one picture card at a time for

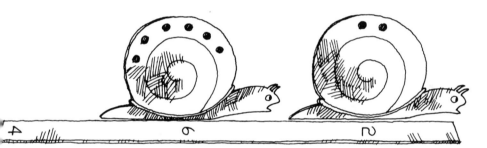

Figure 117

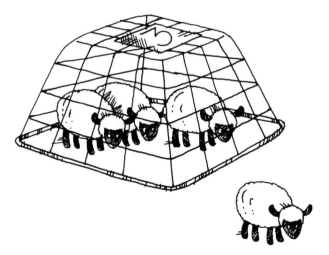

Figure 118

Figure 119

her to match with the corresponding number card from her stack. She sits on this throne as long as she can provide the correct answer. When she misses, the child who gave her the card to be matched takes the stack and attempts to find the correct numeral. If he succeeds he becomes the "King."

Number Bingo.   Make a bingo card for each child with the numerals 1 to 5 along the top, as shown in Figure 120. Make a set of number cards, each depicting a number of items (for example, one dog, two trees, two carrots, three girls, and so on). There should be four number cards for every numeral on each bingo card. Arrange a pile of number cards and have the children take turns selecting them. One child places her first number card in the appropriate column on her bingo card (for example, two trees would be placed in the two column). The second child picks the next number card from the pile and does the same. The goal is to see who can be the first to fill in any row or column on a bingo card.

Math Telescope.   Clean out a used plastic detergent bottle and decorate the outside using marking pens, stickers, or adhesive felt. Cut a 2-inch slit into the top as indicated in Figure 121. Prepare a set of cards narrow enough to slide through the slit but long enough to stick out about three inches. You should construct ten such cards, one for each numeral. Write the numerals at the bottom. At the top of each card make dots corresponding to each numeral. Insert the card into the bottle and ask the children to tell or show you the numeral that corresponds to the number of dots sticking out of the detergent bottle. Have the child check to see if he was correct by peering into the "telescope" bottle where the numeral at the bottom of the inserted card will appear.

I Love Worms.   Cut out ten colorful fish, write the numerals 1 to 10 on them, and tape or paste each fish onto a milk carton or can. (See Figure 122.) Cut out fifty-five worms from colorful paper. Ask the children to arrange the containers in proper numerical order and place the corresponding number of worms into each "bait container."

Circle Games. Cut a number of 5-inch circles from tagboard. Divide each circle into four sections and draw a set of objects within each section, as shown in Figure 123. At the edge of each section, write three numerals, one of which represents the number of objects in that set. Have the children attach a clothespin

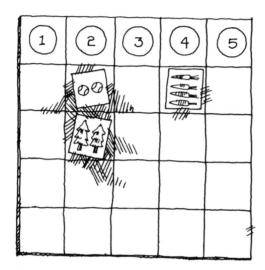

Figure 120

Figure 121

Figure 122

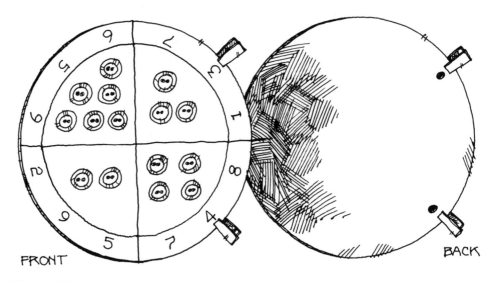

FRONT

BACK

Figure 123

to the numeral that matches the objects. Place a dot on back of the correct responses so the children can check their answers.

It's Raining Numbers.   Make a large tagboard umbrella as illustrated in Figure 124. Divide it into ten sections, and draw one raindrop in one section, two in another, and continue until you reach ten. Attach a magnet strip to each of the ten sections. Make ten cards each with a numeral from 1 to 10, and attach a magnet strip to each. Have the children count the raindrops on each section and place the corresponding numeral card onto each.

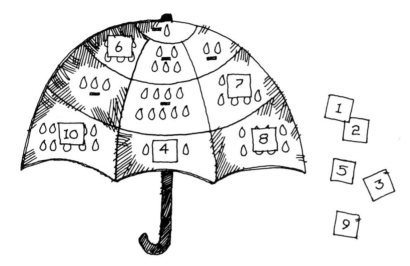

Figure 124

Go Fishing.   Trace a series of tailless fish shapes on sturdy tagboard. Cut out the shapes and staple them together, except for the tail end, thus making fish-shaped envelopes. (See Figure 125.) Draw a number of silhouetted fish on each envelope. On the tails, which are strips of paper that can be slid into the opening of each fish, write corresponding numerals. The child can "catch" the fish, write the numeral or select a numeral card corresponding to the number of silhouetted fish, and check her response by pulling out the tail.

Pin the Tail on the Donkey.   Draw a donkey from heavy tagboard and attach it to a bulletin board. Glue a magnet strip to the middle of the donkey's back. Cut out ten colorful pieces of construction paper and draw from one to ten dots on them, as shown in Figure 126. Attach a magnet strip to the back of each. These will serve as "riding blankets." Cut out ten tails, each tail displaying a numeral from 1 to 10. The children may play in pairs or the teacher may play the game with a small group.

Have one person put a "riding blanket" on the donkey. Another child must then choose the tail with the corresponding numeral and pin it to the bulletin board at the proper place.

Counter Game.   Two or three players may play this game. Give three or four plastic counters to each player. For every turn, each player puts zero, one, two, three, or four counters into his hand and makes a fist. Then each player must guess the total number of counters held by all the players. Once all the guesses are made, the children open their hands, count the counters, and see if anyone made a correct guess. The children continue in this way until interest wanes.

Number Wash Line.   Cut a variety of pieces of laundry from colorful construction paper. (See Figure 127.) Put a numeral and corresponding number of dots on each. Have the children look at the laundry and hang the individual items in order from one to ten.

All Mixed Up.   Hang a numeral (from 1 to 10) on each child and have them form a line so the numerals are in order. Play some music and have the children move around freely so they get all mixed up. When sufficiently mixed, shut off the music and ask the children to get back in numerical order. When they have done so, they call out their numeral.

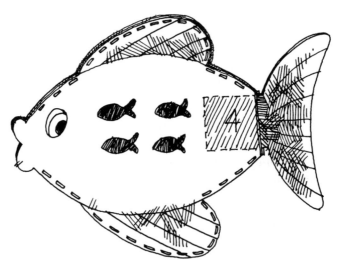

Figure 125

Figure 126

Number Story.   Make enough large numeral cards so that your children will each have one. Create a short story in which all of the numerals can be used. The children hold up their numeral as it is used in the story. For example, "On a fine spring morning, *one* pretty robin was hopping along the ground looking for food. The robin had *three* hungry babies waiting in the nest . . . "

Counter Toss.   Fold down the top of a large brown grocery bag and place it on the floor. Put a unit block in the bottom to keep it from falling over. Use masking tape to mark the floor an appropriate distance from the bag (decide what is most reasonable for your group), and encourage the children to try to toss as many plastic counters from the mark into the bag as they can. Count the number each child tossed into the bag. How many missed the bag?

Classroom Inventory.   Have the children take an inventory of everything in the classroom. Keep a written record of the results on a large chart: How many tables? Chairs? Windows? Cubbies? Bulletin boards? Easels? Puzzles? How many shoes are all the children wearing? Socks? Shirts? Record the numbers on a large chart as they are counted.

Writing Numerals.   Write the numeral on the chalkboard as you say this rhyme:

One, one, stands up straight and gets ready to run.
Two, two, a graceful swan swimming in the zoo.
Three, three, a curvy road always bothers me.
Four, four, a fancy kite getting ready to soar.
Five, five, a little bee buzzes to its hive.

Say the rhyme a second time and ask the children to write the numeral in the air. Say the rhyme a third time as the children trace their fingers over sandpaper or cardboard numerals.

Figure 127

SCIENCE

How can you be sure you are providing a rich variety of science experiences for your children? If you willingly answer children's questions and help them find answers about their physical environment, you are teaching science. In order to teach science successfully, these guidelines may help:

1. Guide the children to solve their own problems.
2. Become aware of your children's interests.
3. Plan many opportunities for informal learning and spontaneous discoveries.
4. Provide scientific experiences (not magical "tricks") so that children are encouraged to explore their world and make exciting new discoveries.

The following science activities can help stimulate interest in the child's physical environment.

Magnets

What Is a Magnet?   Spread a mixture of sand and small nails on a table top. Ask the children to move a small magnet slowly through the mixture. They will see that the magnet does not attract the sand but only the nails, because they are made of iron or steel.
Challenge: Put a nail in a glass of water and ask the children to think of a way to get it out without getting their fingers wet. (They will want to use the magnet.)

What Will a Magnet Attract?   Put several objects into a large box. Include magnetic objects made of iron and steel, as well as nonmagnetic objects such as those made from wood, rubber, plastic, or tin. Provide a magnet and a divided box where the children can separate the magnetic from the nonmagnetic objects, as shown in Figure 128. Direct the children to place each object on the table, touch the magnet to the object, and separate the objects into magnetic or nonmagnetic.

Make a Magnet.   Give the children a 2-inch nail and ask them to see if they can use it as a magnet to attract some iron filings. Once they see that it cannot be done, instruct them to take a magnet and rub their nail a few times with it in only one direction. Then ask the children to see if they can pick up the iron filings with their nail. What happens when we rub the nail ten more times?

Magnet Boat Race.   Make some racing boats according to these directions, which are illustrated in Figure 129:

1. Bend one end of a paper clip and stick it into a cork.
2. Cut a triangle out of colored paper and paste it onto a pin to make a sail. Stick the pin into the cork on the opposite side from the paper clip.
3. Tape or glue a small magnet firmly to the end of a wooden dowel.

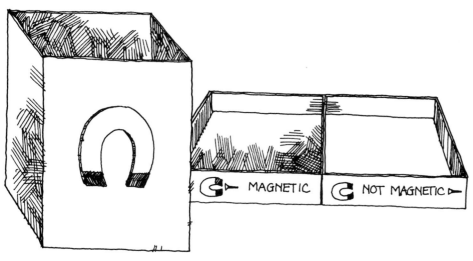

Figure 128

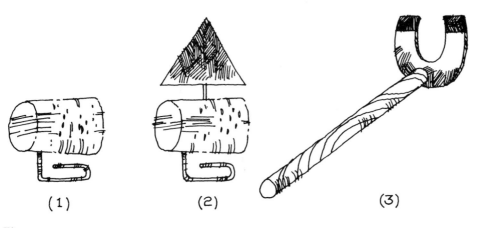

(1)   (2)   (3)

Figure 129

Fill a pan with water and put it up on two piles of blocks, making sure the pan is level. Have the children float their boats in the water, maneuvering them beneath the pan with the magnet rods. Raising a pan of water and keeping it that way is a tricky feat in most rooms with young children, so use this activity in an area of the room where spills can be cleaned quickly with minimum disturbance to the staff.

The Sun Rises. The children will discover that a magnet can attract a magnetic substance without touching it when you set up the following experiment.

Support a bar magnet on a laboratory ring stand and clamp it securely. Glue or tape a smiling sun face to a paper clip, making it not much larger than the clip itself. Tie the clip to a string as shown in Figure 130. The string should be long enough so that it just misses touching the magnet.

If the sun face is placed on the base of the ring stand, the children can pick it up toward the magnet. The sun face should be held in position, suspended in the air by the magnet.

Magnet Puppets. Hammer small nails into small wooden dolls or glue metal washers to the bottom of plastic dolls. Decorate a show box and use the bottom as a puppet stage. (See Figure 131.) Have the children make the puppets move by manipulating a magnet beneath the stage.

Plants

Seed Germination. Place a damp paper towel, cotton wad, or sponge in the bottom of a clear jar or dish. Sprinkle some lawn seed on the pad. Keep the pad moist and watch the seeds germinate.

How Plants Get Water. Put a sponge into a clear glass jar and place some radish seeds between the sponge and the glass. Moisten the sponge, and be sure to keep it moist. Place the jar in a warm place until the seeds sprout. The children can observe that the plants send out roots to absorb the moisture that is so essential to their lives. (See Figure 132.)

Sock Plot. Ask your children to bring in old socks from their parents that are ready to be thrown away. Take the children to a grassy field with weeds and grass

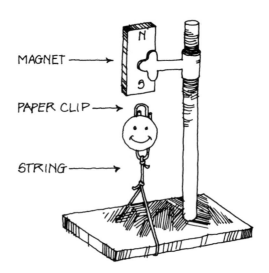

MAGNET

PAPER CLIP

STRING

Figure 130

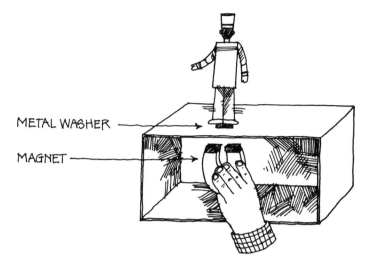

METAL WASHER

MAGNET

Figure 131

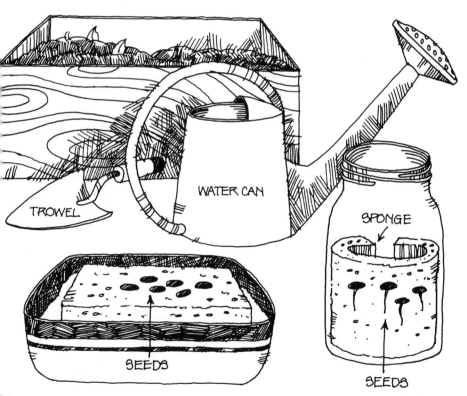

TROWEL

WATER CAN

SPONGE

SEEDS

SEEDS

Figure 132

high enough to reach their knees (fall is the best time for this trip). Have the children put the old socks over their shoes and run or walk through the field. Then have them take off the socks and examine them. Discuss the things that are stuck. Back in the classroom, put three to five socks in the bottoms of flat plastic boxes (or line cardboard boxes with plastic film). Cover the socks with potting soil and keep the mixture watered. In seven to ten days, a good number of young plants should begin to emerge.

Potato Head.   Start with a large potato. (See Figure 133.) Scoop off the top and line the shallow hole with a wet paper towel, sponge, or blotting paper. Stand the potato in a large dish of water. Sprinkle the wet paper towel with grass seed as shown in Figure 133B. Keep the towel moist at all times. Shortly, the seeds will begin to sprout and the "potato head" will begin to grow "green hair." Furnish cloves to the children so they can add eyes, nose, and mouth to their potato creature's face.

Which Way to Go?   Plant bean seeds in pots and water them daily. After the seeds have sprouted, select one plant to put in a box with a window cut out of one end. That window should be the only light source for the plant. Have the children observe how the plant bends toward the window and continues to grow in that direction. (See Figure 134.)

Green or Pale?   Plant bean seeds in two separate containers and allow the plants to sprout. Keep one pot in direct sunlight on the window and cover the other pot with a paper bag. Continue this procedure for about two weeks, removing the bag for observation purposes only. After that time, the uncovered plant should be green, robust, and healthy, while the covered plant is stunted and pale. Help the children understand the importance of sunlight to the healthy growth of plants.

May I Have a Drink, Please?   Have the children stir some food coloring into a glass of water. Slice a piece of celery across the bottom, and allow the children some time to examine the stalk. Let the celery stand in the tinted water for about one hour. The celery stalk will change color as the water travels upward.

Take the celery out of the water, slice it, and examine the stalk again. Try the same experiment with a carrot or a white carnation.

PAPER TOWEL→   ←GRASS SEED

A   B

Figure 133

My Sweet Potato.   Carefully wash a fresh sweet potato and suspend it in a jar of water so it is about one-half to two-thirds above the water. The potato can be supported with toothpicks as shown in Figure 135. Have the children observe the emergence of an attractive new plant.

Terrarium.   Place a handful of charcoal at the bottom of a glass container—this will keep the soil from getting "stale." Put in some pebbles or sand; make it as colorful and attractive as you can. Fill the container with good, rich potting soil and plant a variety of dwarf or slow-growing plants. Arrange pieces of rock, toy animals, driftwood, or a variety of other items to enhance the terrarium's attractiveness. Sprinkle the garden lightly and cover with a glass lid.

More Plant Ideas

☐ Bring in many different kinds of flowers. Have the children compare color, shape, smell, size, and so on.

☐ Encourage the children to classify plants or flowers according to color, shape, and so on.

☐ Visit a nursery. Arrange for the children to purchase a small plant or seeds to grow once they return to the classroom.

☐ Observe the formation of seeds on plants, especially in the fall. Go outdoors and collect as many different kinds of seeds as possible.

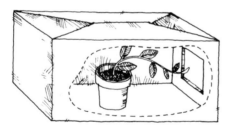

Figure 134

Figure 135

- [ ] Plant a variety of seeds—grass, flower, bean, or whatever your choice. Keep the ground moistened. Continue observing the differences in growth among the different seeds.
- [ ] Grow a fruit-bearing plant such as a tomato or pepper plant. Examine the seeds within the fruit. Dry the seeds and plant them so the children can see the plant go through its life cycle from seed to plant to flower to fruit to seed again.
- [ ] Visit a farm or orchard. Highlight the fact that fruits and vegetables are grown there for us to eat.

Animals

The following animals are appropriate for the preschool classroom (see Figure 136). With good care, they should become some of the most interesting and valuable science materials in your classroom.

Ants   provide long periods of entertainment for young children as they tunnel through the soft dirt in a jar or purchased ant farm. Fill a ventilated jar with loose soil and dampen it lightly. Cover the side of the jar with dark paper to encourage the ants to tunnel out to the sides. Sprinkle some sugar on the soil and put in the ants. Check the jar in a few days. Ants are easy to care for; simply feed them some tiny food scraps and dampen the soil periodically.

Caterpillars   or their cocoons can be found in autumn clinging to the leaves of bushes, trees, or weeds. If the caterpillar is found, be sure to pick a large number of leaves of the type on which it was feeding to keep it alive until it spins itself into a cocoon. If the cocoon is found, keep it attached to the branch or twig and carefully bring it into the classroom to be stored in a cool, relatively moist area until the butterfly or moth emerges. The monarch butterfly's caterpillar or cocoon (chrysalis), which is found on milkweed, is an exceptionally good insect for the children to observe.

Earthworms   can be purchased as bait at a fishing store or are readily found in soft soil, especially after a period of rain. They can be easily kept in an aerated (i.e., not airtight) container filled with a mixture of loose earth and coffee grounds. Children can watch them tunnel into the dirt and create passageways similar to those of ants. Let the children handle the earthworms if they wish; the rough texture and squiggly feelings in their hands especially delight many youngsters.

Tadpole   eggs look like small marbles of clear jelly with a tiny dark dot in the center. They can be found along the edge of a pond and can be easily scooped up and placed into a container full of water. When the tadpoles hatch, they eat either the algae and microscopic organisms found in the pond water, or goldfish food. Young tadpoles spend all of their time completely submerged in the water, but as they grow and develop legs, they need to get out of the water. A large rock or floating piece of wood serves their purposes. However, be careful to supply a mesh screen to cover the top of the container or you will have trouble keeping the tadpoles inside. When the tadpole completely loses its tail, it becomes a frog and requires different food from the tadpole—tiny bits of fish, meat, or leafy vegetables, and especially live insects such as flies, gnats, or worms. The special needs of a frog make it nearly impossible to keep it in the classroom, so it might be best to return the developed frogs to the pond in which they were found.

Goldfish   are perhaps the easiest fish to care for in the preschool classroom as they require much less special care than do tropical fish. Goldfish, or any other kind of fish, rarely survive for any length of time in a small goldfish bowl, so purchase an aerated aquarium for any fish you plan to keep.

When setting up the aquarium, be sure to wash it with plain water—no soap! Add successive layers of sand and coarse gravel to the bottom and secure some live plants into this base. Put a small jar or plate on the gravel so that excessive dust cannot be stirred as you slowly add water. Hook up an aeration

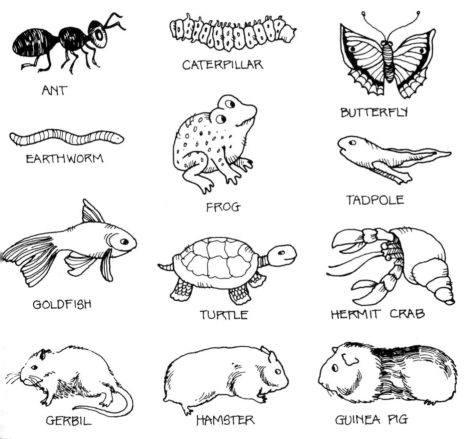

Figure 136

and filtration system so that a proper balance will be ensured. Allow the aquarium to settle for a few days while the chlorine and other harmful chemicals dissipate. Snails, catfish, and other scavengers help control algae and waste materials. If all precautions are heeded, very little additional care is needed.

Tropical fish   such as guppies, swordtails, mollies, and platys are much more difficult than goldfish to care for, but they possess some unique characteristics that make them much more desirable. Besides being very colorful, these fish are live-bearers rather than egg layers, which allows the children to actually observe the young fish emerging from the mother at birth. But since the adult fish will devour the babies in a short period of time, provide either a dense growth of plants or a special breeding tank in which the small fish can be separated from the adults.

Turtles   were found in nearly every preschool classroom until recently. They became less popular when it was discovered that some carry salmonella, a serious intestinal disease. Nevertheless, you can keep turtles successfully in your class-room if you are careful. The best way to ensure that the turtle you choose is a safe one is to buy it from a reputable pet shop.

Turtles are very easy to care for. They eat worms, ground beef, some vegetable greens, and small insects. Turtles *must* eat in the water, so all foods must be placed somewhere the turtle is able to submerge its head while eating.

The hermit crab   is an increasingly popular classroom animal because it requires so little care and is so fascinating for young children to observe. These tiny creatures can be bought in a pet store or large department store. They use abandoned shells for their homes, and children love to watch them carry their homes on their backs as they move from place to place.

Keep your hermit crabs in a well-ventilated box or plastic container. Spread coarse gravel at the bottom of the container and scatter a few empty shells on the surface. Except for a diet of almost any type of food scraps, these amusing creatures need little or no additional care.

Gerbils   are clean, playful animals requiring little care, so they make an almost ideal classroom pet. Active and gregarious, they must be kept in pairs or they will die of loneliness. Gerbils are usually kept in a wire cage or aquarium with a screen on top. The cage is lined with newspaper and cedar shavings, which form a hygienic bed for the gerbils' wastes. Gerbils delight in gnawing on the shavings and shredding the newspaper until they have collected material for their sleeping quarters: they completely cover themselves with the shredded newspaper and shavings mixture as they sleep. The gerbil cage should include a special water bottle, an exercise wheel, and an aluminum can for small moments of privacy. Do not buy a plastic gerbil cage or accessories made from plastic as gerbils will gnaw and chew through anything softer than metal or glass.

Gerbils reproduce readily and often have a litter every month or two. Children delight in watching the mother and father care for the tiny pink babies, but the frequency of reproduction often results in extreme crowding. You will be better off selecting two gerbils of the same sex unless you have an extra cage for the babies.

Feed the gerbils a mixture of grains, cereals, breads, or vegetables such as carrots or lettuce. A hanging water bottle with a tubular extension provides what little water these desert animals need.

Hamsters, like gerbils, can be purchased very inexpensively at pet stores. An old aquarium fitted with a wire mesh screen at the top makes an ideal home for hamsters and gerbils alike. Hamsters are very similar to gerbils and require the same basic care. The main reason some teachers select gerbils rather than hamsters is that hamsters are nocturnal animals and usually sleep during the hours when the children are in school. Gerbils, however, are often awake and active during the hours of the normal school day.

Guinea pigs, in contrast to the active gerbil and hamster, are very quiet, docile animals who are content to cuddle and snuggle in a person's arms. Their cage should be similar to the gerbil cage, but with more shavings or straw to absorb greater amounts of moisture. Because guinea pigs eliminate much greater amounts and in greater frequency, their cages must be cleaned more often. Guinea pigs are vegetarians and especially enjoy eating lettuce, apples, grass, or commercial guinea pig food from the pet store.

Tender Loving Care

In order to obtain the greatest value from having animals in the preschool classroom, there must be a constant watch for their health and safety. A teacher's lack of concern in this area may foster a feeling of disrespect in the children, which often results in abuse of the animal followed by its injury, sickness, or death. If the children are to respect animal life, they must learn to understand and appreciate suitable environments and patterns of care. They must understand that all living things depend on each other for survival.

Hatching Eggs. Nothing is more rewarding than helping to bring forth a new life, so hatching eggs can be a very satisfying experience for preschool children. Waiting for the appointed day and watching the chicks struggle on their wobbly legs as they begin life outside the shell is an experience beyond compare.

Before you begin an egg hatching project, make sure you have good homes for the hatchlings—our lesson in life can be quite ineffective if we do not properly provide for the care of our chicks after they emerge. Children in the class may volunteer (with parents' written approval); also check with farmers and hatcheries. If homes are ensured, you may wish to embark on this sequence.

1. Begin the project during a period of time when there are at least three uninterrupted weeks of school. It is best to start on a Tuesday or Wednesday since the chicks will arrive about twenty-one days after you begin the incubation process. Never start on Monday or Friday because the eggs might hatch on Sunday or Saturday.

2. Be sure to obtain *fertilized eggs* from a farmer or hatchery. Grocery store eggs will not develop into chicks.

3. Some teachers prefer to buy incubators because the temperature and humidity levels are precisely maintained in those units. However, when you help the children make their own, the project takes on added meaning. To make an incubator, buy a styrofoam ice chest and slice two 4-inch-square openings—one in the side and the other in the lid. Cover the holes with transparent plastic food wrap, and duct tape the plastic securely to the box. The children will use these as viewing holes throughout the project. Place a flat metal tray (a frozen dinner tray works fine) into the box and cover it with an aluminum of plastic screen. Then cut a hole in the center of the box opposite your window (about three inches below the top) large enough to allow an empty light socket with an attached cord to be squeezed into the styrofoam. Fit a bulb (25-watt) into the socket and plug it in. Fill the tray with water (eggs require high humidity) and put a thermometer on the inside of the box near where the eggs will be placed. Test your incubator for a few days to make sure it maintains a constant temperature of 101 to 103 degrees Fahrenheit. If the temperature reads higher, make a few holes in the box lid. If it reads lower, try to regulate it with a bulb of higher wattage.

4. Place the eggs on the screen covering the flat tray.

5. Begin turning the eggs on the second day of incubation and continue until two days before the eggs are scheduled to be hatched. You must help the children turn the eggs for the same reason you turn yourself while sleeping—to relieve pressure. A hen instinctively uses her beak to turn the eggs in her nest. The developing embryos will not grow with strength and vigor if they are not turned regularly. Establish a reasonable turning schedule. Although the eggs must be turned at least three or four times a day, children readily accept this responsibility. The eggs should be turned 180 degrees each time i.e., the "up" side will be the "down" side after the turn. Some teachers like to mark an "X" on one side and an "O" on the other as a way of visually keeping track of how the eggs are turned.

6. Constantly check the humidity within the box. It is important to keep the metal tray filled with warm water at all times. You must regularly monitor the temperature, too. Be sure it is maintained within the 101 to 103 degree range.

7. At about the tenth through twelfth day, hold the eggs in front of the light from a filmstrip projector. You should be able to see the embryo if there is one. You should even be able to see the heart beat. If you do not see the shadow of the embryo, the egg is not fertile and will not hatch. Dispose of it Fertility is rarely 100 percent in eggs. Fertility often varies from 55 to 95 percent depending on the condition of the chickens. This is an excellent opportunity to discuss the rate of failure in nature for other animals as well

8. Watch the eggs hatch! The children will be fascinated by the slimy appearance and helplessness of the newly hatched chicks. They will expect fluffy, yellow

chicks most often pictured in their storybooks. It will take about two hours for this to happen. Don't be in a hurry to take the chicks out of the incubator. Chickens can survive for two days without food or water. The yolk of the egg is drawn up through the navel into the stomach of the baby bird before it hatches so nourishment is provided while the chick fluffs out, gains strength, and becomes active enough to seek food. In general, chicks are taken from the incubator after twenty-four hours.

9. Place the chicks in a brooder and provide them with suitable food and water. Starter mash for chickens is available at pet or feed stores. Place some mash in a small, flat container (jar lids do fine) and some fresh water in another container. Do not let the feed or water run out. A large nonflammable box or an empty aquarium make good brooders. You will need to shine a small lamp into the box to achieve a constant temperature of about 95 to 98 degrees Fahrenheit. Be sure the brooder gives the chicks enough room to roam freely from the warmest sections (near the light) to the cooler parts. Temperatures can be regulated downward about a degree per day until the chicks gradually become adjusted to the natural temperature and environment. (This usually takes about two weeks.)

10. Talk to the children about the care of chickens taken from the brooder. The entire experience not only helps children develop responsibility and a reverence for life, but also motivates them to try other types of science projects.

More Animal Activities

Water Microscope.   Cut three circles from the sides of a small plastic pail with a good sharp knife. The circles should be large enough to accommodate a child's hand, but not so large as to make the pail weak. (See Figure 137.) Get a piece of plastic wrap slightly larger than the top of the pail and fit it over the top. Keep it in place with a snug-fitting rubber band or string. Pour tepid water (not cold) slowly onto the plastic until it sags into the shape of a lens. View tiny insects (or other objects) through this magnifying glass by inserting them under the plastic-wrap lens through the holes in the side of the pail. Allow specimens to feed on food scraps while the children observe.

Look for Underwater Animals.   Get a large juice can for each child and cut out both ends. Cut a piece of cleaner's plastic wrap and cover one end of the can. Secure the wrap with a strong rubber band. Leave the other end of the can open as shown in Figure 137).

Have the children put their can, wrap-end first, into a stream to view the rocks, vegetation, or animal life there through the opening. The wrap acts as a magnifying lens as the water pushes it up, allowing the children to see things at the stream's bottom in bigger-than-life proportions.

Insect Zoo.   Small, simple cages containing insects give children an opportunity to watch the habits of small animals and to view their developmental changes. Cages are easily made and can be adapted to a variety of insects; see Figure 138 for two examples. Keep the insects for a day and then release them to nature.

JUICE CAN

CLEAR
PLASTIC
WRAP

Figure 137

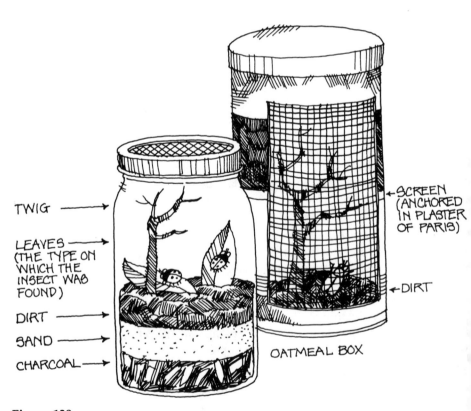

TWIG

LEAVES
(THE TYPE ON
WHICH THE
INSECT WAS
FOUND)

DIRT

SAND

CHARCOAL

SCREEN
(ANCHORED
IN PLASTER
OF PARIS)

DIRT

OATMEAL BOX

Figure 138

Bird Feeder #1.   Make a hole through the center of two jar lids by hammering a 3-inch nail through both. Put the nail through one lid, through a large chunk of bread, cake, or doughnut, and then through the other lid. Bend the pointed end of the nail to keep it from pulling through the bottom lid. Tie a string below the nail head and hang up the feeder.

Bird Feeder #2.   Tie a long string onto a pine cone. Smear the cone with gobs of peanut butter and roll in bird seed. This quick "feeder" is ready for hanging and for attracting numbers of birds to your playground.

Water

Is Water Heavy?   To develop the concept that water has weight, use a scale and two cups. Place an empty cup on one side of the scale and ask the children to notice what happens. Then fill the second cup with water and place it on the other side of the scale. Again, have the children notice what happened to the scale. Ask, "Does a cup weigh more when it is filled with water or when it is empty?"

What Kind of Water is Heavier?   Fill two glasses two-thirds full of water and place them on the scale so the children can see that they weigh the same. Take them off the scale and dissolve two tablespoons of salt in one glass. Put both glasses back on the scale and compare.

Place one egg in the clear water and another egg in the salt water. Have the children observe that the egg will float in the heavier water (salt water), while it sinks in the lighter water (plain water).

Stick a thumbtack in the rubber eraser of each of two pencils. Ask the children to predict which will float: the pencil placed in the salt water or the pencil placed in plain water?

Sink or Float?   Children learn that some things float in water while others do not with this simple experiment. Fill a dishpan with water and make available a variety of objects: Ping-Pong ball, golf ball, pencil, key, spoon, jar lid, twig, button, leaf, and so on. Direct the children to place the objects, one at a time, into the pan of water. Then, have the children classify the objects as those that float or sink by placing them in appropriate trays.

More Water Experiments

Fill a glass with water. Ask the children to look at themselves in a mirror through the glass of water, as shown in Figure 139. What do they see?

Put some water in a glass. Put a rubber band around the glass to mark the top of the water line. Leave the water in the glass for one full day. What happened? (Illustrations of this experiment and those that follow are included in Figure 140.)

Figure 139

Figure 140

❑ Fill a dishpan with water. Blow up a small balloon, and hold it on the water. Now push it down slowly. What happens as you try to push it completely under?

❑ Put a different amount of water into each of four glasses. Tap each glass with a wooden dowel. Do they all make the same sound?

❑ Put a few drops of cooking oil into a glass of water with a dropper. What happens to the oil?

❑ Put some water in a dish and put a nail in the water. Wait a few days. What happens?

❑ Fill a glass to the top with water. Drop a marble in. Does the water spill over? Have the children guess how many more marbles it will take before the water spills over. Then they can try it and see.

❑ Fill a glass half full of water. Put a pencil in the water. Let the children look at the pencil and describe what they see.

❑ Fill a can with water—make sure it is filled exactly to the top. Put the can in the freezer. Wait until the next day and look at the can. What happened?

Miscellaneous Science Activities

Homemade Telephone. Get a length of tubing (an old garden hose will do), push a funnel into each end, and use string or rubber bands to hold the tubing securely to the funnels. Have a child talk into one end while a second child listens at the other by holding the funnel to her ear. (See Figure 141.)

Figure 141

Homemade Stethoscope (or Three-Party Telephone).   Get three pieces of rubber tubing and put a funnel at one end of each. Use a Y joint to join the three pieces of tubing together, and tie all connections with string or rubber bands. One child can hold the "earpiece" (two funnels) to his ear while another holds the third funnel near a vibrating object.

An additional benefit of this activity is that the children may overcome any fear of the doctor's stethoscope by listening to their own heartbeats.

Spool Racers.   Put a medium-sized rubber band through the hole in a spool (the rubber band should be slightly longer than the spool); attach the loop at one end of the spool to a short carpet tack. (See Figure 142.) Put a long match stick or dowel through the loop at the other end. Have a child hold the spool in one hand and wind up the stick with the other. When the tension seems just right, have the child put the racer on the floor and let it go.

Clothespin Wrestling.   Arrange the children in pairs. Give each child in a pair a clothespin of a different color. Have the children hook their clothespins together with a rubber band and wind them up (not too tightly) by turning the clothespins in opposite directions. (See Figure 143.) When let go, the clothespins will twist and bump all over the place, but one will eventually land on top of the other— the winner!

Weather Forecaster.   Children can begin to predict changes in the weather by making their own barometers. Use a wide-mouth jar (olive or peanut butter jars will do) and cut a piece of balloon to fit over the mouth. Stretch the balloon so it fits tightly, and fasten it to the jar with string or rubber bands. Glue a soda straw to the balloon, making sure that the straw is positioned in the center of the balloon. Make a simple scale such as the one illustrated in Figure 144; space the

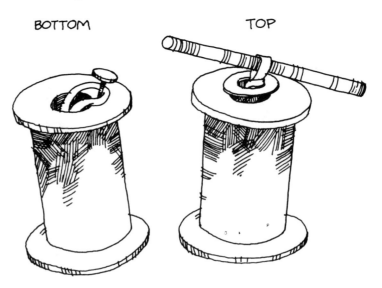

BOTTOM   TOP

Figure 142

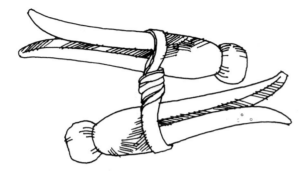

Figure 143

markings evenly about ¼-inch apart. The straw will point to various parts of the scale as the air pressure (and the balloon) rises and falls to indicate changes in the weather.

Crystal Garden.   Place enough aquarium charcoal on a pie tin to cover the bottom. Mix together ½ cup water, ½ cup salt, ½ cup liquid bluing, and 1 cup ammonia, and pour the mixture slowly and carefully over the charcoal, making sure all the charcoal gets wet. Then drip a few drops of blue, green, and yellow (not red) food coloring over the charcoal. The next day you should find a colorful crystal garden growing in your classroom.

Silly Stuff.   This project can get a little messy so first put some newspapers on your table. In a small bowl (a 1-pound margarine tub is ideal), mix ½ cup cornstarch and 3 tablespoons water. This will make a strange substance which is semiliquid and semisolid. Rest your finger on the surface and it will sink as if into quicksand. Poke your finger into it and it will feel solid. You and your children can experiment and have messy fun, yet it is easily cleaned up!

Racing Colors.   Put about ½ inch of water into a tall glass jar. Cut three narrow strips (about ¾ inch) of paper towel and attach a paper clip to the end of each. Then, above one clip put a yellow food coloring dot, above another put an orange dot, and above the third put a purple dot. Hang the strips in the jar so that the clips touch the water, and tape the ends to the outside of the jar. (See Figure 145.)

The color dots will separate into their component colors as the water moves up the paper towel, so the children can observe that these three colors are made up of different ones.

COOKING

Preparing food is a learning activity that not only fulfills the goal of feeding children but also explores the emotions and attitudes surrounding food. Children come to the early childhood setting with experience in being fed, but often with little or no experience in helping prepare food. Thus they may find it difficult to

Figure 144

Figure 145

understand that a meal must be prepared, and does not merely appear on the table through some sort of supermarket or parental magic.

Cooking gives children many meaningful opportunities not only to learn about food preparation, but also to be exposed to other valuable lessons such as

□ Following directions.
□ Listening to instructions.
□ Learning new words.
□ Working as a group member.
□ Learning about foods.
□ Maintaining a safe, healthful environment.

☐ Keeping track of time.
☐ Measuring ingredients.
☐ Observing changes in the state of matter.
☐ Understanding the principles of good nutrition.

Suggested Cooking Program for Young Children*

One may remain longer on some skills or eliminate others that do not apply to the program. It is not necessary to actually cook with heat to have a successful cooking program. Do not confuse the children by asking them to do too many different things in one day.

1. Explore cooking tools with water (cups, bowls, beaters)
2. Measure and pour with dry ingredients (rice or corn meal)
3. Taste fresh fruit (one type at each session)
4. Compare fresh fruits (yellow, green and red apples)
5. Dipping (raw vegetables in sauce or liver in flour)
6. Scrubbing with brushes (carrots, celery or radishes)
7. Tear, break, snap (lettuce for salad, beans, peas)
8. Pouring (mark cups with rubber bands at stopping point)
9. Stirring and measuring (cocoa, carrots with mayonnaise)
10. Shaking (baby food jars with cream for butter, food coloring and coconut)
11. Spreading with table knives (butter, honey, cheese)
12. Rolling with both hands (cheese balls, meat, liver sausage)
13. Juicing with hand juicer (oranges, lemons)
14. Peeling with fingers (cooked eggs and potatoes, shrimp)
15. Cracking raw eggs (progress to scrambled or fried)
16. Cutting with table knife (progress from soft food to hard)
17. Grinding with hand grinder (peanut butter, cranberries)
18. Beating with eggbeater (eggnog, meringue)
19. Peeling with scraper (carrots mostly but may try potatoes)
20. Grating with hand grater (cheese, carrots, fresh coconut)

You may wish to start the cooking program with item 3 while having materials available from the first and second items off and on during the year. In general, two-year-olds can progress through item 15. Most three-year-olds can continue through item 18, and most four-year-olds are capable of mastering all of these skills. You may find that older fours also can cut with sharp knives with proper supervision.

*Ferreira, Nancy (1973). Teacher's guide to educational cooking in the nursery school—an everyday affair. *Young Children, 29,* 31–32.

A Dozen Rules for Preparing Food

1. Be sure you know the recipe thoroughly before you start. Follow it carefully; do not make any changes.
2. Gather together all of the ingredients, tools, and utensils. Be sure you have enough utensils for all the children to use one.
3. Use child-sized, unbreakable tools and utensils.
4. Use standard measuring cups and spoons.
5. Explain to the children that they will be helping prepare food. Make sure they *and* all adults wash their hands before beginning to prepare anything.
6. Place all foods to be sliced on a cutting board—do not cut *anything* in the hands. If slicing something that can roll around (eggs, onions, etc.), the adult first cuts it in half. Place the flat side down on the cutting surface and the children can continue slicing. The adult may need to do any peeling or chopping in advance.
7. When pouring, place the containers on a flat surface.
8. After you taste something, wash off the spoon before using it again.
9. Allow time for discussion—talk with the children about what is happening. Describe the activity; talk about the sights, smells, tastes, touches, and sounds of the experience.
10. Wipe up at once anything that spills on the table or floor. Wet spots become very slippery.
11. Cleaning up is part of the cooking experience. The children will enjoy helping you get the area back in shape.
12. Take your time. Don't rush with what you are doing. Have fun, for if the children have a hand in making it, they will usually enjoy eating it even if the food is slightly burned or speckled with egg shells.

Food Groups

Prepare a large bulletin board display that is divided into four sections. (See Figure 146.) Label each section with the name of a food group and provide a few pictures or illustrations of foods that would be classified into each group. Children can be encouraged to draw their own illustrations or to cut out magazine pictures of foods that would be appropriate for each section. Let them take turns mounting their choices in the proper sections.

Balanced Meals

Arrange a grocery store corner in your classroom. Display empty boxes, cans, and other food packages. Also cut out pictures of meat, cheese, or poultry from magazines and glue them onto empty styrofoam meat trays. Provide a few toy shopping carts. Ask small groups of children to go to the grocery store to buy the items they will need for a balanced meal.

☐ *Meat Group.* Two servings daily from this group are recommended. Lean meats, fish, poultry, eggs, and cheese are all good sources of protein, fat, and vitamins.

☐ *Milk Group.* Children should have about one quart of milk daily. Other dairy products such as cheese and ice cream may also be considered as milk products. These foods are good sources of protein, fat, calcium, phosphorus, and vitamins.

☐ *Vegetable and Fruit Group.* Four servings daily from this group will provide an excellent source of vitamins and, to a lesser extent, carbohydrates and minerals. At least one of the recommended four servings should be a food which is high in vitamin C, such as oranges or fruit juices fortified with vitamin C.

☐ *Bread and Cereal Group.* Four servings daily from this group are suggested as they provide the primary source of carbohydrates. Foods from this group provide some protein, vitamins, and minerals.

Send letters home explaining that your class will be participating in a program to encourage eating balanced meals—those that include foods from each of the four categories. At the end of the week, ask the children to discuss the different kinds of foods they ate from the four groups. Then give each child a special reward—the official "I'm a Food Nut" badge illustrated in Figure 147. He or she will wear it with pride!

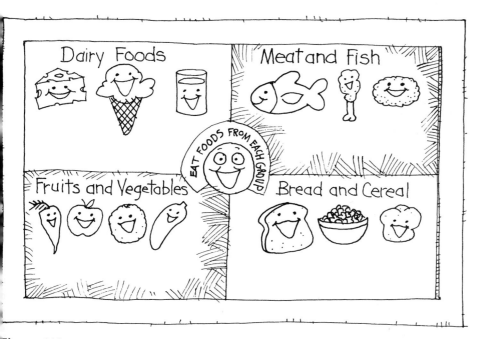

Figure 146

Figure 147

Simple, Uncooked Recipes

Raw Fruits and Vegetables

Help the children become familiar with basic principles of food preparation as they scrub the food, peel or cut it, take out the seeds, taste it raw. This can lead to a comparison of raw and cooked fruits or vegetables. These skills are basic to the preparation of the following foods.

Fruit Salad

¼ apple
¼ banana
¼ pineapple
2 orange sections
1 walnut half, chopped

Cut or dice each of the ingredients and stir together. (Makes an individual portion.)

Apples and Peanut Butter

Cut a small apple in half. Scoop out the seeds and fill the hole with peanut butter.

Special Candy

2 tablespoons peanut butter
2 tablespoons honey
¼ cup dry milk (powdered milk)

Mix all ingredients and roll in small balls. For added flavor roll in chocolate sprinkles.

(For larger quantities use ½ cup peanut butter, ½ cup honey, and 1 cup dry milk.)

Tasty Turtles

Set out as many round crackers as you wish for the children in your room. Spread some peanut butter on each cracker. Press a walnut half onto the peanut butter and use raisins or other dried fruit to make the head and feet of the "tasty turtles."

Raisin Snacks

2 cups peanut butter
1⅓ cups raisins
1 box crackers or vanilla wafers

Combine peanut butter and raisins and spread on crackers or wafers. (Makes enough spread for about 15 children.)

Uncooked Candy

2 cups honey
2 cups peanut butter
4 cups dry milk
1 cup shredded coconut
½ cup chopped walnuts

Combine all ingredients in a large bowl. Roll into small balls and serve. (Makes about 60 or 70 candy balls.)

Health Snack

Provide separate containers of banana slices, yogurt, and wheat germ. Encourage the children to dip a slice of banana into the yogurt and then into the wheat germ. This makes a delicious and healthful snack.

Summer Fruit Salad

1 cup fresh pineapple, in small chunks
1 cup fresh pitted cherries
2 cups fresh grapefruit, sectioned
2 cups pears, cut into squares
3 cups peaches, cut into squares
1 cup fruit juice

Stir the ingredients together and serve individual portions. (Makes about 18 one-cup servings.)

Stuffed Celery

Wash and dry one stalk of celery per child. Stuff each stalk with peanut butter.

Lettuce Roll-Ups

Wash and dry one leaf of lettuce per child. Spread the leaf with peanut butter, and roll it up.

Granola Candy

2 tablespoons granola
1 tablespoon peanut butter
½ tablespoon dry coconut

Mix ingredients well and add extra dried fruit or nuts if desired. (Should form 4 or 5 granola candy balls.)

Celery Boats

Cut pieces of celery into 3- or 4-inch pieces. Fill the centers with cream cheese or another favorite spread. Have a box of triangular crackers available, or cut cheese into triangular shapes as shown in Figure 148. The children can push a cracker or cheese into the spread to make a sail.

People Sandwiches

Cut people shapes out of bread slices with a cookie cutter. The children can spread butter or peanut butter over the shapes and then use raisins to make the facial features. (See Figure 149.)

Individual Lemonade

Squeeze ½ a lemon into ½ cup water and add 2 teaspoons sugar. Stir well and serve.

Figure 148

Figure 149

Individual Tomato Juice

1 small tomato
2-inch piece of celery
1-inch piece of onion
sprig of parsley

Dip tomato into hot water and peel. Cut peeled tomato into small pieces and place in blender. Add celery, onion, and parsley. Blend and serve.

Ice-Pops

Freeze ice cubes made from real fruit juices.

Pleasant Punch

1 can chilled pear nectar
1 can chilled unsweetened pineapple juice
1 tablespoon lemon juice
1 cup chilled ginger ale
vanilla ice cream *or* fruit-flavored sherbet (optional)

Combine all the fruit juices and ginger ale. For an extra treat, top each serving with a small scoop of ice cream or sherbet. (Makes enough to serve 15 children.)

Jelly Milk

Pour cold milk into an almost empty jelly jar. Shake it vigorously. Drink the flavorful mixture!

Figure 150

Peanut Butter

2 cups roasted peanuts
2 tablespoons cooking oil
salt

Ask the children to help you shell the peanuts. (Have a few extra for the children to taste before they are turned into peanut butter.) Pour the oil into a blender and add the shelled peanuts. Cover the blender and run at low speed until the peanuts are chopped into tiny pieces. Then, turn the blender to medium speed until the nuts and oil blend into a smooth paste. Add a pinch of salt to taste.

Butter

1 cup cold heavy whipping cream
¼ teaspoon salt

Place the cream into as many individual baby food jars as you will need to accommodate groups of two to three children. Have them take turns shaking the jars. When the butter forms, drain off the buttermilk and put the butter into a bowl. Press out the excessive buttermilk with a spoon. Add ¼ teaspoon salt per cup of cream. Serve with crackers. Encourage the children to taste the drained off buttermilk.

Mayonnaise

2 eggs
¼ teaspoon dry mustard
¼ teaspoon salt
dash pepper
1 tablespoon lemon juice
1 cup cooking oil

Have all ingredients at room temperature. Break the eggs into a blender, throwing away the shells. Add the mustard, salt, pepper, lemon juice, and half of the cooking oil. Turn on the blender for 30 seconds at medium speed (or until the mixture thickens). If you wish, the children can take turns mixing the ingredients with an eggbeater instead of using the blender. Slowly add the rest of the oil and continue beating until the mixture is thick again.

Cooking Recipes

Initial cooking projects should be fairly simple and involve all the children who wish to join. Most teachers begin with simple recipes such as the ones described in the first part of this section and then move on to those that require higher degrees of sophistication.

Hint: When cooking, try to use unbreakable glass pots and pans so the children can see what's happening during the cooking process.

The recipes in this section are described in terms of tablespoons and cups. However, some centers will soon be measuring foods by the metric system and will use terms such as milliliters and liters instead. If you care to experiment in these new measures, Table 2 may be handy.

Vanilla Cookies

1 cup shortening
2 cups sugar
6 tablespoons milk
2 teaspoons vanilla
3 eggs, beaten
5½ cups unbleached flour
1 teaspoon salt
3 teaspoons baking powder

Cream shortening while gradually adding sugar. Mix together milk, vanilla, and beaten eggs. Combine flour, salt, and baking powder. Add flour and milk mixtures alternately to the creamed shortening. Mix well. Chill for about one

Table 2

Standard		Metric
1 teaspoon	=	5 milliliters
1 tablespoon	=	15 milliliters
1 cup	=	240 milliliters
1 pint	=	473 milliliters
1 quart	=	946 milliliters
1 pound	=	0.454 kilogram

hour and roll dough out. Children can cut out the dough with cookie cutters or create their own designs. Bake at 375 degrees for 15 minutes. (Makes about 7 dozen cookies.)

Stained Glass Cookies

½ cup butter or margarine, softened
½ cup sugar
½ cup honey
1 egg
1 teaspoon vanilla extract
2½ cups unsifted flour
1 teaspoon baking powder
½ teaspoon baking soda
½ teaspoon salt
2 packets (12 ounces each) lollipops

Thoroughly blend margarine, sugar, honey, egg, vanilla. Stir in flour, baking powder, baking soda, salt. Cover and chill several hours.

On foil-covered baking sheets draw shapes using a dull pencil. Roll small dough pieces on a lightly floured board into long ropes about ¼ inch thick. Use to form cookie outlines on the foil.

Crush each candy color separately. Spoon crushed candy inside dough ropes.

Bake at 350 degrees about 6 minutes or until candy is melted and cookie is lightly browned. Cool completely. Remove from foil. (Makes about 6 dozen cookies.)

Single Pizzas

Provide one split English muffin for each child. Cover the muffins with tomato sauce and sprinkle with mozzarella cheese. Place them under the broiler until the cheese melts.

Soft Pretzels

4 cups flour
1 tablespoon salt
1 tablespoon sugar
1 package dry yeast
1½ cups warm water
2 eggs (beaten)
1 cup kosher salt

Combine flour, salt, and sugar. Stir in yeast, which has been activated in warm water. Knead the dough until it's smooth and elastic. Give each child a small ball of dough to form a pretzel in any shape desired. Brush dough with the beaten egg and sprinkle with kosher salt. Bake for 20 minutes at 425 degrees. (Makes about 12 pretzels.)

Applesauce

8 apples, pared and quartered
1 cup water
½ cup brown sugar
¼ teaspoon cinnamon
⅛ teaspoon nutmeg

Heat apples in water until boiling. Reduce heat and simmer 5 to 10 minutes until tender; stir periodically and add water if necessary. Mash apples with a potato masher and add the remaining ingredients. Stir. Heat to boiling and remove from stove. (Makes about 8 cups applesauce.)

Banana Biscuits

2 ripe bananas
1 tablespoon shortening
1 cup flour
1½ teaspoons baking powder
1½ teaspoons brown sugar
1 teaspoon lemon juice
pinch of salt

Mash bananas in bowl. Sift together flour, baking powder, and salt. Cut in shortening. Add lemon juice. Make a dough by combining the mashed bananas and flour mixture. Roll out on a floured pastry board; cut into 2½-inch rounds. Prick tops of rounds with fork and place on greased, floured cookie sheet. Bake at 350 degrees for 10 minutes. (Makes 12 biscuits.)

Flying Saucers

Hard boil enough eggs (10 to 15 minutes) so there will be at least half an egg for each child and cool them in cold water. Peel the eggs and cut them in half the long way. Remove the yolks and mash them together with mayonnaise and a bit of salt and pepper. Fill up each egg white with the mixture. Cut circles of pumpernickel bread slightly larger than the eggs with a cookie cutter and spread cream cheese on each piece. Put the eggs, upside down, on top of the cream cheese and bread to make the flying saucers.

Chicken Soup

3 to 5 pound chicken
1 whole onion
1 bay leaf
1 tablespoon parsley flakes

1 clove garlic, whole
1 carrot, diced
1 stalk celery, diced
1 teaspoon salt
dash pepper
1 package alphabet noodles

Wash the chicken and place in a large pot with enough water to cover. Heat to boiling, skimming fat and residue from the surface. Reduce heat, add all remaining ingredients but the noodles, and simmer until chicken is tender (about 2 hours). Remove onion, garlic and bay leaf; also remove the chicken and cut the meat from the bones. Replace chicken, add cooked noodles, and serve. (Makes about 18 one-cup servings)

Vegetable Soup

6 pounds beef shanks
3 quarts water
1 bay leaf
dash pepper
1 teaspoon salt
2 cups diced carrots
1 cup diced celery
1 onion chopped
2 1-pound cans tomatoes
1 cup fresh peas
1 cup corn
1 tablespoon parsley flakes

Cover shanks with water in a large pot and heat to boiling. Reduce heat; add bay leaf, salt, pepper, and parsley. Simmer about 2 hours until the beef is tender.

Remove the shanks from the stock and separate the beef from the bone. Add meat and remaining ingredients to stock and simmer until all vegetables are tender. (Makes about 18 1-cup servings)

Health Snack

2 cups Kix
2 cups Cheerios
2½ cups pretzel sticks
1½ cups mixed nuts
⅓ cup butter, melted
½ teaspoon garlic salt
½ teaspoon celery salt

Heat oven to 250 degrees. Mix nuts, pretzels, and cereal on large, flat pan. Blend seasonings with butter and pour over the mixture. Bake for 30 minutes, stirring with wooden spoon after 15 minutes.

Mountains of Other Recipes

Look for these recipes in your favorite cookbook:

popcorn	potato pancakes	spareribs
Jell-O	corn bread	(barbecued)
hamburgers (on the	doughnuts	peanut butter
grill in good	cakes	pizza
weather)	cupcakes	popcorn balls
hot dogs	Chinese mixed	sloppy Joes
potato salad	vegetables	chowder
tossed salad	grits	spanish rice
coleslaw	guacamole soup	gingerbread
macaroni salad	kabobs	cookies
scrambled eggs	ice cream	turkey and
bread	apple cider	stuffing
muffins	grilled cheese	stew
French toast	sandwich	tacos
waffles	mashed potatoes	tamales
pancakes	meat loaf	tortillas
hot cereals	meatballs	ambrosia
	cornmeal mush	baked bananas

Planning and Organizing a Cooking Experience

Guide Sheet

Because cooking activities often get very hectic and confusing, many teachers write up a basic outline of the procedure. A sample form is provided in Figure 151.

Send-Home Notes

Because children will often eat foods they helped prepare, but won't touch them otherwise, some teachers like to send home the recipe. A sample note is included in Figure 152.

Class Recipe Chart.   Choose a recipe that reflects the skills and interests of your children and organize the steps as visual images. (See Figure 153 on page 264.) Draw the steps in sequence on a large sheet of tagboard and print, in upper- and lowercase letters, the related direction beneath each illustration. Encourage the children to explain the directions as the cooking process evolves.

Original Recipe Book.   "Get one scoop of flour, a scoop of salt, and one cup of hot water. Mix them in a pan. Crack three eggs and put them in the pan. Stir it

COOKING PROJECT

Date _____   Project _____

Whole-group activity   Small-group activity

1. Purpose for the project:
   New food experience   Observing texture changes in
   Fun experience   cooking
   Language development   Noting similarities and
   Following directions   differences
   Cooking skills   Small muscle skills
   Sensory experience   Learning about different foods
   Listening experience   Encourage experimentation
   Observing changes in matter   Social experience

2. Cooking supplies needed:

   _____ _____ _____

   _____ _____ _____

   _____ _____ _____

   _____ _____ _____

3. Ingredients needed:

   _____ _____ _____

   _____ _____ _____

   _____ _____ _____

   _____ _____ _____

4. Step-by-step procedure:

   a. _____   f. _____
   b. _____   g. _____
   c. _____   h. _____
   d. _____   i. _____
   e. _____   j. _____

Figure 151

March 16, 1980

Dear Parents,

We made a tasty tossed salad in school today! We would like to share our recipe with you. You will need these vegetables:

2 cups iceberg lettuce
1 cup raw spinach
½ carrot, thinly sliced
¼ cucumber, sliced
¼ onion, diced
2 radishes, sliced
¼ green pepper, sliced
1 tomato, sliced

Wash or scrub all of the vegetables. Tear the lettuce and spinach leaves and place them into a large bowl. Add each of the other ingredients. When all have been added, toss them until the salad is evenly mixed. Store the salad in the refrigerator until it is to be served. Then prepare this dressing and pour it over the top.

Mix: 2 cups mayonnaise
1 cup sour cream
4 tablespoons finely chopped green onion

The salad was delicious!

With love,

Mrs. Hollister's Five-Year-Old Group
Sunnydale Day Care Center

Figure 152

up. Cook it about three hours. Be sure to flip it over all the time. Put it on a plate and eat it." According to one kindergartner, this is a recipe for scrambled eggs. You will obtain a number of these humorous, yet sincere, recipes when you ask your children to explain, in a step-by-step fashion, the steps their parents take in making a favorite dish. Write the directions for the children and ask them to illustrate them. Copy the recipes and compile them into "books" that can be taken home or placed in a parent center at school.

Figure 153

Personal Recipe Cards.   At times, a recipe may be appropriate for individual children to complete independently. Place the necessary ingredients in the order they will be used on a long table. Lay a numbered, illustrated direction card next to each ingredient; encourage the children to begin with the #1 card and continue in sequence to the end.

PROMOTING GOOD HEALTH

The basic premise underlying a healthy early childhood setting is that caregivers and children can exercise control over many of the environmental factors that affect their health. The role of the adult should be to help children develop and maintain habits and attitudes that promote good health while exhibiting appropriate behaviors and attitudes herself. The following suggestions, developed by the National Association for the Education of Young Children (NAEYC), are offered to help ensure a state of physical well-being.*

Step 1: Prevent the Spread of Germs

Infectious illnesses are often spread by people who do not look or feel sick. People are often contagious *before* they show any sign of illness. If you wait to keep germs from spreading until after someone is sick, it's already too late.

We cannot see the germs that make us sick, but they are all around us. They are found in common body fluids from the nose, eyes, and mouth: sneezes, coughs, and even that cute drip on a baby's chin! They are on hands that have touched places where germs are plentiful: bottoms, diapers, used tissues, trash cans, and foods. When people breathe, eat, or touch items contaminated by these germs—in the air, on food, or on surfaces—illnesses are spread.

The basic solution to reduce the risk of illness is really quite simple. Germs thrive in warm, wet, and stuffy places. Clean, dry places are much less likely to harbor them. You can help keep germs from spreading by keeping your hands and your surroundings as clean and dry as possible. Here's how.

Wash your hands properly and frequently. Use warm running water and *liquid* soap. (See Figure 154.) Lather well, scrubbing between fingers and under the nails. Rinse thoroughly, letting the water run back into the sink, not down to your elbows. Dry your hands on an individual paper towel. Avoid touching any unclean surfaces with your clean hands. The trash can lid, door handles, and sink faucet are all likely places for germs. Keep your paper towel handy if you must touch any of these surfaces after washing your hands. Throw the towel away after a single use.

Always wash your hands *before* you eat or handle food as after handling raw meat. Always wash your hands *after* you use the toilet, assist a child in toileting, change a diaper, wipe a runny nose, or contain a sneeze or cough with a tissue. If you can equip sinks with elbow- or foot-operated faucets, do so.

Parents, teachers, and children alike should learn these easy steps to keep germs away. Water play is one of children's favorite activities, so most children eagerly learn the proper way to wash their hands. Gentle reminders can help children develop habits of cleanliness that will help them stay healthy throughout their life.

Keep the air fresh. Air out classrooms and other common areas daily. Open bedroom and bathroom windows at home. Make sure children play outdoors every day. Fresh air is invigorating and gives children a chance for very active play, too.

Moisture is a key ingredient. Use a dehumidifier in summer if rooms feel damp or the bathrooms have mildew. Adding humidity in winter can help make

---

*McCracken, J. B. (1988). *Keeping healthy*. Washington, D.C.: National Association for the Education of Young Children.

Figure 154

breathing more comfortable. Cool vapor humidifiers are preferable and should be cleaned with a bleach solution daily.

Allow ample space between furniture.   Ample space between cots, cribs and other furniture helps to prevent the spread of germs in the air. Children should not sleep too close together. In group programs, leave enough room between cots so you can comfortably walk between them. Stagger children's heads and feet if cots are lined up. Arrange cribs at angles to keep children from touching each other. Keep play areas as spacious as possible so children are not all cramped together or crowded in one spot.

Clean and sanitize.   Toys, furniture, and areas for diapering, toileting, and eating should be sanitized regularly. Make a solution of ¼ cup bleach per gallon of water, or 1 tablespoon per quart if a smaller amount is more convenient. (See Figure 155.) Keep this solution handy in a spray bottle. After you clean away visible dirt, spray the solution on the diaper changing table, children's toilets, tabletops, high chair trays, cupboard tops, doorknobs, telephones . . . wherever germs could hide. Spread the spray thoroughly and allow it to air dry. Mix up a fresh solution daily so that bleach evaporation does not make the solution too weak.

Wash all eating utensils, dishes, and hard plastic toys in a dishwasher if possible. If not, wash them well, rinse them in the bleach solution, and allow them to air dry. This is especially important for toys that have been mouthed by infants and toddlers. You need to wash objects whenever they have been in contact with body fluids and *at least* twice a week. Daily is preferable.

Sheets for cots and cribs, dress-up clothes, and other fabric items should be laundered at least once a week. Hats for the dress-up corner are best if they are

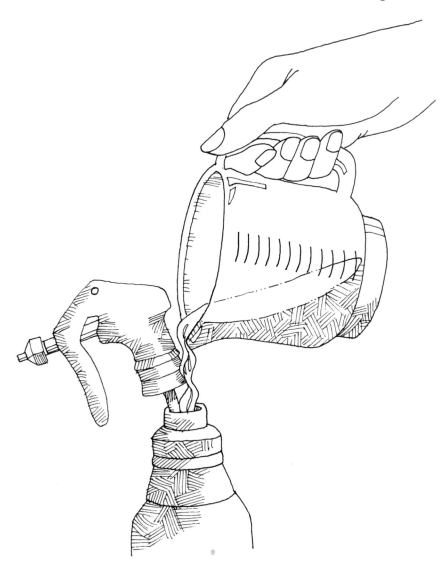

Figure 155

made of plastic or other easily washable materials. Wigs, loose woven shawls, and other fragile items are not practical.

When caring for a child in diapers, establish a diapering routine that includes carrying a soiled child away from other children, keeping the child from contact with your clothes, using a disposable cover on the changing table, and discarding the soiled diaper in a covered, lined container. Be sure to clean the changing table and spread the bleach solution thoroughly over the surface after each use, *in addition* to discarding the disposable cover. Thoroughly wash your hands as the last step. Child-care programs may want to consider the use of disposable gloves for diapering. This practice is helpful but not essential. (See *Healthy Young Children: A Manual for Programs*, published by NAEYC, for details.)

Accidents frequently happen with young children—they dribble their lunch on themselves, don't make it to the bathroom on time, cut their knee, or vomit on a nearby child. Keep extra changes of clothes available, and remove the soiled clothes whenever such accidents occur. Soiled clothing should be wrapped in a plastic bag and returned to parents for laundering at home.

Learn how to cough and sneeze correctly, and teach children to do the same.   Keep those tissues handy! Always use a tissue to catch a sneeze or cough or to wipe a runny nose. Then toss the tissue away and wash your hands. Never share tissues. When you cough or sneeze, turn away from people and direct it toward the floor. If the cough or sneeze is a surprise, cover it with a bare hand, then wash immediately. Be sure not to touch anything on the way.

Keep personal items apart.   Children's toothbrushes should be stored in holders with their bristles up and open to the air. They should not touch one another. Toothbrushes should never by shared with other children, nor should combs, hairbrushes, hair ornaments, food, or clothing be shared. Hats and mittens should be clearly labeled to be sure they are put on the right child. Cots and cribs should be used by only one child unless the bedding is changed each time and the sides wiped with the bleach solution. Label cots and store them so bedding does not come into contact with that of other children.

Step 2: Require Certain Immunizations

All children entering a group program should be immunized against these diseases at the appropriate ages: diptheria, tetanus, pertussis. Haemophilus influenza type b (Hib) disease, poliomyelitis, measles, mumps, and rubella. Some state laws may grant religious or medical exemptions. Otherwise, programs should exclude children who are not properly immunized. Partial immunizations do not provide complete protection against disease. Programs and physicians are urged to follow the latest recommendations of the American Academy of Pediatrics of immunization schedules.

Step 3: Report Illness

Parents and programs both have the responsibility to communicate with each other about issues surrounding children's, parents', and teachers' health. Whenever anyone is at risk, all of you are at risk.

What parents should do.   All parents whose children attend group programs have the responsibility to know about and follow the program's policies regarding illnesses. Ask your child's teacher or the program director for a copy of the health policies before you enroll your child. Come immediately when you are called to pick up a sick child. Always notify child-care providers when your child is ill.

Call to let the provider know why your child is absent and how long you expect the child to be out. Follow the program's policies about returning after recovery (see the next section). Provide the signed forms if medicine must be administered when the child returns.

What programs should do.   Programs also have an obligation to parents. Put your health policies in writing. Base your decisions on current information, such as that found in *Healthy Young Children*. Enforce policies fairly for everyone. Post notices and prepare take-home memos for parents about common ailments.

Teachers who know the children in their care will often notice changes in children's health from one day to the next. This information should be shared with parents. "Jamie seemed to be just a bit out of sorts today. Several of our children have been out with the flu. You might want to keep an especially careful eye on him tonight."

Some states have laws that certain diseases must be reported to the state department of public health. Maintain a current list of these diseases, and call the health department for advice on problem illnesses.

☐ Hepatitis, meningitis, AIDS, and sexually transmitted diseases, for example, must be reported for each case. Often the health care provider files the report, but may not let the health department know that the child attends an early childhood program.

☐ Other diseases such as flu, mononucleosis, conjunctivitis, or pneumonia are only reported if an outbreak (e.g., three or more children or staff) or an epidemic (many cases in a short period of time) occurs.

☐ Special requirements may apply if the illness is caused by contaminated food.

Step 4: Exclude Some Children, Staff, or Parents

Medical research is always providing new answers and raising new questions. Contrary to popular belief, there are really very few illnesses that require exclusion from a group care program. [Exclude children and adults with these illnesses and symptoms: meningococcal disease, Hib disease, diarrhea with fever and/or vomiting, chicken pox, and Hepatitis A. Other diseases may have waiting periods after treatment begins or may require special precautions. *Consult your local health authority.*]

With many illnesses, people have either already exposed others before they became obviously ill (colds) or are not contagious at some point after beginning treatment (strep throat, conjunctivitis, impetigo, tuberculosis, ringworm, parasites, head lice, and scabies). In some cases, staff or children may be present only if special precautions are taken. Those who are carriers of viral illnesses such as cytomegalovirus and herpes can and should be allowed to attend.

Parents must be aware that program policies may contain specific reasons for exclusion beyond medical requirements. Some programs are not staffed or equipped to care for even mildly ill children who are irritable and cannot fully participate in the day's events. Other programs can accept children with mild colds or the flu, for example. All policies should be based on current medical information, and should be reviewed from time to time by health professionals, parents, and teachers to assure that they are still appropriate.

Staff certainly cannot care adequately for children if they are not feeling in tip-top shape. Ample sick leave and the availability of health insurance are essential staff benefits in early childhood programs.

Step 5: Be Prepared

Programs and parents can take steps to make preventing and handling illnesses as hassle-free as possible. Programs can:

☐ Insist that staff and children follow handwashing procedures and all other health guidelines. Keep lotion within easy reach for dry hands.

☐ Post the phone numbers and policies of the local board of health and the state department of public health.

☐ Never admit children without current immunizations. Check children's health status at least once each year.

☐ Remind parents of health policies.

☐ Prepare information sheets in advance so that parents will know what to do about common illnesses.

☐ Routinely assess children's health and recommend appropriate action.

☐ Inform parents whenever a contagious disease occurs in the program.

   Parents can:

☐ Follow program policies, especially with regard to picking up ill children, exclusion, and immunization schedules.

☐ Inform staff if children have been exposed to a contagious disease elsewhere (perhaps another child in the family has chicken pox).

☐ Follow recommended procedures when children are exposed.

☐ Always leave any changes in your emergency numbers. Inform staff if you are at a different number even for just a day!

Nobody wants to be sick. Parents, teachers, and even young children can all take responsibility for making sure that we don't spread contagious disease and that we all help to keep each other healthy.

HOLIDAYS

Holidays are special days for nearly all children, but observances may differ from group to group. A Christmas celebration, for example, could be a deeply religious event in one household while an occasion for party and frolic in another. That is what makes it so difficult to choose ideas for this section of the book. Regardless of how they're celebrated, though, holidays are special days for all of us. Study your families carefully and choose those activities which will enrich and deepen their celebrations.

Halloween

Halloween is among the most favorite of all children's holidays. They love the fun and excitement of dressing in costumes and going from door to door searching for special treats. The holiday has its roots long before the time of Christ when the Celts and Druids lived in the British Isles and Northern France. These people were awed by the forces of nature which they were unable to explain—destructive storms, droughts, and wind, for example. They worshipped these forces and often had special ceremonies to appease them. One of these special ceremonies took place on October 31, for that day was the last day of the year and signalled the start of winter. The Celts and Druids were especially fearful of winter because they thought that the associated shortening of days was caused by the killing of the sun by evil forces of darkness. They tried to appease these evil forces by building huge fires on the night of October 31 so the sun would come back. We know the days get longer after mid-December because of the position of the earth, but the Celts and Druids believed that the phenomenon occurred because of their ceremonies.

The Celts and Druids also believed that October 31 was a day of special spiritual nature. Ghosts and witches were supposed to have come back to earth then. And, because they were afraid of the huge fires, the ghosts and witches were said to have tried pleasing the evil spirits by setting big tables with good things to eat. The ghosts would become angry if the treats were not there and ended up doing fearful, nasty deeds to the people. To rid themselves of the ghosts and witches after their feast, the Celts put on masks and costumes so they could lead them out of town. Our traditions of "trick-or-treating" and dressing in costumes is believed to have its origin in these practices.

Christians had developed early beliefs that duplicated many of the Celtic and Druid convictions. For them, November 1 was called "All Saints' Day"—a special time to recognize the church's list of saints. ("Hallow" means saint, and so "Halloween" is short for "All Hallows Eve.") Today Halloween is a time of fun, decorations, and food. It can hold a special place in school when you offer imaginative games and activities. Here are some suggestions.

Halloween Mask.   Place a paper shopping bag over each child's head and carefully mark where the eyes are. Take off the bag and cut out the eyes. Provide a variety of "junk" materials, crayons, or paint that the children may use to create their ghoulish masks.

Marble Spider Web.   Supply each small group of children with a plastic spoon, a box bottom or lid (at least 9" × 12"), a sheet of black construction paper large enough to fit inside, a cup of white paint, and enough marbles so that each child has one. Taking turns, each child carefully drops his marble into the cup, spoons the marble onto his paper, and rolls it around. A weblike appearance should result. Help the children add spooky spiders to their webs by inserting pipe cleaners into styrofoam balls. (See Figure 156.)

Rice Jack-O'-Lantern.   Provide each child with about ⅛ cup of rice in a small plastic bag. Help them to add six drops of yellow and two drops of red food coloring to the rice. Seal the bag tightly and ask the children to shake it vigorously. Then, they spread the rice to dry on a paper towel.

As the rice is drying, the children trace and cut out from black construction paper the eyes, nose, and mouth of a jack-o'-lantern face. Give each child a small, plastic, margarine-type lid that has a prepunched hole at the top. The children spread glue over the entire inside section of the lid, sprinkle it with their orange rice, and pat it down. Then, they turn over their lids and allow the loose rice to fall off. Finally, keeping the hole of the margarine lid at the top, the children glue their jack-o'-lantern facial features in place, as shown in Figure 157. After threading a piece of black or orange yarn through the hole, the children can wear these rice jack-o'-lanterns as necklaces.

Halloween Tablecloth.   Use a white sheet for the tablecloth, and cut a variety of Halloween shapes out of sponge—witches' hats, jack-o'-lanterns, ghosts, and so on. Offer black and orange tempera paint, and let the children take turns choosing shapes, dipping them into the paint, and stamping them onto the sheet. Use the sheet as your "Halloween feast" tablecloth, or as a decoration.

Guess the Goblin.   Blindfold a "witch" and position the other children ("goblins") in a circle around the designated child. Have the goblins take turns making spooky noises while the witch tries to guess who it is. If she guesses correctly, the witch and goblin switch places.

Bert- and Ernie-O'-Lanterns.   Pattern jack-o'-lanterns after two favorite Muppet characters—Bert and Ernie. Find an oval shaped pumpkin for a Bert-O'-Lantern and a round pumpkin for an Ernie-O'-Lantern. There are two ways that you can make Bert- and Ernie-O'-Lanterns. One way is to paint on the features and glue on yarn or the type of black fur found in craft departments for the hair and eye brows. Use orange construction paper for the ears. Another way is to carve out

Figure 156

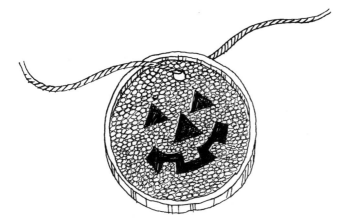

Figure 157

the features, using half-circle pumpkin cutouts for the ears and the same materials suggested above for the hair. Put a small flashlight inside to make the Bert- and Ernie-O'-Lanterns glow.

Halloween Fingerplays, Songs, and Action Rhymes

Special songs and rhymes add to the magic of all holidays. Here are some special ones for Halloween.

The Funny Old Woman

A funny old woman in a pointed cap
(Clap hands together over head)
On my door went rap, rap, rap
(Knock on door)
I was going to the door to see who was there.
(Open door)
When off on her broomstick she rode through the air!
(Point up)

Five Little Jack-O'-Lanterns

Five little jack-o'-lanterns sitting on a gate,
(Start with fingers closed)
First little jack-o'-lantern said, "My it's getting late."
(Raise one finger, continue to raise additional fingers as indicated)
Second little jack-o'-lantern said, "Who goes there?"
Third little jack-o'-lantern said, "There are witches in the air."
Fourth little jack-o'-lantern said, "It's only Halloween fun."
Fifth little jack-o'-lantern said, "Let's run, let's run!"

When puff went the wind, out went the light,
   (*Hide hand behind back*)
Away ran the jack-o'-lanterns on Halloween night.

Hi Ho for Halloween
(Tune of "Farmer in the Dell")

The old witch had a broom
The old witch had a broom
Hi Ho for Halloween
The old witch had a broom.

The old witch had a cat
The old witch had a cat
Hi Ho for Halloween
The old witch had a cat.

The old witch met a ghost
The old witch met a ghost
Hi Ho for Halloween
The old witch met a ghost.

And the ghost will catch *you*
And the ghost will catch *you*
Hi Ho for Halloween
And the ghost will catch *you*.

Two Little Ghosts

A very old witch was
Stirring a pot.
   (*Stirring motion*)
Ooo—ooo. Ooo—ooo!

Two little ghosts said
   (*Hands on hips, bend over as if looking in pot*)
"What has she got?"
Ooo—ooo. Ooo—ooo!

Tiptoe, tiptoe, tip
   (*Fingers creep forward*)
Boooo!
   (*Raise hands over head and jump up*)

Halloween's Coming
(Tune of "London Bridge")

Halloween will soon be here
Soon be here
Soon be here
Halloween will soon be here
Look out, children!

Witches on a broom will soon be here
Soon be here
Soon be here
Witches on a broom will soon be here
Look out, children!

Howling black cats will soon be here
Soon be here
Soon be here
Howling black cats will soon be here
Look out, children!

Goblins in the dark will soon be here
Soon be here
Soon be here
Goblins in the dark will soon be here
Look out, children!

Skeletons will soon be here
Soon be here
Soon be here
Skeletons will soon be here
Look out, children!

Trick or treaters will soon be here
Soon be here
Soon be here
Trick or treaters will soon be here
Look out, children!

Strange things happening will soon be here
Soon be here
Soon be here
Strange things happening will soon be here
Look out, children!

Jack-O'-Lantern

Jack-O'-Lantern, Jack-O'-Lantern, you are such a funny sight;
As you sit there in the window, looking out in the night.
You were once a yellow pumpkin growing on a slender vine.
You are now a Jack-O'-Lantern, see the candlelight shine.

Pumpkin Bells
(Tune of "Jingle Bells")

Dashing through the street
In our costumes bright and gay,
To each house we go,
Laughing all the way,

Halloween is here,
Making spirits bright—
What fun it is to trick-or-treat
And sing pumpkin songs tonight!

Oh Mrs. Witch!

Oh Mrs. Witch, Oh Mrs. Witch, tell me how you fly.
I fly on a broomstick all through the sky.
Oh Mrs. Witch, Oh Mrs. Witch, tell me what you see.
I see a little jack-o'-lantern looking at me.
Oh Mrs. Witch, Oh Mrs. Witch, tell me what you'll do.
I'll ride on a broomstick and I'll scare *YOU!*

Witch

If I were a witch
    (Make high peaked hat, fingers touching high over head)
I'd ride on a broom
    (One fist rides on top of other, waving through the air)
And scatter the ghosts,
    (Wave arms)
With a zoom, zoom, zoom.

Halloween Recipes

"Witches Brew."   Heat a cup of apple cider and top it with a scoop of orange sherbet. Add a cinnamon stick to this popular potion!

"Skeleton Snack."   Make a skeleton head from a pear half and raisins as illustrated in Figure 158.

"Pumpkin Seeds."   After scooping the seeds from a pumpkin, wash and dry them thoroughly, being careful to separate the seeds from the membrane. Mix 2 cups seeds with about 2 tablespoons of melted butter (or cooking oil) and a

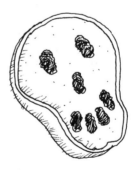

Figure 158

teaspoon of salt. Spread the seeds out on a cookie sheet and bake at 350 degrees until light brown (usually for 15 to 20 minutes). Stir them from time to time.

Thanksgiving

In 1621, the Pilgrims at Plymouth with their leader, William Bradford, observed the first Thanksgiving feast with the Wampanoag (WAHM-peh-NOH-ag) Indians and their leader Massasoit. The Pilgrims were thankful for the help they received from the Wampanoags, who shared their seeds and showed the Pilgrims how to use strange new foods such as corn, squash, and pumpkins, as well as how to prepare food for the winter. More than fifty Pilgrims and in excess of ninety Indians were present. Thanksgiving was proclaimed a national holiday in 1863 by President Abraham Lincoln after a strong seventeen year campaign by the prominent writer, Sarah Josepha Hale (who, among other famous works, wrote "Mary Had a Little Lamb"). Today, we celebrate Thanksgiving by having a big dinner (usually with turkey) with family, relatives, and friends. Choose from the following recipes and projects to plan some special Thanksgiving activities with your class.

Popcorn Balls.   The Pilgrim children were held spellbound during the first Thanksgiving when the Indians heated corn above a fire until the kernels popped into white puffs. They were further delighted when maple syrup was poured on the popped corn to make a treat similar to our popcorn balls. Use the following recipe to make popcorn balls or other fancy popcorn decorations.

½ cup sugar
¼ cup butter or margarine
½ cup light corn syrup
½ teaspoon salt
8 cups popped corn

Simmer all ingredients except popped corn over medium heat, stirring constantly. After about three minutes, remove from heat and pour over popped corn. Stir with a wooden spoon until corn is well coated. Cool slightly. Have the children dip their hands in cold water (or coat them with butter) and shape the popcorn into balls. Place on waxed paper to cool thoroughly. To make decorations, press popcorn into well oiled molds in seasonal shapes such as turkeys or Pilgrims.

Thanksgiving Dinner.   Although turkey is the main course of most Thanksgiving dinners today, deer meat (venison) was the central food of the first Thanksgiving feast. The Pilgrim women preparing the first feast planned a meal of wild turkey, geese, clams, and fish. But, when Massasoit realized more food was needed, he sent several of his men into the forest for deer.

If you know a hunter who can spare some meat or live near a specialty store that stocks venison, prepare venison stew. Children can be asked to bring in vegetables such as potatoes, carrots, celery, onions, and peppers; they can then wash, peel and cut their vegetables. Cut the meat (3-pound breast or shoulder roast) into small cubes and dredge it with flour. Brown the meat slowly in hot oil and add water and seasonings. Stir, cover, and simmer at a low temperature until the meat is tender, about 45 minutes. Add the diced vegetables and cook until tender. Serve with rolls and milk. The Indians might like to bring fresh fruit for dessert.

If you want to add gravy to your stew, follow this procedure after browning the meat. Remove meat and all but 2 tablespoons of the drippings. Blend in 1 or 2 tablespoons of flour. Stir until the mixture is thick and smooth. Continue to stir constantly and cook slowly while adding the rest of the drippings. Strain the gravy before adding the meat and vegetables.

Thankful Booklet. Discuss the questions, "What were the Pilgrims thankful for?" "What are you thankful for?" The children can make a special "Thankful Booklet" consisting of four pages: I am thankful for myself (draw self); I am thankful for my family (draw family); I am thankful for food (children search through magazines, cut out pictures of their favorite foods, and paste them on the page); and I am thankful for the place I live (draw house, apartment, etc.). You may want to make this activity more open-ended by inviting the children to contribute their own pages of what they are thankful for.

Turkey Trip. Many preschoolers think of turkey as a big white blob that comes in a plastic package and turns up later well browned on a platter. Visit a turkey farm and introduce them to the real thing in all its feathered glory. Study the birds carefully; view them from different angles. Listen to the birds gobble. Collect turkey feathers to bring back to school. Note how they differ from those of a chicken. Examine turkey eggs and compare them to chicken eggs.

Thanksgiving Placemat. Have your children design placemats for their families that can be used for the big meal. Cut old grocery bags into rectangles about 12' × 18". Show the children how to fringe the ends and then let them decorate a mat for each member of their families. (See Figure 159.)

Brown Bag Skins. Open grocery bags at their seams and flatten them out. Cut them into shapes similar to old bearskin rugs. The children can paint or draw designs on the surface.

Indian Corn Gobbler. Glue down a simplified, black yarn turkey design on heavy cardboard, as illustrated in Figure 160. Squeeze glue into different sections and ask the children to fill them in with colored kernels of Indian corn.

Thanksgiving Centerpiece. Prepare a number of different colored sheets of construction paper on which turkey feather shapes have been outlined and a set of tan sheets of construction paper on which turkey heads have been outlined. Have the children cut out the feathers and head, coloring the head to add features. Ask the children to stuff a lunch-size paper bag with newspaper. Tie the end shut with a string. Have the children glue the head to the tied end of the bag and glue the feathers to the other end, as shown in Figure 161.

Figure 159

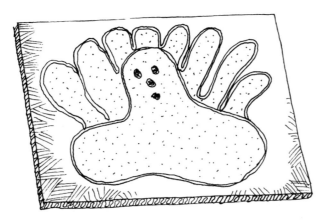

Figure 160

Hand Pattern Turkeys.   Give each child a large sheet of drawing paper. Help them to trace their own hand with thumb outstretched and fingers spread apart. The children then draw a turkey's head and feet on their turkey bodies. They cut out the turkey and decorate it with crayons, paint, beads, discarded feathers, or any other similar materials. (See Figure 162.)

Thanksgiving Fingerplays, Songs, and Action Rhymes

Add to the enjoyment of Thanksgiving by using a number of spirited songs, fingerplays, and action rhymes. Here are a few suggestions.

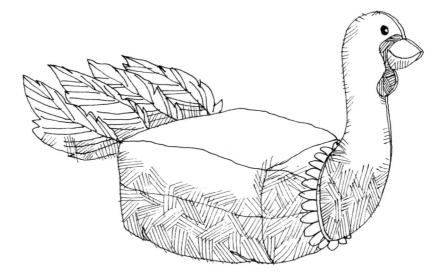

Figure 161

Figure 162

Happy Thanksgiving Day

This little Pilgrim went for a walk,
This little Indian wanted to talk.
This little Pilgrim said, "How do you do?"
This little Indian said, "How do you do?"
They looked at each other as if to say,
"I'm glad you're here, Happy Thanksgiving Day!"

Dan Turkey

I have a turkey
    (Hold fingers together, extended forward to touch thumb)
His name is Dan.
He has fine feathers,
They are colored tan.
We wobbles when he walks,
    (Walk hand)
And he gobbles when he talks,
    (Raise finger from thumb to "talk")
And he opens up his tail
Into a great big fan.
    (Open hand with fingers spread apart in fan position)

Five Turkeys

Five big turkeys, perched on a gate.
The first one said: "It's getting very late."
The second one said: "Do you see a man?"
The third one said: "He has a roasting pan!"
The fourth one said: "Let's run very fast."
The fifth one said: "Until Thanksgiving's past."
They all talked it over and agreed they were right.
And away through the air they all took flight!

Thanksgiving Dinner
Tune: "Are You Sleeping?")

We eat turkey, we eat turkey. Oh, so good. Oh, so good.
Always on Thanksgiving. Always on Thanksgiving.
Yum, yum, yum. Yum, yum, yum.

Mashed potatoes, mashed potatoes. Oh, so good. Oh, so good.
Always on Thanksgiving. Always on Thanksgiving.
Yum, yum, yum. Yum, yum, yum.

Pie and ice cream, pie and ice cream. Oh, so good. Oh, so good.
Always on Thanksgiving. Always on Thanksgiving.
Yum, yum, yum. Yum, yum, yum.

Homemade biscuits, homemade biscuits. Oh, so good. Oh, so good.
Always on Thanksgiving. Always on Thanksgiving.
Yum, yum, yum. Yum, yum, yum.

Turkey dressing, turkey dressing. Oh, so good. Oh, so good.
Always on Thanksgiving. Always on Thanksgiving.
Yum, yum, yum. Yum, yum, yum.

Mr. Turkey

Mr. Turkey's tail is big and wide.
    (Spread hands wide)
He swings it when he walks.
    (Swing hands back and forth)
His neck is long, his chin is red.
    (Stroke chin and neck)
He gobbles when he talks.
    (Open and close hand)
Mr. Turkey is so tall and proud.
    (Straighten self up tall)
He dances on his feet.
    (Make fingers dance)
And on each Thanksgiving Day,
He's something good to eat.
    (Pat stomach)

Five Little Pilgrims

Five little Pilgrims on Thanksgiving Day.
The first one said, "I'll have cake, if I may."
The second one said, "I'll have turkey, if it's roasted."
The third one said, "I'll have chestnuts, if they're toasted."
The fourth one said, "I'll have pumpkin pie."
The fifth one said, "Oh, cranberries, I spy."
But before they ate their pie, or the turkey, or the dressing,
They bowed their heads for
The first Thanksgiving blessing.

Christmas

Although a treatment of the religious aspects of Christmas may not be permitted in many public schools, private schools do allow teachers to offer related activities.

Christmas is the Christian celebration of the birthday of Jesus. Most churches celebrate the holiday on December 25, some two weeks later on January 6.

The story of Jesus' birth is well-known. Joseph had to participate in a census in the city of his ancestors, Bethlehem. Bethlehem was known as the city of

David. He took with him his wife, Mary. When they arrived in Bethlehem, there was no room for them to stay in an inn, so they found shelter in a stable. There Mary gave birth to her firstborn son. She made a bed for him in a manger.

Nearby, shepherds were watching their sheep when an angel appeared to them. The glory of the angel frightened the shepherds, but the angel calmed them and told them to be happy because Jesus had been born. He told them to look for a child lying in a manger.

At the same time, three kings from the East traveled to Jerusalem, following a star that they said foretold of Jesus' birth. When they found Jesus, they gave him gifts of gold, frankincense, and myrrh.

Christmas customs go back to celebrations and rituals performed long before Jesus' birth in Bethlehem. Early Christians used to celebrate the holiday on January 6, but it was changed to December 25, which was an ancient pagan holiday, the birthday of the sun. Some Christians still celebrate Christmas on January 6, commemorating the day the three kings brought their gifts to Jesus.

Today, observances of Christmas include the giving and getting of gifts. The individual most commonly associated by the children with gifts is St. Nick, or Santa Claus. As a young, rich man in Asia, Nicholas decided to secretly give gifts to other people each Christmas. No one knew Nicholas was the giver of these mysterious gifts until he went away forever and the gifts ceased to come. Then the people themselves began to give gifts secretly in the name of St. Nicholas (later Santa Claus). This secretive magic of Christmas still lives on all over the world.

Gifts for the Animals. Cut stale bread with Christmas cookie cutters; make a hole in each bread shape and thread with yarn. Spread the shapes with peanut butter and dip them in bird seed. Then hang the bread on a tree for the birds and other small animals. (See Figure 163.)

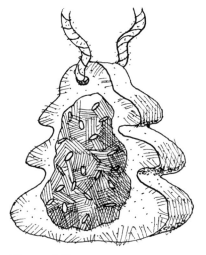

Figure 163

Old Fashioned Christmas Trees.   String popcorn, bake cookies, wrap candies, and hang fresh fruit (apples, pears, or oranges) on the branches. Some of the fruit should be covered with cloves. Fruits were the first ornaments used on Christmas trees and the cloves symbolize the spices brought by the Three Kings who visited Jesus.

Wrapping Paper.   Provide sheets of newsprint, tempera paint, and sponges cut into a variety of seasonal shapes. Children use the sponges by dipping them into the tempera paint and dabbing them up and down to make wrapping paper.

Egg Carton Bells.   Cut apart egg cartons into individual cups so that each child has one; punch a hole in the top of each. Have the children paint the cups and decorate them by sprinkling glitter on the wet paint. Allow the ornaments to dry. Help the children roll pieces of aluminum foil into small ball shapes. Ask the children to wrap one end of a pipe cleaner around the ball. Then, help them push the opposite end of the pipe cleaner through the shell and hook the end to make a hanger, as illustrated in Figure 164.

Window Tree.   Have the children cut triangles from green construction paper and use a paper punch to make holes in it. Glue a brown rectangle on the bottom to be the trunk. Have the children tear small bits of colored tissue paper (about the size of a fingernail) and paste them behind the holes. Add a cutout foil star. Tape the trees up in the window and the "ornaments" will glow.

Napkin Ring Gifts.   The children cover sections of cardboard tube with glue and paste on colorful wrapping paper. The tubes are then trimmed with yarn borders as shown in Figure 165.

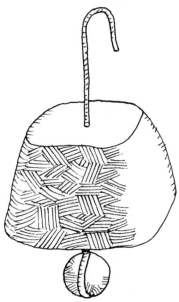

Figure 164

Figure 165

Serving Trays.   Save a number of styrofoam produce or meat trays; wash them thoroughly so they will not harbor harmful bacteria. Brush with thin school glue and paste on scraps of green and red fabric. Varnish when the glue is dry.

Table Tree.   Children cut paper squares in five graduated sizes (eight of each size) and punch a hole in the middle of each. Then they stick a plastic drinking straw into an empty spool. They push the squares (largest to smallest) onto the straw, turning the squares so sides of each do not directly coincide above or below one another.

Tissue Christmas Tree.   Provide small, tree ornament-sized templates of Christmas tree shapes. Have the children trace around the templates on green construction paper and cut out the forms. They can then glue crumpled odds and ends of varied colored tissue paper on the trees. If they paint over the tissue with watered-down school glue, the ornament should shine.

Piñatas.   The piñata, a large papier-mâché ornament filled with candies and toys, is a Mexican tradition. Hung from the ceiling, it is struck with a stick by blindfolded children until it yields its contents for all to enjoy.

A simple piñata can be made from a large paper bag decorated with animal designs or crowns. The crowns reminds us of the Three Kings. Streamers of green and white symbolize the colors of the Epiphany season. Tied at the top and attached to a long cord, it can be raised and lowered from the ceiling until broken open by a lucky child.

Epiphany Eve.   In Spain, the nacimientos or manger scene is lighted on Noche-buena, or the Good Night (Christmas Eve). But on Epiphany Eve (January 5) the custom is for families to seek the Magi (the Wise Men) by staging great parades to the edge of town. Foods are carried for the Kings and their animals. The Magi are found in the nacimiento in the village church. Simulate the events of this joyful time by recreating your own parade with the children.

Epiphany Cake.   In England, Epiphany Eve is known as the Twelfth Night—the last evening of Christmas and the traditional time to take down the holiday decorations. It is also the last chance to celebrate the Christmas season. As the decorations come down, carols, games and food, including the Epiphany Cake, are enjoyed by all.

Epiphany Cake, a spice cake with white frosting and green crowns, has three beans baked into it as well as other objects such as a coin for wealth or a ring for marriage. The beans represent the Magi. Each person who discovers a bean in his or her slice of cake is crowned with a paper crown. The Kings of the evening lead a festive procession while singing "We Three Kings."

Songs, Fingerplays, and Action Rhymes

Although many of your Christmas activities will involve traditional carols, the following suggestions may be used to add some fresh ideas to your repertoire.

Christmas Bells

Five little bells hung in a row.
The first one said, "Ring me slow."
The second one said, "Ring me fast."
The third one said, "Ring me last."
The fourth one said, "I'm like a chime."
The fifth one said, "Ring me at Christmas time."

Five Little Children

Five little children pop into sight.
They peek out their window
On the cold, cold night.
The first one said, "I think I see the snow."
The second one said, "We'd better whisper real low."
The third one said, "Oh, I just can't wait."
The fourth one said, "I hope Santa's not late."
The fifth one said, "Did you hear that."

The five little children ran to their beds;
Hopped under the covers and peeked out their heads.
They saw a strange figure all covered with snow,
They heard a strange sound—
It was Ho! Ho! Ho!

Here's Our Little Pine Tree
(Tune of "I'm a Little Teapot")

Here's our little pine tree
  tall and straight.
Let's find the things
  so we can dec-or-ate.
First we want to put
  a star on top!

Then we must be careful
     the balls don't pop!
Hang on all the tinsel
     shiny and bright.
Put on the canes
     and hook them just right.
Finally put some presents
     for you and me.
And we'll be ready
     with our Christmas tree!

Christmas Presents

See all the presents by the tree;
Some for you
          (Point to neighbor)
And some for me.
          (Point to self)
Long ones,
          (Hands spread)
Tall ones,
          (Measure with hand from floor)
Short ones, too;
          (Measure shortness)
And here is a round one
          (Make circle with arms)
Wrapped in blue.
Isn't it fun to look and see,
All of the presents by the Christmas tree?
          (Point hands to shape tree)

Christmas Is Here

Here is the wreath that hangs on the door.
          (Circle arms over head)
Here is the fir tree that stands on the floor.
          (Triangle with thumbs, forefingers)
Here is the book from which carols are sung.
          (Palms up like open book)
Here is the mantel where stockings are hung.
          (Fold arms in front)
Here is the chimney that Santa comes down.
          (Put hands over head, touching fingers)
Here is the snow that covers the town.
          (Fingers flutter down)

Here is a box in which is hid
     (Close right fist with thumb inside and put left hand on top)
A Jack that pops up, when you open the lid.
     (Lift left hand and pop up thumb)

Santa's Reindeer

One, two, three, four, five little reindeer
     (Pop fingers up one by one)
Stand beside the gate.
"Hurry, Santa," said the five,
"So we will not be late!"
     (Make fist)

One, two, three, four, five little reindeer;
Santa said, "Please wait!"
"Wait for three more little reindeer,
And then that will make eight."
     (Hold up eight fingers)

Santa is Back

Two merry blue eyes,
     (Point to eyes)
A cute little nose,
     (Point to nose)
A long, snowy beard,
     (Make motion as if stroking beard)
Two cheeks like a rose,
A round, chubby form,
     (Make large circular motion around stomach)
A big bulging sack.
     (Shoulders bent, hands holding heavy sack)
Hurrah for old Santa!
     (Clap hands)
We're glad that he's back.

Santa's Chimney

Here is the chimney,
     (Make fist, enclosing thumb)
Here is the top.
     (Place palm of other hand on top of fist)
Open the lid,
     (Remove top hand quickly)
And out Santa will pop.
     (Pop up thumb)

Las Posadas

Some Hispanic Americans celebrate *Las Posadas* beginning on December 16 as a reenactment of Joseph and Mary's trip to Bethlehem. The celebration often includes the whole community in feasts, parades, and other festivities. Much of the celebration is like Christmas, but special customs characterize Las Posadas; chief among these is a nightly search of homes to see where statues of Joseph and Mary could be housed. Prearranged, such a home is found on the ninth night (Christmas Eve) where coffee, punch, wine, tortillas, tamales, and other special foods are served. Special experiences designed to communicate the characteristics of Las Posadas include the following:

❏ Make *piñatas*. Fill them with wrapped candy or nuts and small unbreakable toys. Children are blindfolded, spun around one by one a time or two, and given a chance to swing the stick to break the piñata.

❏ Invite a Hispanic American parent to your classroom to explain Las Posadas.

❏ Prepare tortillas, tamales, or other traditional foods.

❏ Read stories of Las Posadas to the children. (See *Nine Days to Christmas* by Marie Hall Ets and Aurora Labastida; New York: Viking, 1959.)

❏ Provide materials and costumes for the dramatic play area so the children can play out the events of Las Posadas.

Hanukkah

A long time ago, the Jews of Israel were not free people. They were ruled by cruel King Antioches from Syria, who planned to take away their religion. He wanted the Jews to believe in the Greek religion, so he sent soldiers to the Jews' most holy place, the Temple in Jerusalem, destroyed the holy things, and made it a place of Greek worship.

The soldiers killed many people and burned many homes. A brave Jewish man, named Judah the Maccabee, led a small Jewish army—the Maccabees—in a fight against the King and his soldiers. After three years, the King and the Syrians were defeated on the 25th of the Hebrew month of Kislev.

After the Maccabees chased the Syrians from the holy temple, they began the hard job of rebuilding it. They needed oil to light the lamps as they worked, but all they could find was enough oil to burn for one day. But something wonderful happened—the oil burned for eight days, until new oil could be prepared. It was a miracle. That is why Hanukkah is now celebrated for eight days and we light the Hanukkah menorah for eight days. Hanukkah means "Rededication," because the Maccabees rededicated the Temple and cleansed it. It is celebrated each year on the 25th day of the Hebrew month *Kislev* which falls in November or December.

Lighting the Menorah.   A menorah is a candelabrum that holds nine candles; one is lighted each night for eight nights, until all the candles are lit. The tall middle candle (*shammash*) is lit first and then used to light the others. Small gifts are exchanged each time a candle is lit, songs are sung, and games are played. The burning candles remind Jews of their fight for freedom. It is a happy time for Jewish people.

Here are the blessings that are recited over the Hanukkah menorah:

☐ Baruch ata adonai, eloheynu melech ha-olam, asher kidshanu b'mitzvotav, vitzivanu l'hadlik ner shel Hanukkah.
(Blessed are you, O Lord Our God, King of the Universe, who has sanctified us through your commandments and commanded us to light the Hanukkah lights.)

☐ Baruch ata adonai, eloheynu melech ha-olam, she-asa nisim la'avoteynu bay-amim heheym ba-zman hezeh.
(Blessed are You, O Lord Our God, King of the Universe, who did wonders for our ancestors in former times at this season.)

☐ (On the first night only) Baruch ata adonai eloheynu melech ha-olam, she-hecheyanu v'ki-y'manu v'higianu la-zmen hazeh.
(Blessed are You, O Lord Our God, King of the Universe, who has kept us in life, sustained us, and brought us to this time.)

Hanukkah Treats.   Jelly doughnuts are enjoyed greatly at Hanukkah. Another food eaten on Hanukkah is latkes, potato pancakes, because they are made with oil, as are the doughnuts. Here is the recipe for latkes:

4 large potatoes
1 small onion
2 eggs
3 tablespoons flour
1 teaspoon salt

1. Grate the potatoes and onions finely and put them in a bowl.

2. Add the eggs, flour, and salt and mix well.

3. Drop tablespoons of the batter into hot oil in a frying pan. Fry until crisp and brown on both sides.

4. Remove from oil and drain on a paper towel.

5. Eat while warm with sour cream or apple sauce.

Makes 6 to 12 pancakes.

The Dreidel.   Children play with a dreidel on Hanukkah. The dreidel is a spinning top that has four sides, each of which is decorated with a Hebrew letter. Dreidels can be made by inserting a wooden dowel through a styrofoam block and holding it in place with glue. The four sides of the dreidel should have the symbols shown in Figure 166. Collectively, the symbols read, "A Great Miracle Happened There." Play the game by giving each child the same number of nuts, raisins, or pennies. Each child puts one of these in the middle. Taking turns, the children spin the dreidel. If the dreidel lands on Shin, the player puts an object in the middle. If it lands on Hay, the player takes half the objects. If it lands on Gimel, the player

Figure 166

akes everything from the middle. And, if it lands on Nun, the player does nothing. Whoever gets the most is the winner.

The Dreidel Song.   A favorite Hanukkah song is this tune which is sung by the children as they use their dreidels.

I have a lit-tle Drei-del, I made it out of clay And when it's dry and rea-dy Then Drei-del I shall play O Drei-del Drei-del Drei-del I made it out of clay O Drei-del Drei-del Drei-del Now Drei-del I shall play.

Kwanzaa

wanzaa (Kwan-zah) is an African-American celebration during which black families and friends come together, give thanks for, and celebrate their African heritage. Kwanzaa was first observed on December 26, 1969 as a seasonal gathering of black people in California under the leadership of Dr. Maulana Ron

Karenga, a scholar and philosopher. The celebration was not intended as a religious holiday, but as a time for blacks to gather together to remember their past and to rejoice in their present and future.

Kwanzaa is a Swahili word meaning first fruits. Swahili is the official language of Kenya, a nation in East Africa. Celebration of the "first fruits" of harvest has always been traditional in Africa; it is a time to come together and rejoice. These celebrations sometimes last weeks. In recreating this African spirit of gathering and celebration, Kwanzaa was established as a holiday to fall on December 26 of each year so that black people could come together to celebrate their achievements as a people, to rededicate themselves to greater achievements, and to look forward to fuller, more meaningful lives.

Kwanzaa activities begin December 26 with the *mkeka* (straw mat) on which all the items for the celebration are placed. The *mkeka* (mah-KAY-kah), which represents the land, is put on a low table or on the floor. A wooden candleholder *(kinara)* for seven candles (the candles are red, black, and green), along with fruit and corn *(muhindi)*, is placed on the *mkeka*.

One candle is lit each day until the seventh, when the center and final candle is lit. Each one is labeled with one of the seven principles of blackness *(nguzo saba)*, which are guidelines to be followed all year: *Umoja* (unity), on the first day; followed by *Kujichagulia* (self-determination); *Ujima* (collective work); *Ujamaa* (cooperative economics); *Nia* (purpose); *Kuumba* (creativity); and *Imani* (faith) on the final day.

The *kinara* represents the original stalk from which all people sprang and each *muhindi* represents a child. The kernels are the children and the stalk the father. At each meal during Kwanzaa, a candle is lit, a principle is discussed, and everyone drinks from the unity cup.

Kwanzaa is primarily for children. Studying the seven principles is designed to give them an idea of who they are and their responsibility as adults. For example, the sixth day of Kwanzaa (*Kuumba*, on December 31) is the *karamu* (kerrah-MOO), or feast. It begins with the lighting of the seventh candle and continues all night with singing, dancing, storytelling, and feasting. On the last day, *zawadi* (presents), such as books or something made by the parents, are given to the children. The *zawadi* represent the fruits of labor of the parents and rewards to children for their accomplishments.

Kwanzaa Feast.   A Kwanzaa meal consists of delicious and nutritious foods. Most families create their own special dinners, each of which contains foods that symbolize special characteristics of black people in America. Some popular selections include:

- [ ] *Blackeyed peas:* Their black color symbolizes Africa, the mother continent.
- [ ] *Rice:* Their white color symbolizes the slave ships that brought Africans to America.
- [ ] *Collard greens:* Green symbolizes rebirth and cultural awareness.
- [ ] *Cornbread:* The yellow-orange color symbolizes the sunrise of a new day.

Karamu Games.   Five or more children may play "Big Leopard and Mother Hen." One player is the Big Leopard, another is the Mother Hen, and the other players are the baby chicks. The chicks form a line behind Mother Hen, each holding the player in front around the waist. They sway and chant, "Who is coming?" Big Leopard stands in front of the line growling, "I am coming for you!" Mother Hen chants, "The leopard comes to catch my babies!" At that point, the leopard grabs at the chicks. The chicks fall to the ground when the leopard approaches. The leopard tries to catch a chick before it falls. If he or she can do that, the chick gets taken to the leopard's den. The game continues until all chicks are caught.

Valentine's Day

This holiday is especially appropriate for young children because it deals with one of the most pervasive attributes of the young child's life: love. The time-honored tradition of sending and receiving Valentines makes this day especially valuable for studying the mail system. The children can make valentine cards for their parents out of precut hearts and put them into envelopes which the teacher stamps and addresses (if the children cannot do it themselves). Then, a trip to the post office, where the children can see the envelopes cancelled and routed into the proper channels, can be a valuable field trip activity. Other appropriate Valentine's Day activities include a Valentine's Day party where the children prepare heart-shaped Jell-O molds, cakes, or cookies for treats. Valentines can be exchanged, but be sure that each child brings one for every member of the class. Since most of the children will be unable to read or write, it is not necessary to address the cards, though children who can write their own name will want to sign their cards.

Craft activities can be used to design a gift to take home for a parent or other family member. Provide heavy cardboard tracers for one large heart and one small heart. The children trace around the large shape onto white construction paper and around the small shape onto red construction paper. They then glue the red heart on top of the white heart, and decorate the entire project with glitter, stickers, or frilly paper.

Easter

Usually signalling the coming of spring, Easter is a delightful time of the year for the preschool child. Buds are popping out on the trees, bulbs poke their way through the cold ground, and birds twitter as they build their nests. An awareness of these wonders of nature helps the child later understand the religious significance of Easter and Passover when and if those holidays are observed by her family. However, at this early period of their lives, children seem more concerned about the Easter Bunny, little chicks, and candy. Therefore, they should be given opportunities to enjoy the season through a variety of fun activities in the classroom. Some suggestions follow.

- ☐ Eastertime signals the beginning of spring and the reawakening of plant and animal life. Have the children plan their own flower or vegetable gardens, select the seeds, and look after the plants as they grow.
- ☐ This is an excellent time to introduce pets to your classroom, if you do not yet have any. The care and feeding of pets is an important part of any child's preschool experience.
- ☐ Color hard-boiled eggs with a food dye solution. Refrigerate the eggs. At an Easter party, the children can peel the eggs and eat them. Use the discarded shells for a group art activity—make a mosaic design by gluing colored egg shells onto construction paper.
- ☐ Read or tell stories (one good choice is *The Runaway Bunny* by Margaret Wise Brown; New York: Harper & Row, 1977) or sing special Easter songs such as "Peter Cottontail".
- ☐ Hatching chicken or duck eggs in a classroom incubator is both challenging and enjoyable. (See pages 239–241 for instructions.)

PARENT-SCHOOL RELATIONSHIPS

Today, nursery schools and child-care centers are viewed as partnerships between families and teachers. This implies a relationship where parents and teachers share in the services provided to the children. Parents do not "dump off" their children at school and forget about them, but have a continuing responsibility to become involved in the program. We examined some techniques of parent involvement in the earlier "First Day of School" section; here are some others.

General Ideas for Conferences

To create a warm environment that encourages comfort and ease, consider the following suggestions:

- ☐ Play soft, easy listening music in the background.
- ☐ Cover your conference table (not your desk) with a suitable tablecloth; or, you may wish to cover the table with butcher paper and ask each child to sign his or her name (if your children can do so) and draw a picture. The parents will enjoy searching for their child's work.
- ☐ Put a vase of fresh or silk flowers on the table to add a colorful touch.
- ☐ Provide comfortable chairs.
- ☐ Have some of the child's special work in a folder near the parent's chair.
- ☐ Have refreshments available. You may wish to bake some cookies with you children the day of (or the day before) the conferences. Put these out with a fresh pot of coffee or tea to greet the parents.

Make sure parents outside your room will be comfortable if your conference schedule begins to run five or ten minutes late. Provide a comfortable seating area with a cozy chair and table. Arrange photos of the children involved during the daily routine, materials appropriate for casual reading, and/or articles from magazines that deal with current issues in early childhood education: the value of play, early academic stimulation, nutrition, and so on.

Often parents are not aware that you are meeting with others and walk into your conference while your conference is in progress. To prevent what could be an embarrassing situation, make "Busy, Please Wait" or "Ready, Please Come In" signs that can be hung from or posted on your classroom door.

Start and end your conferences on a positive note. Parents should have a good feeling about their children, so a positive attitude is important. Send each parent away with a "Happy Note." Make a smiley face note for each child, as illustrated in Figure 167. Write his or her name on it, and identify a special area of strength for that child. Encourage the parents to take home the notes and share them with their children.

Use a process of *active listening* as you speak with parents. You can do this by accepting what the parent says. Also, you can communicate your interest in the following ways:

☐ *Establish favorable body language.* Your facial expressions (smiles, frowns, looks of surprise, etc.) and posture (looking directly at the speaker) communicate your degree of interest.

☐ *Paraphrase what was said.* By rephrasing what the speaker said we invite the person to tell us more. (For instance, "You don't feel that Julio should play with dolls.")

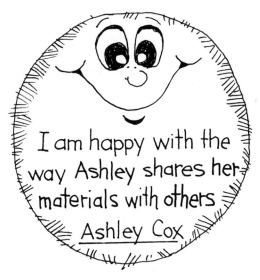

I am happy with the way Ashley shares her materials with others
— Ashley Cox

Figure 167

□ *Feed back feelings.* This is a way to acknowledge the parents' strong feelings and encourage them to tell us more. ("You feel awkward when Julio brings out his dolls in front of the other boys . . . Would you rather he played outdoors?")

Refrain from using educational jargon at the conference. "Educationese" such as "Your child's ability to perform seriation skills appears to be maturing," might better be said, "Your child's ability to put items in sequential order seems to be improving." Jargon often creates a barrier between parents and teachers, so always phrase your questions and comments in ways easily understood by nonprofessionals.

Be ready to answer the questions most often asked by parents at conferences: "How is my child doing in his schoolwork?" "Does my child behave?" and "Does my child get along with the other children?"

Try to ask open-ended, nonthreatening questions during home or school visits, conferences, or other informal or formal contacts. This is just a partial list, but it may spur you to develop your own.

1. "How does _____ feel about school?"
2. "How does _____ help with duties around the house?"
3. "How does _____ get along with his brothers and/or sisters?"
4. "What special interests or skills does _____ have?"
5. "Have there been any sudden, upsetting experiences (illness, death, and so on) affecting _____ ?"
6. "Does _____ seem to enjoy participating in activities with other children?"
7. "How does _____ let you know when he's angry? happy? sad? interested? frustrated?"
8. "What do you and _____ enjoy doing most together?"
9. "What have you found to be the most successful way of controlling _____ 's behavior?"
10. "What do you think _____ should be doing in school?"
11. "What would you like _____ to be when he/she grows up?"
12. "What things do you do with _____ at home that you would like to see continued at school?"

Newsletter

The importance of parent involvement in the child's education often leads teachers to prepare periodic messages, usually in the form of a newsletter, as a communication link between home and school. Such newsletters serve three basic objectives: (1) they keep parents informed about routine classroom activity; (2) they help stimulate the parents' interest in their children's activities; and (3) they provide suggestions that help reinforce and extend school learning at home.

The content of preschool newsletters varies, but the following topics have been used successfully:

1. Names, addresses, and phone numbers of other children and their parents in the group.
2. Suggestions for activities similar to those tried in school.
3. Short lists of appropriate books for young children.
4. Recipes for finger paints, play-dough, paste, or food projects the children have experience with.
5. Words to favorite songs or fingerplays.
6. Short suggestions on such topics as dental health, thumb sucking, sleeping problems, fears, or personal grooming.
7. Ideas for promoting reading, mathematics, and other cognitive skills.
8. Toy buying guides—especially around the Christmas season.
9. Suggestions for activities that can be undertaken during vacations, car trips, or other situations where children need extra stimulation.
10. Information regarding fees, health services, the school calendar, school policies, and special activities planned for the school year.

A sample newsletter is illustrated in Figure 168.

In addition to newsletters, consider sending special notes to thank parents for their efforts in helping their children. (A sample is included in Figure 169.)

V TO PLAN AND START A GOOD EARLY CHILDHOOD PROGRAM

If you're thinking about opening a child-care center, preschool, employer-supported child-care facility, or other high quality early childhood program, you will need to be familiar with the major steps involved in planning and starting programs that will benefit children, their families, and your community. Starting a nursery school or child-care center is a formidible task; though ultimately rewarding, at first it may seem overwhelming. The following plan was designed by the National Association for the Education of Young Children to help you do a better job of managing the process by detailing the many responsibilities and procedures involved in starting a new program.

Explore the Market*

1. *Find out what the child-care needs are in your community.* What programs are available now? What ages do they serve? Are parents satisfied with the quality of the care?

Which families need good early childhood programs? What are the ages of the children? When is the care needed? What locations would be most convenient for parents?

PRESCHOOL
◆NEWS◆

REMEMBER...

November 15
all morning

Field Trip
to Turkey
Farm

November 26-30

NO SCHOOL
THANKSGIVING
BREAK

Encourage interest in reading by...

● asking your child to "read" a familiar sign or label.
● requesting your child to find a special book he or she wants you to read.
● reading stories to your child.
● helping your child to follow a recipe or direction sheet as you complete a task.
● asking your children to tell you what they have tried to "write."
● encouraging your child to "read" traffic signs.

Here's a rhyme the children enjoyed today. Maybe you'd like to try it at home.

> Here's a ball. (Make a small circle with thumb and index finger on each hand.)
>
> And here's a ball. (Make a larger circle by using both thumbs and index fingers.)
>
> And a great big ball I see. (Make huge circle with both arms.)
>
> Shall we count them? Are you ready?
>
> One! Two! Three! (Make each circle as you count.)

Figure 168

298

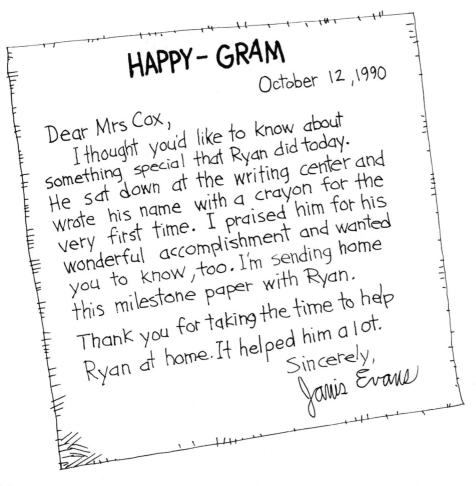

HAPPY - GRAM

October 12, 1990

Dear Mrs Cox,
    I thought you'd like to know about something special that Ryan did today. He sat down at the writing center and wrote his name with a crayon for the very first time. I praised him for his wonderful accomplishment and wanted you to know, too. I'm sending home this milestone paper with Ryan.

Thank you for taking the time to help Ryan at home. It helped him a lot.
                    Sincerely,
                    Janis Evans

Figure 169

Many communities have child-care resource and referral agencies that can provide valuable assistance in this regard. Local government planning offices may also be an information source.

2. *Obtain a copy of all licensing requirements.* What state or local regulations (child-care, education, zoning, fire, building, health) apply to the type of service you are planning? How will these regulations affect funding? Opening date projections? The children and families served? Facility planning? Staff selection? Community relations?

3. *Observe a variety of local programs for young children.* How do the programs seem to meet the needs of the children? Their families? The staff? Are the

programs accredited by the National Academy of Early Childhood Programs? What can you learn from their experiences?

How are the programs supported? How could a new service be coordinated with existing programs?

Plan the Business

1. *Decide how the program will be funded and governed.* Will the program be nonprofit, employer-supported, funded by state or local agencies, or a profit-making corporation?

   Who will determine policies and budgets? A board comprised of parents or agency/employer representatives? The proprietor(s)? A director?

   What items will be included in the program budget? Mortgage or rent? Staff salaries and benefits? Utilities? Supplies? Taxes? Insurance? Which items will be contributed/funded by other sources?

2. *Secure the service of specialists.* Will an early childhood specialist be needed as a consultant for planning? Will a lawyer be needed to file for incorporation? For purchase or lease of property?

   Should an accountant set up a record-keeping system for income and expenditures, including worker's compensation, social security, unemployment compensation, and taxes?

   What insurance is needed? Liability? Health and accident for children and staff? Fire and theft?

   Will architects or contractors be needed to build or renovate a facility? Do they have expertise in designing environments for young children?

3. *Identify funding sources.* Where will start-up funds be obtained? How much money will realistically be needed to cover fees for professional services? Purchase or lease of land and a building? Construction or renovation expenses? Classroom, office, and food-service furniture, equipment, and supplies? Publicity about the program? Initial staff training and services?

   How much working capital is available to cover operating expenses until the program income is sufficient to do so? Have opportunities for local grants, partnerships, and venture capital been explored? What level of enrollment is necessary to meet expenses?

   What fundraising efforts can be used for start-up costs? for operating expenses? As a basis of regular program support? For improvements, repairs, and replacement of equipment in the future?

4. *Prepare an annual budget.* What portion of income will be from parent fees? Other sources?

   What are anticipated expenditures? Salaries? Substitutes? Staff benefits? Taxes? Licensing fees? Marketing? Fees for other professional services? Mortgage or rent? Supplies? Utilities? Fundraising expenses? In-service training? Transportation?

5. *Secure a facility.* Is the area zoned for this type of facility?

   Is the location convenient to family neighborhoods, major employers, schools, or transportation centers? How will location affect the services provided? Should transportation be provided?

   What renovations will be necessary to meet all state and local regulations and assure a high quality program?

Plan the Program

1. *Write program objectives.* How will the program serve families? Children? The community? What ages of children will be served? How will groups be determined? Do program goals represent the best current knowledge about how young children grow and learn? About the roles of early childhood teachers and families? What longterm goals will the program strive for?

2. *Prepare job descriptions and schedules.* What will be the responsibilities of the director? Teachers? Assistant teachers? Nutritionist? Social worker? Maintenance staff? Cook? Drivers? Office personnel? Others?

   Will staffing patterns enable teachers to care for small groups of children? To provide the individualized attention young children need? To provide needed continuity for children? Do schedules allow paid time for staff planning and coordination? For staff breaks to keep energy levels high? How will children's arrival and departure times affect staffing and the program?

3. *Set major policies.* What ages of children will be served? What enrollment requirements must be met? How will parents be involved? How will parent fees be collected? Will sliding fee scales or scholarships be provided? How will the program handle sick children or staff? What hours will children attend? What holidays will be observed? How will difficulties with parents or staff be resolved? How will staff be evaluated? How will the program be evaluated? What requirements will be made for transportation and field trips? How will emergencies be handled?

4. *Recruit and retain competent staff members.* What community resources (NAEYC Affiliate Groups or other early childhood networking organization) can offer assistance in locating potential staff?

   Do staff have the educational and work experience necessary to provide a developmentally appropriate program for children? Do staff enjoy working with young children and their families? Are they healthy and energetic?

   Are staff salaries and benefit packages based upon educational qualifications and experience? Do salaries adequately reflect levels of job responsibility? Will ongoing opportunities for professional development and career advancement be provided to staff?

5. *Develop a high quality program for children.* How will the program be designed? Will the program be appropriate for the age groups served and implemented with attention to the needs and differences of the individual children enrolled?

How will room arrangement, furniture, equipment, and play materials affect the quality of the program? Will curriculum planning reflect understanding of the ways young children learn best?

For further information about providing a high quality program, see NAEYC's resources catalog and the resources listed below.

For further information about specific procedures for starting a program in your community, contact your state licensing agency, your local resource and referral agency, the president of the nearest NAEYC Affiliate Group, or the NAEYC Information Service.

Selected Resources

Many of the resources listed below are available from NAEYC. To order, specify the publication number and send appropriate payment to NAEYC, Publication Sales, 1834 Connecticut Avenue, N.W., Washington, DC 20009. Orders less than $20 must be prepaid. There are no shipping charges on prepaid orders.

General Information

Young Children—NAEYC's bimonthly journal offers the latest information on early childhood practice, theory, and research. Subscriptions are included as a membership benefit. For more information about becoming a member, contact NAEYC.

Child Care Information Exchange—Excellent bimonthly magazine specifically designed for child-care program directors, with regular features on finance, staffing, computers, and other administration topics. Subscription rate is $35 per year. Contact: Exchange Press, P.O. Box 2890, Redmond, WA 98073. (206) 882-1066.

Developmentally Appropriate Practice in Early Childhood Programs Serving Children From Birth Through Age 8, S. Bredekamp (editor), 1987. NAEYC #224, $5. Specific guidelines on implementing developmentally appropriate practice, with chapters addressing infants, toddlers, and preschool and school-age children.

Quality in Child Care: What Does Research Tell Us? D. Phillips (editor), 1987. NAEYC #140, $6. Monograph discusses recent research that defines quality in early childhood programs and describes how it can be measured.

Accreditation Criteria and Procedures of the National Academy of Early Childhood Programs, S. Bredekamp (editor), 1986. NAEYC #920, $6. The Academy Criteria address all aspects of a high quality early childhood program.

Child Care: Facing the Hard Choices, A. J. Kahn and S. B. Kamerman, 1987. Dover, MA: Auburn House. Analysis of child care services in America today and choices for shaping the future.

Getting Started

A Guide to Child Care Regulations in [your state], 1987. Developed by Work/Family Directions; distributed by NAEYC, #720, $3 per state (please specify state when ordering). Summarizes key licensing requirements for centers and family day care in your state.

Facility Design for Early Childhood Programs Resource Guide, NAEYC #789, $5. Provides contract information for organizations and experts involved with the design of early childhood learning environments, plus an extensive annotated bibliography.

Planning Environments for Young Children: Physical Space, S. Ktritchevsky & E. Prescott with L. Walling, 1977. NAEYC #115, $2.50. See how organization of space can prevent classroom traffic jams and even diminish discipline problems.

GOOD TOYS AND ACTIVITIES FOR YOUNG CHILDREN

Approximate age	What Children Are Like	Types of Toys and Worthwhile Activities
Birth to 3 months	Begin to smile at people, coo Follow moving person or object with eyes Prefer faces and bright colors Reach, discover hands, kick feet, lift head Suck with pleasure Cry, but often are soothed when held Turn head toward sounds	Rattle, large rings, squeeze or sucking toys Lullabies, nursery rhymes, poems Bright pictures of faces hung so baby can see them Bells firmly attached to baby's wrist, ankle, booties Cardboard or vinyl books with high-contrast illustrations to stand in baby's view Brightly patterned crib sheets Mobile with parts visible from baby's position
4 to 6 months	Prefer parents and older siblings to other people Repeat actions that have interesting results Listen intently, respond when spoken to Laugh, gurgle, imitate sounds Explore hands and feet, put objects in mouth Sit when propped, roll over, scoot, bounce Grasp objects without using thumbs, bat at hanging objects Smile often	Soft doll, texture ball Toys that make noise when batted, squeezed, or mouthed Measuring spoons, teething toy Cloth or soft vinyl books with bright pictures to grasp, chew, and shake Pictures of faces covered in plastic, hung at child's level; unbreakable mirror Fingerplays, simple songs, peek-a-boo Socks with bright designs or faces

Note: Each child develops at a different pace, so most suggestions overlap age groups.

Source: Toys: Tools for Learning, 1985, Brochure #571. Copyright 1985 by the National Association for the Education of Young Children. Reprinted by permission.

Approximate age	What Children Are Like	Types of Toys and Worthwhile Activities
7 to 12 months	Remember simple events, form simple concepts Identify themselves, body parts, voices of familiar people Understand own name, other common words Say first meaningful words Explore, bang, or shake objects with hands Find hidden objects, put objects in and out of containers Sit alone Creep, pull themselves up to stand, walk May seem shy or become upset with strangers	All of the above *plus* Rag and baby dolls, stuffed animals, puppets Container for large beads, blocks, balls Nesting toy or plastic containers Board books to read, old magazines to tear Recordings of voices, animal sounds, music Wooden blocks, large soft blocks Water toys that float Rubber or large plastic balls Soft plastic or wood vehicle with wheels Games like peek-a-boo
1 to 1½ years	Imitate adult actions Speak and understand more words and ideas Enjoy stories Experiment with objects Walk steadily, climb stairs Assert independence, but strongly prefer familiar people Recognize ownership of objects Develop friendships, but also play alone Are beginning to understand what adults want them to do, but do not yet have the ability to control themselves	All of the above *plus* Surprise or music box Puzzles, 2 to 6 large pieces with knobs Books/recordings with songs, rhymes, simple stories, and pictures Wide watercolor markers, nontoxic fat crayons, large blank paper Geometric, unit, or cardboard blocks People and animals, vehicles; wood or rubber Pounding bench Sand and water play: plastic measuring cups, boats, containers, washable doll Large cardboard box to crawl in Toys that jingle or move when used Kitchen cupboard of *safe* pots, pans, lids, and utensils
1½ to 2 years	Solve problems Speak and understand even more Show pride in accomplishments, like to help with tasks Exhibit more body control, run Play more with others Begin pretend play	Self-help toys; sorting box, holes with pegs Large spools or beads to string Books with large colorful illustrations, short stories Soft dough clay, bells, drum Small broom, sponge, camera, pots and pans Shopping cart, wagon, steerable riding toy; toy telephone, washable doll
2 to 3½ years	Enjoy learning new skills Learn language rapidly	Wood puzzles with 4 to 20 pieces

Approximate age	What Children Are Like	Types of Toys and Worthwhile Activities
2 to 3½ years (continued)	Are always on the go Have some sense of danger Gain more control of hands and fingers Frustrated easily Act more independent, but are still dependent, too Act out familiar scenes	Pegboards, sewing cards, stacking toys, picture lotto, dominoes Picture/story book about familiar things, poems Classical, folk, children's music Finger or tempera paint, ½" brushes, blunt scissors, white glue Unit blocks and accessories, wood train set with large pieces Hammer (13 oz. steel shanked), soft wood, roofing nails, nailing block Triangle, wood block, texture- and sound-matching games Wagon or wheelbarrow, large rubber ball, riding toy Washable doll with a few clothes, doll bed Dress-up clothes (hats, shoes, shirts), hand puppet
3½ to 5 years	Have a longer attention span Act silly, boisterous, may use shocking language Talk a lot, ask many questions Want real adult things, keep art projects Test physical skills and courage with caution Reveal feelings in dramatic play Like to play with friends, do not like to lose Share and take turns sometimes	Puzzles with more pieces, simple card or board games Smaller beads, parquetry blocks, small objects to sort Flannel board with pictures, letters, study numbers and letters More detailed books, simple science books Sturdy record/tape player, book and record sets Potter's clay, easel, narrower brushes, thick crayons, chalk, paste, tape and dispenser, collage material More unit block shapes and accessories, realistic model vehicles Construction set with smaller pieces Woodworking bench, saw, sandpaper Sand and water play; egg beater, muffin tin, vehicles Xylophone, maracas, tambourine Roller skates, plastic bat and balls, balance board Bowling pins, ring toss, bean bags and target

Approximate age	What Children Are Like	Types of Toys and Worthwhile Activities
3½ to 5 years (continued)		Planks, boxes, old tires Child-sized stove or sink, toy telephone, play food, cardboard cartons, more dress-up clothes, dolls, carriage, and accessories Airport, doll house, other miniature settings; finger or stick puppets
5 to 8 years	Grow curious about people and how the world works—by 7, are beginning to understand other people's feelings and that varying viewpoints and life-styles exist Show an increasing interest in numbers, letters, reading, and writing—by 7, most understand adding and subtracting if real objects and real situations are often used, can really read, and can draw/write/spell stories (in their own ways) Become more and more interested in a final product as they move toward 7 Gain more confidence in physical skills Like grown-up activities—by 7, show interest in jobs admired adults do Use words to express feelings and to cope; still may need adult help to calm down—by 7, many children are able to help others plan group activities and solve social problems Become more outgoing, play cooperatively, need to make many choices and decisions and to initiate independent activities; also need time to play alone Still need reassurance and affection Need protection from the competitive stress-producing world many of today's children find themselves in, and warmly enthusiastic adult support for what they can do and do "right"	All the toys for 3- and 4-year-olds *plus* More complex puzzles More difficult games, including board and card games Yarn, big needles, mesh fabric, weaving Magnets, balance scales, magnifying glass, math games made for 5- through 7-year-olds with pieces to handle Books with chapters, favorite stories children can read and books adults can read to children (even 7- and 8-year-olds), children's recipe books, diaries for the older children to write in privately Watercolors, stapler, hole punch, chalkboard, oil crayons, paint crayons, charcoal, simple camera, film More unit blocks, props, hollow or attribute blocks Brace and bits, screwdriver, screws, metric measure Sand and water play: food coloring, pump, funnel, containers Harmonica, kazoo, guitar, recorder Outdoor toys: playground ball, tetherball, jump rope, Frisbee, bicycle, roller skates Cash register, typewriter, other dramatic play props Nature activities 7- and 8-year-olds are beginning to be interested in hobbies, group and team games, clubs, and time to "hang out" and talk with friends

ACTIVITIES FOR INFANTS LISTED BY SKILL AREA

PHYSICAL SKILLS

ACTIVITIES FOR TODDLERS LISTED BY AGE

ACTIVITIES FOR YOUNG CHILDREN
LISTED BY SKILL AREA

CONCEPTUAL SKILLS

COOKING SKILLS

CULTURAL SKILLS

DRAMATIC PLAY

LANGUAGE SKILLS

SPEAKING

LARGE MUSCLE SKILLS

BASIC BODY MOVEMENTS

BODY IMAGE

CREATIVE MOVEMENT ACTIVITIES

LITERACY SKILLS

MATHEMATICS SKILLS

MUSIC SKILLS

PLAY SKILLS

READING SKILLS

SCIENCE SKILLS

SELF-CONCEPT AND SOCIAL SKILLS

SMALL MUSCLE SKILLS

WRITING SKILLS